MUSICAL MEANING IN *Beethoven*

MUSICAL MEANING IN

Advances in Semiotics

Thomas A. Sebeok, *General Editor*

Robert S. Hatten

Beethoven

Markedness,

Correlation,

and Interpretation

Indiana University Press: Bloomington *&* Indianapolis

Publication of this volume was assisted by a grant from
The Pennsylvania State University.

The paper used in this publication meets the minimum requirements of
American National Standard for Information Sciences—Permanence of
Paper for Printed Library Materials, ANSI Z39.48-1984.

Manufactured in the United States of America

Library of Congress Cataloging-in-Publication Data
Hatten, Robert S.
  Musical meaning in Beethoven : markedness, correlation, and
interpretation / Robert S. Hatten.
    p.   cm. — (Advances in semiotics)
  Includes bibliographical references and index.
  ISBN 0-253-32742-3 (cl : alk. paper)
  1. Beethoven, Ludwig van, 1770-1827—Criticism and interpretation.
2. Music—Semiotics.   I. Title.   II. Series.
ML410.B4H28   1994
780'.92—dc20   93-26001
             1 2 3 4 5   99 98 97 96 95 94

To my parents

Contents

Part II. Historical and Theoretical Perspectives

FOREWORD

by David Lidov

Robert Hatten integrates perspectives from semiotics, music theory, and music history to construct a new mode of interpretation of Beethoven's late style. As a novel synthesis of these three disciplines pursued with exceptional rigor and thoroughness, this book will interest specialists in each of the fields it draws together. The argument will be easier to follow for musical scholars who are new to semiotics than for literary and semiotic scholars who have little background in music theory, but the latter, if they do what is necessary to master it, will earn surprising rewards. We are becoming able, with such studies as this one, to antici-pate a comparative vista on the process of signification which does not take natural verbal language as its yardstick.

The title phrase "Musical Meaning" should be understood in that context. The book is written in words and uses words to construct its conceptual scaffolding, but what we acquire in the end is not a transla-tion from music to language. Language serves rather to disclose aspects of the anatomy and physiology of content relations established by music alone and unavailable to any other medium. We can be more precise than that: "musical meaning" here refers to the contents of the compo-sition, not the performance of music. There is a mysterious conjunction and disjunction between these two. The musically competent reader will recognize that the interpretations Hatten develops refer to precise man-ners of hearing the music which cannot be conveyed in sound except in a performance which is sensitive to and committed to the understanding espoused. At the same time, it will be equally evident that the contents perceived and explicated are potentials of the composition as scored, that they are not interchangeable from one piece to another or available to the performer to add to the music arbitrarily, like some new relish for an old recipe.

The method of analysis is complex. Hatten's point of departure is the linguistic theory of marking. Markedness theory originated in phonology but has emerged as one of the most, perhaps the most, widely applicable and enduring models of cognition to appear in the linguistic, structuralist, and semiotic investigations of this century. Markedness theory proposes that wherever humans draw distinctions (right/left, man/woman, etc.) these tend to be asymmetrical: One side tends to be more richly evaluated (positively or negatively) and more special; the other, to lend itself more to abstraction and sometimes to represent the divided whole (as was until recently the case with "man" in English). Hatten was quick to recognize the fundamental character of this theory and had the original insight that the principle could be applied to structures that do originate in binary oppositions. Music differs from speech in that its articulatory foundation begins with scales rather than contrastive pairs, but Hatten is able to identify guiding threads of binary contrast even in such subtly modulated terrains as harmonic doubling and figuration. Drawing on Michael Shapiro's extensive demonstrations that marked pairs of signifiers correlate in our understanding with respectively marked pairs of contents, he is able to forge a new logic of interpretation.

A second point of departure is the reconstruction by Leonard Ratner of a repertoire of stylistic references in Classical music that he calls "topics." Topics are richly coded style types which carry features linked to affect, class, and social occasion such as church styles, learned styles, and dance styles. In complex forms these topics mingle, providing a basis for musical allusion. In projecting this vocabulary forward in time to take account of Beethoven's cultural milieu and personal propensities, Hatten takes full advantage of our knowledge of Beethoven's literary interests and song texts to portray his highly individual grounding for a stylistic lexicon.

The foregoing might suggest merely a sophisticated system of pigeonholes for musical items, but I have indicated only the foundations of Hatten's hermeneutic. The heart of his theory is a concept of musical "troping." The notion of a "trope" derives from literary theory and resonates with our structural understanding of tonal music as a hierarchy of embellishments, but the term is used in a strict technical sense here which retains these other affiliations only as fortunate connotations. Specifically, a trope occurs where one expressive sign is used to modify or transform the effect of a second. There are two salient consequences of this conception. One, which Hatten elaborates carefully in his study, is that it permits him to trace the path of each work as a unique trajectory rather than as a simple collection of standard parts. The other, which is external to the analysis itself, is that it returns us to sound. Once we deal with music as a movement among ideas rather than as a mere collection of them, it is self-evident that our sensitivity to the weight of each color and the balance of their combinations restores an authority to our sensory immersion in their sound that might have seemed—momentarily—usurped by verbal exegesis. The critical notion of troping thus becomes our ultimate guarantee of aesthetic deference in the whole theoretical structure; again, it is not a translation.

In modern music theory the task of developing a systematic description of relationships between structure and values began with Leonard Meyer's *Emotion and Meaning in Music* in 1956. The project has not advanced rapidly since then, but the present work seems to me a major advance. Hatten has chosen a complex musical style as the territory in which to develop his novel approach and has worked cautiously. At a time when many despair that there is nothing fresh to say about the most important classics, his studies provide a new impulse for their reinterpretation. As his paradigm is subtle and very different from any now popular in academic research, the reader is well advised to approach it with a patient and open mind. Ultimately, it should assist our studies not just in music but across the nonverbal arts.

PREFACE

This study is the product of a decade's work on issues raised by my dissertation, "Toward a Semiotic Model of Style in Music: Epistemological and Methodological Bases" (1982). Although my semiotic framing of a concept of style provided a foundation for the study of expressive meaning, I was still rather formalist in my inability to move beyond "meaningful syntax" and explain expressive meaning in a more complete sense. An extended footnote on markedness, a concept I had discovered in 1980 through the work of Michael Shapiro, appeared in Chapter 6 of the dissertation; but it would be another two years before I began to address the consequences of markedness theory, enlarging my investigation to build a broader base for markedness in music. In so doing, I have moved far beyond the limits of the dissertation to deliver what it could only promise: a semiotic model of style that embraces expressive as well as formal meaning.

But a model needs exemplification, by a style (since different theoretical applications are demanded by different styles) and by analyses of individual works (since general style meanings must be further interpreted as manifested in unique contexts). My concern to provide examples of subtler interpretation, yet at the same time ground those interpretive insights in a coherent theory, led me to limit my primary examples to one composer's style. Beethoven was a natural choice, given the expressive richness of his music, especially evident in his late style. The decision to focus still further on piano sonatas and string quartets was based on my commitment to musical meaning on its own terms, without reliance on texts or preexistent programs. Analyzing late works of Beethoven, including one fugal movement, could dramatize the importance of expressive meaning by addressing some of the greatest works in the category of "absolute" music, a designation that has lost much of its original spiritual significance and had become roughly equivalent to "autonomous" in our more formalist century. My choice of movements, however, was also conditioned by the kinds of issues they could best illustrate, as a series of related and progressively reinforcing examples.

I have left open how one might apply the broader model to other composers, since the reconstruction of styles and the formulation of a theory appropriate to each style are mutually dependent enterprises. Applications may differ in significant ways from style to style, but I trust the general model introduced here can provide a useful foundation for other historical and even ethnomusicological investigations.

In conceiving and developing a model of musical expressive meaning, I have been profoundly influenced by the work of the Peircean linguist and literary theorist Michael Shapiro of Brown University. Shapiro's groundbreaking work on asymmetry in poetry (1976) was my introduction to the theory of markedness, and *The Sense of Grammar* (1983) was my inspiration for grounding markedness in a Peircean semiotic. His personal mentorship, beginning in 1985, was an invaluable asset in my adaptation and application of markedness theory in music. Ed Battistella, student of Shapiro's first NEH summer seminar, wrote the accessible primer on markedness from which I drew some of the definitions and examples in a later revision of Chapter 2.

The first version of the present study, including all of its basic theoretical claims, was completed in 1989. Since 1990 four books on semiotics or hermeneutics of music have appeared that are relevant to important issues I have addressed independently in my own work (Jean-Jacques Nattiez, 1990; Lawrence Kramer, 1990; Carolyn Abbate, 1991; and Kofi Agawu, 1991). In addition, several essays on aspects of Beethoven's work have recently appeared, and many anticipate or provide further evidence for claims I make about expressive meaning in Beethoven (notably *Beethoven's Compositional Process*, edited by William Kinderman, 1991; and *Beethoven Forum* 1, 1992). I have inserted extended notes in appropriate locations to these and other sources that appeared after the book was virtually complete. Given the particular style and organization of my theoretical exposition, I have not attempted any further integration of these recent studies into the body of my work. Updating references is an inevitable problem for any book that deals with current theoretical topics, but in this case I am deeply grateful for such distinguished company. When I began work as a music theorist on the issue of expressive meaning in music, the climate for speculation in the United States was still rather chilly. That this has changed immeasurably is due in large part to the impact of these and other musicologists.

In my own field, I am also grateful for the efforts of several fellow theorists, notably Fred Maus, Marion Guck, and Robert Snarrenberg, for their pioneering efforts in music narrative and metaphor in discourse about music. Shared papers at meetings in Iowa City and Melbourne, Australia, as well as at meetings of the Society for Music Theory, helped strengthen our resolve in the face of neglect or dismissal. Another vital source of inspiration and support for my work has come from yearly meetings of the interdisciplinary Semiotic Society of America, where I first launched many of the trial balloons that led to portions of this book and profited from the penetrating critiques of David Lidov and William Dougherty.

Eero Tarasti of the University of Helsinki has been a spiritually close, if geographically distant partner in the music semiotic enterprise. Indebted to the work of Greimas and the Parisian school of semiotics, he approaches issues of expressive meaning and topical analysis in ways that are often complementary to my own. Through his offices I have met many Europeans working in music semiotics, and have had fruitful exchanges with many (notably, Márta Grabócz) who share my vision that expressive interpretation is not only an integral part of musical competence but amenable to theoretical inquiry.

I have also been inspired by the work of Leonard B. Meyer, Eugene Narmour, Charles Rosen, Leo Treitler, David Lidov, and many others with whom I have shared ideas about musical meaning. Robert Gjerdingen commented in caring detail on an earlier draft of the book; and David Lidov, Patrick McCreless, William Dougherty, and Edward Williams (Graduate Research Dean at Penn State) offered valuable advice at various stages.

Leonard B. Meyer and Eugene Narmour provided intellectual and moral support during my Mellon postdoctoral fellowship year at the University of Pennsylvania (1985–86), where I began work on this project. I would like to express my deep appreciation to the Mellon foundation; a year to think and read without regard to disciplinary boundaries or academic schedules is the most precious gift a scholar can receive. The University of Michigan funded two graduate research assistants, Robert Snarrenberg and Ken Logan, who edited and commented on earlier drafts of chapters (1986–87). The Pennsylvania State University provided funding for preparation of the text and figures, attractively finished by Paul Zelinka and David Geyer respectively. In addition, a publication subvention from Penn State supported preparation of the numerous musical examples. I am deeply grateful for these various forms of support.

No one can spend time with Beethoven and fail to be moved by the very real spiritual content of his music. It has been my privilege to explore the theoretical basis for such understanding: the consistency with which we infer expressive meanings from musical structures. But there is always more to artistic interpretation than can adequately be theorized, and I trust I have respected the further significance each of us brings to an experience of Beethoven's music.

This book was written during a time of great personal sorrow and disturbance in my life, which has given me a greater understanding of the courage that, at some level, Beethoven's works always exemplify. I do not mean this as naive hero-worship, but I freely acknowledge the inspiration of Beethoven's example, as well as his works, in the struggle to encompass a subject that by its very nature is elusive, and thus controversial.

I wish to thank my family and my close friends for their support in other parts of my life, without which I could not have completed this work. Finally, I am grateful to Lesley, who always understood the heart's motivation, and who encouraged me to write for the future.

MUSICAL MEANING IN *Beethoven*

Introduction

I have concentrated in this study on what has variously been called expressive (as opposed to formal), semantic (as opposed to syntactic), extramusical (as opposed to purely musical), or even programmatic (as opposed to absolute) meaning. Unfortunately, each of these oppositions is misleading in some respect, and I offer them here simply to provide an initial orientation for the reader. In proposing a model for musical expressive meaning, I have explored other oppositions that have given me a more helpful orientation to the problem of interpretation, but I have not been able to dispense with some of the terminology of the past. I am concerned with *how* music has expressive meaning and not merely with *what* that meaning might be. Is there an underlying consistency to expressive interpretation? Can we speak of a stylistic competency for expressive meanings in music, and if so, how can it best be mapped? How does one draw upon that stylistic competency to reconstruct historically appropriate interpretations?

Furthermore, can it be shown that expressive considerations motivate compositional choices? If so, can those motivations also help explain style growth and change? Partial answers to each of these questions are to be found throughout the following chapters, with the Conclusion and Glossary providing two perspectives on the larger model in its entirety.

Unlike recent theories of musical structure (e.g., Lerdahl and Jackendoff, 1983), I have not attempted to formalize this model as a systematic theory, nor have I proposed a comprehensive set of rules by which one might on the one hand generate stylistically appropriate interpretations, or on the other, empirically test the results. There is a place for such theories, but I would argue that there is equally a place for the kind of modeling and theorizing that may be found in this book. I am committed to a *semiotic* approach, which I construe as involving both structuralist and hermeneutic approaches to the relationship between sound and meaning. A *structuralist* approach, in this construal, is concerned with mapping associations (*correlations*) of structures and meanings in a manner that reveals their oppositional organization. *Markedness* is a semiotic valuation of oppositional features that, as will be explained in some detail beginning in Chapter 2, accounts for relative specification of meanings, the coherence of meanings in a style, and the emergence of meaning within an expanding style competency. A *hermeneutic* approach is concerned with interpretation beyond the more general oppositional meanings secured by correlations. Although guided by stylistic correlations, hermeneutic inquiry expands the theoretically stable bases of a structuralist modeling to encompass the subtlety, ambiguity, and allusive richness implied by any truly artistic competency. The hermeneutic approach to interpretation also goes beyond purely structural methods in its *abductive*, or hypothetical, "leaps of faith," construing potential meanings on the basis of any available evidence—from any relevant source, and at any level or organization. Thus, hermeneutics is not essentially systematic or deductive, although its results may well be amenable to a later structural explanation, and indeed must be if those interpretations are to expand the systematic base of style understanding.

Since I believe that expressive meanings, and the stylistic competency they presuppose, were a part of Beethoven's compositional process (whether consciously or tacitly), I maintain that expressive meanings are as purely musical as the forms and structures that serve to distinguish them. And since I believe that such meaning can often be inferred consistently, even in Beethoven's nontexted, "absolute" music, it should be clear that my quarry is not an overdetermined or overly specific program but rather frameworks of conventionally encoded expressive states and processes. These, in turn, serve to organize and constrain the widely varying individual interpretations of a listener historically informed in a musical style.

That I have chosen Beethoven for my development of the model should come as no surprise, since his music has lent itself to extensive investigation along expressive as well as structural lines. In building upon a wealth of accepted knowledge as well as recent discoveries about Beethoven's highly dramatic and increasingly configured expressive "language," I can forego many of the digressions that would be required for a less well-known style in order to establish historical or cultural plausibility. On the other hand, I have at times taken pains to belabor an obvious interpretation in order to provide a perhaps not-so-obvious explanation for its stylistic coherence. And I have pursued the cultural roots of a less familiar concept, that of *abnegation*, for which the Appendix provides extensive literary justification.

Historically, Beethoven's highly dramatic and increasingly expressively configured musical "language" has been subject to numerous interpretations, ranging from the overly literal (Arnold Schering's bizarre attribution of literary works as hidden programs) to the metaphysical (J. W. N. Sullivan's musings on Beethoven's spiritual development). In every case, critics are responding to something very real in their experience of the music, but without a stylistic theory consistently tying expressive interpretations to structural features, those impressions may appear less than convincing. My aim is to provide a stronger theoretical—indeed, semiotic—basis for the explanation of commonly held convictions, as well as to expand the range of stylistically informed interpretations.

It is not my intention, however, to investigate the history of Beethoven reception or to debate the sequence of theoretical and aesthetic stances in the eighteenth or nineteenth centuries.[1] Nor, on the other hand, am I proposing a general theory or "language of music" equally applicable to all tonal styles (as in Deryck Cooke, 1959). I have concentrated on one style because theories of musical meaning must be stylistically constrained to have validity. Nor have I attempted to survey or critique the numerous semiotic approaches to music that have appeared in the past twenty years, as can be found in an illuminating recent guide to the field (Monelle, 1992).[2] Finally, I am not attempting to establish a scientific approach to music cognition, although I would claim that any account of music cognition that ignores the kind of meaning dealt with here will be impoverished from the start.[3]

Instead, I am developing a modern theory of meaning compatible with Peircean semiotic theory, and applying that theory to the historical reconstruction of an interpretive competency adequate to the understanding of Beethoven's works in his time. I am not proposing specifically modern interpretations in themselves. Although a semiotic theory may be more capable of dealing with expressive meaning than were the aesthetic theories of Beethoven's time, my aim is a more contemporaneous explanation of expression in Beethoven—for which Beethoven, or Czerny, or E. T. A. Hoffmann left but a series of tantalizing clues in their respective letters, comments, or essays on the music.

A semiotic approach need not pretend to exclusivity, however; it can and should draw freely from available historical and theoretical scholarship. Thus, my results need not be incompatible with those of traditional formal or Schenkerian analyses. Rather, I view my approach as an indispensable complement, providing insights often unavailable from a formalist perspective, and extending the limits of musical understanding by offering a wider range of hypotheses for the explanation of musical structures.

I have purposefully selected a style whose expressive aspects have been featured in recent scholarship (see the Preface), since well-established speculation is always the best base for further leaps of the imagination. Core studies by Charles Rosen (1972, 1980) and Leonard Ratner (1980) on the Classical style in general, and notable work on aspects of Beethoven's music by a wide range of musicologists cited in chapters to follow, have furthered the interpretation of formal structures in terms of their cueing of expressive content at all levels in Beethoven's works. I think I offer something new to that effort, but the reader can benefit as much as I have from the rich network of expressive meanings already established for these works (with varying degrees of acceptance by theorists and musicologists, to be sure). It is also heartening to see at least occasional reference to the term *semiotics* in recent work that I would construe as implicitly semiotic in its concerns.

The organization of the book reflects my methodological strategies. In Part I, four chapters of close analytical interpretations (1, 4, 6, and 8) are interspersed with four chapters elaborating the theoretical foundations of my interpretive claims (2, 3, 5, and 7). Thus, what might appear speculative in an analysis is often more fully established as a correlation in the theoretical chapters which follow. The distinction between correlation and speculative interpretation, however, is clearly dependent on one's perspective within an ongoing theoretical investigation. A correlation is, in one sense, merely an interpretation that has been codified by the systematic formulation of those structural oppositions ensuring its consistent recognition from work to work within a style.

Some aspects of an interpretive analysis, however, may not be conducive to establishment in terms of stylistic correlations. Indeed, the subjective range of further interpretations is beyond theoretical accounting in any systematically specific fashion. I freely acknowledge the limitless range of *subjective* (personal, or private) interpretations, while necessarily limiting my focus to the reconstruction of plausible *intersubjective* (shared, or sharable) interpretations, insofar as they are based upon an emerging model of Beethoven's stylistic competency.

In a broader sense, my hermeneutic work (historical and speculative pursuit of potential meanings) is but a sample of how the basic semiotic model of markedness might be applied in a stylistically and individually sensitive way. I hope that this study may also serve as an illustration of the interdependency of hermeneutic and structuralist approaches in recovering a more complete artistic competency. But I trust that one broader implication of my semiotic approach will not be missed: the model of markedness can be useful for the study of musical styles whose meanings are far less specific than those I have claimed for Beethoven.

One of the major theoretical claims of the book (introduced early on, but fully developed only in Chapter 10) is that the same semiotic mechanism, markedness, underlies both musical meaning and stylistic growth. Michael Shapiro (1983) claims that markedness qualifies as a universal in any human semiotic system, whether linguistic, sociological, or artistic. It is only at this rather abstract theoretical level that I would recognize a unifying, and perhaps universal semiotic mechanism underlying the creation and interpretation of musical stylistic meaning.

PART

I

Interpretation and Theory

I

A Case Study for Interpretation

The Third Movement of Op. 106 (*Hammerklavier*)

Presuppositions

Interpretation is the beginning and the end of all musical understanding. Whether as performers, theorists, or historians, we are constantly interpreting sounds through time as meaningful—in other words, as music. The varieties of musical understanding range from the recognition of patterns (one clue to the intentionality behind a musical work) to the reconstruction of a style; from the processing of musical relationships to the adducing of their expressive correlates; from the kinetic energy transmitted by a performance to the abstract speculation occasioned by the contemplation of a work. Each of these approaches to meaning is relevant from a semiotic standpoint.

As a performer and a listener I have experienced emotions and thoughts directly evoked by the music, and I have also known that aesthetic distance from which one recognizes and appreciates expressed states without an empathetic internalizing of actual emotions. Each of these responses is semiotically relevant, as well. I do not value one form of experience over the other, but I recognize that they have more to do with the receptive mode I have chosen than with the categories of meaning delimited by the work. It is the latter that I wish to illuminate.

Furthermore, in choosing to reconstruct a *stylistic competency*[1] that places historical constraints on interpretation, I do not presume to devalue the multiplicity of semiotically interesting approaches to Beethoven arising from later stylistic and cultural universes. Along with recent hermeneutic approaches (L. Kramer [1990], Abbate [1991]), I am interested in aspects of musical expressive meaning that go beyond current norms of musical analysis, and in neglected cultural evidence to the degree that it supports the historical reconstruction of expressive meaning.

But my investigation in Part I is framed by two broader questions, reflecting the alternation of chapters between interpretation and theory. First: since it is impossible ever to prove (in the scientific sense) a given expressive interpretation, can one nevertheless establish an interpretation as highly plausible based on mutually supportive evidence drawn from inside and outside the work? Second: if consensus cannot be reached on particular labels for expressive meanings, can one nevertheless explain the consistency with which one correlates musical structures in a style with expressive meanings? The first inquiry demands a hermeneutic approach (though grounded in prior stylistic competencies); the second demands a structuralist accounting (though generalizing from speculative interpretations of individual works toward the coherent style that can support those interpretations). Each approach depends on the other; together they constitute a music semiotics based on the reconstruction of a stylistic competency.

Elsewhere I have defined artistic style as "that competency in symbolic functioning presupposed by the work, and required for its interpretation as a work of art" (1982). By using the term *competency*, I mean to indicate that style is more than a repository of *types*. As an interpretive competency, style also goes beyond the bald generative capacities of a rule-based grammar. Instead it balances constraints with productive principles and provides flexibility such that apparent violations of lower-level constraints can be compensated at a higher level in order to preserve the consistency of those general principles. Indeed, as

Leonard Meyer (1956, 1973) has taught us, hierarchies of expectations deferred—or implications that are immediately denied only to be ultimately realized—are one means by which tonal music achieves its expressive and dramatic effects. Thus, while style constrains expectancies, it must also provide room for unique strategies of realization.

As a case study of unique strategies within a coherent style, I turn to an interpretation of the slow movement of Beethoven's Piano Sonata in B♭, Op. 106. My construal of expressive and dramatic events moves beyond those predictable merely from Beethoven's choice of sonata-allegro form for the movement. But the hermeneutic investigation will uncover both local and global expressive meanings that are clearly amenable to general formulation as part of a stylistic competency. The following two chapters will demonstrate how these speculative expressive interpretations can be supported by consistent oppositions in a style, thereby achieving the stability of *correlations*.

A Hermeneutic Reading of the Slow Movement of Beethoven's Piano Sonata in B♭, Op. 106 (*Hammerklavier*)

A hermeneutic approach is geared toward the unusual detail, the striking feature, of a work as a clue to its expressive or thematic significance.[2] Formal aspects of coherence include the use of sonata form at the stylistic level (see Figure 1.1) and the motivic descent in thirds at the *strategic* level. Charles Rosen (1972: 407–34) has exhaustively analyzed the latter as thematic for the sonata cycle as a whole, and I will not rehearse that analysis here. Unusual aspects of the form include its remote key of F♯ minor (in the context of a work in B♭ major), its expansive first theme group (with two related themes presented in oppositional textures and juxtaposed by an interruption—the dotted line in the diagram); a strikingly brief transition that moves to VI instead of III (which Rosen explains in terms of the descent-in-thirds motive projected to the larger tonal structure); an apparent modulation to B major near the end of the second group (which is then rationalized as V/ii in D); and the appearance of G major, the Neapolitan, for a final return of the second theme in the coda. The expressive interpretation I propose is able to relate all of these unusual features, along with other, more local events, as motivated parts of a coherent *expressive genre* for the movement.

The opposition between B♭ major and F♯ minor is important with respect to both mode and tonal distance. Minor vs. major mode *corre-*

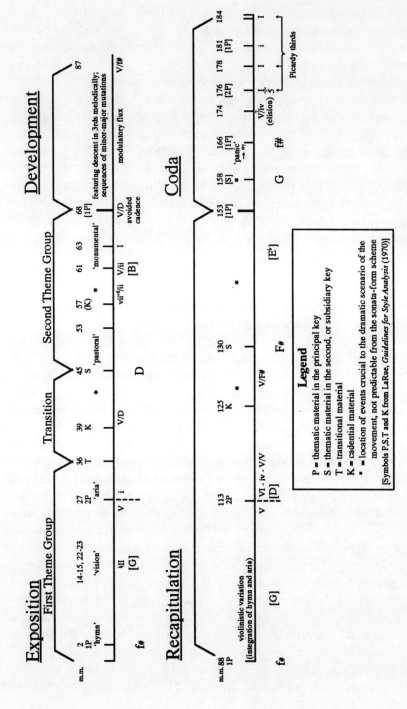

Figure 1.1. Form diagram. Beethoven, Piano Sonata Op. 106, third movement.

lates with tragic vs. nontragic in the Classical style, and distant vs. closely related tonality correlates with extremity vs. normalcy. Thus, the movement can be interpreted, not surprisingly, as extremely tragic.

Another opposition, between monophonic unison and homophonic chordal textures, characterizes the opening (see Example 1.1, mm. 1–

Example 1.1. Beethoven, Piano Sonata in B♭, Op. 106 (*Hammerklavier*), third movement, mm. 1–20.

2). The brevity of the former texture, along with the fact that the latter initiates a self-contained phrase, suggests that the opening bar is to be heard as introductory. In addition to this structural significance, the opening texture correlates with a state of expectancy, suggesting a profound utterance. Janet Levy (1982) has linked such unison textures to the ceremonial or theatrical; they may suggest an "episode 'outside' the realm of the real events of the piece" (528). Her interpretation applies to the role of this curtain-raising measure, in which, not paradoxically, the veil descends as well.

The thick chordal texture that follows is also quite *topical* (Ratner, 1980) in the style, suggesting the high *stylistic register* of a hymn, with its spiritual and solemn connotations. Indeed, this particular hymnic texture is one I would construe as "monumental," a species characterized by primary diatonic triads, slow harmonic rhythm, and a slow tempo. The variation theme of the last movement of Op. 111 provides an extreme case (see Example 1.2, mm. 13–16). One other striking feature of the monumental texture is the primitive effect of chord repetition across the barline to create a stasis that might be interpreted as timelessness (Example 1.1, mm. 16–17; Example 1.2, mm. 15–16).

One might also thus interpret the profound grief of this theme as suggesting a certain objectivity or distance, at least at first. But the contrary motion of lines expanding outward (Example 1.1, mm. 3–5) creates an effect of (expansive) yearning or longing that in turn reveals a more human agency and the dynamics of its will. This effect is enhanced by the parenthetical registral collapse to a diminished seventh chord (m. 5), which signals a reversal in the direction of the contrary motion in m. 6, when the extreme register of the bass is restored. The collapse of m. 5 can be interpreted in terms of its sonor-

Example 1.2. Beethoven, Piano Sonata in C minor, Op. 111, second movement, mm. 13–16.

ity (anxious) and its parenthetical quality, as well as in its undermining of the attempted expansion.

In the context of spirituality suggested by the hymn topic, one might reasonably interpret the event as akin to a spiritual qualm, or tremor of doubt, that besets the previous effort to rise out of the oppressiveness of grief. That obsessiveness is enhanced by the repeated chords in m. 8, and then by the dominant pedal and prolongation of mm. 9–13, where attempts to ascend are trapped within the arpeggiation of, ultimately, a dominant ninth (m. 12). The poignance of these waves of lament is focused by the diminished-seventh suspensions that occur on successive downbeats (mm. 10–13).

With the half cadence in m. 13, a striking harmonic event takes place, as the dominant collapses internally to become vii°⁷/V of the Neapolitan key area. The modulatory "transformation" is enharmonically achieved, which might suggest an interpretation as sudden insight, or epiphany, typical of such surprise modulations in both Classical and Romantic styles.

But there are other oppositions which both support and further define the nature of that sudden insight. The mode changes to major, melody and then accompaniment shift to a higher register, texture is pared down, and harmony is rather static (plagal), with a simplicity that recalls the pastoral. There is also a parenthetical quality to this suspended moment in that it returns to the prevailing mode, texture, and theme after a brief two bars.[3] Interpreting these mutually supportive oppositions leads past the label "nontragic" for major mode, and further specifies the passage as "spiritual" (hymn texture), "serene" (pastoral simplicity of harmony and melody), and "transcendent" (higher register, thinner texture).

One further detail completes the unmistakable associations of this passage: the resolution of the vii°⁷/V to what I call an *arrival six-four*. The sense of transformation to an "elevated" major tonic triad suggests its usage in Liszt, and its rhetorical designation as a "salvation six-four."[4] The opposition of major to minor resembles the effect of a Picardy third, and the cueing of closural stability by the cadential six-four is such that one may exploit it without ever completing the cadence (thus my term, *arrival six-four*). A similar effect, geared to *thematic* resolution at the point of arrival, is found in the coda to the first movement of Op. 101 (Example 1.3), which is analyzed further in Chapter 4. In both cases, the point of arrival has an expressive connotation of transcendent resolution, as opposed to mere syntactic resolution.

Example 1.3. Beethoven, Piano Sonata in A, Op. 101, first
movement, mm. 85–92.

These observations suggest further interpretation of the insight in
mm. 14–15 (in Example 1.1) as a vision of grace in the midst of tragic
grief. Although the brief window is soon closed, it sets up expectations
for the ultimate goal of the movement. An expressive genre that drama-
tizes the move from tragic to transcendent is indeed appropriate for the
movement, as one might surmise from the form diagram in Figure 1.1.
The movement ends with a Picardy third, and the coda features the
spiritual associations of the Neapolitan key area by using it for a transcendent reappearance of the second theme. The second theme is now
transcendent in that it "goes beyond" its stylistic recapitulation in F♯
major, by "transcending" that return a half step higher in the remote
key of G major. This return in the coda is not so much concerned with
syntactic or formal tonal resolution (although the Neapolitan might be
considered a substitute for the stylistic closural effect of a subdominant
area) as it is with the accomplishment of *thematic* resolution. The key of
G has taken on an associative significance for the work, and its return
helps achieve the *thematic* closure required by this expressive genre.

With the larger scheme in mind, let us return to the analysis of the
opening theme. After the brief vision of grace (mm. 13–14), the
deferred cadence in F♯ minor arrives on a weak beat (m. 17), giving way

Example 1.4. Beethoven, Piano Sonata in B♭, Op. 106 (*Hammerklavier*), third movement, mm. 26–31.

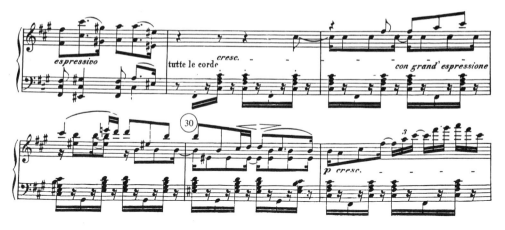

to a large-scale varied return of material from the earlier dominant pro-longation, and leading to a final cadence (Example 1.4, mm. 25–26). The one-measure extension of that cadence in m. 26 is left hanging on the dominant, and a new, aria-like theme emerges from an accompani-mental vamp. Beethoven indicates *tutte le corde* with this theme, which further sets it in opposition to the original theme's *una corda*. But the most striking opposition is between topics: hymn vs. aria. The expressive correlation for this aria is that of a more foregrounded and personal utterance—foregrounded in that the *tutte le corde* melody projects above the accompaniment, and personal in that the solo aria has a color-atura intensity.[5] The aria is set in opposition to the more distanced and objective correlation of the hymn.[6] The *thematic*, instead of an expected *tonal*, opposition at this point suggests a more Romantic than Classical rhetoric. (The opposition of character in turn motivates the schizophre-nic dynamic contrasts in the development section, where juxtapositions of loud and soft dramatize the accelerated descent in thirds.)

Since the transition does not begin until ten measures after the new theme has established itself, a competent listener might have no clear idea of the formal scheme for the movement at this point. Harmonically, the oscillation between tonic and dominant seventh recalls the obses-siveness of the dominant prolongation in the first theme. That oscilla-tion also provides a stable base for an expressive melodic discourse incorporating the suspensions and ninths found in the first theme. Emphasizing that point of similarity, one might consider an alternate interpretation of the theme as an expressively varied counterstatement, eventually leading to a modulatory transition (Example 1.5, mm. 36–38). That formal interpretation, however, might depreciate the productive role of opposition between the two themes—an opposition that is thematic for the movement.

The efficient modulation by chromatic ascent (mm. 36–38) to the dominant of D major (prolonged in mm. 39–44) intensifies the harmonic motion, departing from a static tonic-dominant oscillation in a way that suggests a "willed" effort reaching toward a new state (as opposed to the "unearned," mystical transformation of the earlier modulation to the Neapolitan). When the new dominant is achieved, one might expect stasis to return. Strikingly, the transition's six-measure prolongation of the dominant is highly configured on the surface, filled with expressive poignance in its chromatic and twisting sixteenth-note motive. Mixture adds to the poignance by delaying the arrival of an unclouded major mode until the second theme. The chromatic drift downward, in opposition to the "willed" ascent (mm. 36–38), suggests a kind of yielding in response to unconquerable tragedy.

The most striking example of yielding involves the negation of a chromatic implication (m. 42). The progression is from vii°⁷/V to V$^4_2$, which negates the implication of G♯ in the bass to resolve to A, reversing instead to G♮. The G♮ then resolves normally to the F♯ of a I⁶ chord. To claim that the resolution of G♯ is transferred, or merely elided, would be to accommodate an apparent disturbance to a higher coherence, while perhaps devaluing its dramatic or expressive function.[7] In other words, what matters for interpretation is not simply the voice-leading coherence of the progression, but the expressive effect of its disruptiveness.

This progression not only cues the expressive correlation of "yielding" but suggests an interpretation of resignation.[8] That the resignation is not unproblematic is indicated by the presence of mixture, which helps create the chromatic turn in the alto that clouds the subsequent resolution to I⁶.

Interestingly, the second theme (mm. 44–51) might also be interpreted as resignational, in that it suggests a state of acceptance. The simple, triadic drops in the theme, landing on the "serene" third of the major triad, appear to relinquish the striving of the earlier chromatic ascent. Simple harmonies, parallel thirds, and the major mode all support an interpretation of the pastoral *topic* (see below, Chapter 3).[9]

Example 1.5. Beethoven, *Hammerklavier*, third movement, mm. 36–50.

Example 1.6. Beethoven, "Resignation" (1817), WwO 149, mm. 1–5.

Thematically, the opposition of pastoral to tragic was already suggested by the earlier transcendent vision (Example 1.1, mm. 14–15). This section, however, does not convey a sudden insight, but rather a sober and relatively positive acceptance.[10]

Further evidence for acceptance through resignation comes from a song written by Beethoven in 1817, entitled "Resignation" (WoO 149), and coincidentally in D major (see Example 1.6). The text speaks of the light going out and the need for the persona to be detached—perhaps the reason for major mode instead of the tragic minor mode.[11] Note the similar triadic drops in the melody.

A related melodic line with pastoral simplicity in the harmony is found in another, more famous passage: the "dona nobis pacem" from the Agnus Dei of the *Missa Solemnis* (see Example 1.7). This "plea for inner and outer peace" is later contrasted with a representation of the sounds of war. Thus, the pastoral qualities are appropriately oppositional, supporting cultural associations with a peaceful Arcadia.[12]

The resignational *Hammerklavier* theme is resolved to F♯ major in the recapitulation and (transcendently) resolved to G major in the coda. Given the associations of earlier appearances of the Neapolitan and the resignational acceptance linked with the theme, one might interpret its appearance in the coda as "transcendence through a positively resigned acceptance"—or spiritual *abnegation*.[13] But the *troping*[14] of meaning that leads me to link transcendence with resignation is also supported by the new version in the recapitulation of the vii°7/V-V4/2-I6 progression found in the transition section (Example 1.8, m. 127). The poignant chromatic turn, originally in the alto, has been replaced by a decorated suspension/appoggiatura figure in the tenor. As it echoes through the

Example 1.7. Beethoven, *Missa Solemnis*, Agnus Dei, mm. 96–100 ("Prayer for inner and outer peace").

Example 1.8. Beethoven, *Hammerklavier*, third movement, mm. 125–30.

registers, it recalls the beatific effect of such suspensions in a serene chorale. Transcendence of register, however brief, is supported this time by a subtle but significant change in surface figuration that transforms the earlier diminished sonorites into glowing major ones.

The change is significant, even though it involves what appears to be a mere surface feature and does not alter the basic structural voice leading. But the passage supports the hinging reversal of the expressive genre as a whole. It is here that the move to F♯ major is achieved, not merely syntactically by modulation, but expressively by transformation. Now the second theme, resolved by a tonal return to F♯ major, is also imbued with a sense of spiritual achievement.

Returning to the remainder of the exposition, one can uncover further evidence of the importance of this hinging progression in a series of progressively more distant harmonic and tonal reinterpretations of the G♯-G♮-F♯ voice leading. In m. 53 (see Example 1.9) the second theme is succeeded by a passage that ascends in a very "uplifting" manner.[15] The ascent begins to acquire the character of human aspiration, with increasingly agitated applied diminished sevenths (end of m. 55 through m. 56) exacerbating the "willed" attempt or struggle to regain the transcendence associated with a higher register. The climax is undercut by another diminished-seventh collapse at the end of m. 56. When G♯-G♮-F♯ in the bass is reharmonized it leads more poignantly from vii°7/V-V$^4_2$ to a surprise vii°6/ii evasion (m. 57). The change of register on the surprise diminished chord serves to freeze the action. This interpretation is supported by the *una corda* and sudden change in rhythmic duration. The reinterpreted F♯ in the bass undergoes yet another diminished-seventh collapse in m. 59, after a failed attempt to cadence positively in m. 58. Note how the "arrival six-four" on the second half of m. 58 is undermined by the move from V to vii°7/IV. The resolution to IV in m. 59 is immediately subject to mutation (iv), almost redundantly supporting the tragic undermining of the passage.

One last effort to resolve transcendently in D major by means of the rhetorical arrival six-four is thwarted, this time by a deceptive move that finds G♯-G♮ in the upper voice (middle of m. 60). When G♮ resolves to F♯, it has been transcendently transformed by enharmonic reinterpretation of the diminished seventh chord, leading apparently to B major (m. 61), in a prototypical example of the monumental texture described earlier. The chordal stasis of B major captures the enigmatic aspect of transcendence, and the cadence in D major is accomplished with near mystical simplicity (mm. 62–63). The cadence forces a retrospective interpretation of B major as merely V/ii, but a purely syntactic and synoptic analysis might devalue the expressive drama of B major as a key in its own right. Merely to arrive in a remote key like B major is a significant expressive event, even if the key is not confirmed.

Intepreting this passage in light of the previous efforts toward a transcendent cadence in D major, one can observe how the "earned" arrival

Example 1.9. Beethoven, *Hammerklavier*, third movement, mm. 52–63.

six-fours were thwarted and collapsed, but the "unearned" insight suggested by the modulatory transformation to B major, with its monumentally profound texture, leads magisterially to the goal. The final cadence in D, sought but denied to the will, appears to be achieved through the providential agency of an extrapersonal force.

Looking back over the exposition, one may observe that many of the crucial expressive events occur within sections that are typically devoted to conventional closural material: the end of the transition (mm. 39–44) and the end of the second group (especially mm. 55–63). Beethoven has taken the formal security of these locations for granted in order to pursue some rather exploratory chromatic music. And the importance of these passages for the unfolding dramatic scenario exceeds that which we might attribute to the inherent dramatic rhetoric of sonata form itself. In other words, the process by which the dominant of the new key is achieved is not the point of dramatic focus; instead, the crucial dramatic reversal takes place within the prolongation of that dominant. The *thematic* importance given to material in these locations suggests the kind of growth process which earlier led Beethoven to invest such thematic significance in his introductions and codas (for example, the first movement of Op. 13).

As mentioned earlier, the development section is involved with the opposition between inward and outward expressions, alternating texturally between the descending-third motive and an ascending arpeggiation, and dynamically between vehement *sfs* and *una corda* responses. Tonally, as Charles Rosen (1972: 424–25) has shown, this development mirrors the development of the first movement. Here, the obsessive descent through thirds features colorful modulations and occasional mutations. But the section's rather traditional role in the movement requires less analytical attention.

The recapitulation, on the other hand, begins with a strikingly *integrational* return of the *hymn* theme in a texture that recalls the soloistic intensity of the *aria* theme—here, more suggestive of violin technique with its numerous octave-displaced pitches in the figuration (Example 1.10).[16] The Neapolitan vision of transcendence appears, but less texturally differentiated (Example 1.11, m. 100), furthering the thematic integrational strategy of the return. Upon the varied repeat, the Neapolitan vision receives a more distinctive texture (Example 1.12, mm. 108–109), including an oscillating accompaniment and a sweetening in parallel thirds to support the pastoral as opposed to the tragic.

With the interrupted cadence a tonal shift occurs, and the aria theme returns deceptively in D major (VI of F♯ minor), progressing logically through B minor (iv of F♯) to V/V-V resolving in F♯ *major*. The rewritten progression in the transition section has already been discussed, and the remainder of the recapitulation parallels the exposition. To sum up, it is the integrational, expressively *motivated* recastings of significant

Example 1.10. Beethoven, *Hammerklavier*, third movement, mm. 88–89.

Example 1.11. Beethoven, *Hammerklavier*, third movement, mm. 98–101.

Example 1.12. Beethoven, *Hammerklavier*, third movement, mm. 107–109.

material, not merely the tonal manipulations to place the second theme in F♯ major, that contribute to the drama of the recapitulation.

I have already interpreted the final appearance of the second theme in the coda, where the transcendence of G major combines with the resigned acceptance of the theme to suggest the trope of spiritual abnegation. That state does not hold, but leads to the tragic climax of the movement, an outburst of diminished sevenths and syncopated repeti-

Example 1.13. Beethoven, *Hammerklavier*, third movement, mm. 165–67.

tion in F♯ minor (Example 1.13). The tragic climax is effective partly because of the extremity of its opposition with the juxtaposed theme in G major. In addition, the *subito piano* (*una corda*) that undercuts the violent emotional outburst (m. 166) throws us back into the grieving lament of the depressed first theme, as though there could be no escape.

Interestingly, the return is marked by the unison texture characterizing the one-measure introduction, perhaps suggesting still another integration. In historical fact, we know that the order of composition was just the opposite. Beethoven's last word on this movement was the addition of the opening measure, provided in a letter to his publisher after the movement had already been sent. Understanding stylistically the primal significance of unisons, and strategically the utter desolation of this bare octave return next to the registral density of the outburst, one can infer a reason for preparing this texture from the beginning: to allow it to develop in significance as an enunciation of the profoundly objective.

Although the tragic returns of F♯ minor in mm. 165 and 181 mar both the transcendent resolution in G major and the first attempt at a positive Picardy-third close in F♯ (Example 1.14, mm. 178–80), the extensive breadth of Picardy-third closure (mm. 184–87, as well) supports the interpretation of an overall move from tragic to transcendent. The returns to F♯ minor may be construed as "re-cognitions" of a tragic reality that can neither be defeated nor dismissed, even if spiritual transcendence is possible through abnegation or an extrapersonal agency. The triumph here is not the extroverted heroic victory of the Fifth

Example 1.14. Beethoven, *Hammerklavier*, third movement, mm. 174–end.

Symphony; rather, use of a higher stylistic register projects the drama into the realm of an interior, spiritual struggle.

The fragile status of transcendent closure leaves room for the epic-heroic intellectual struggle of the fugue that follows, which regains the heroic plateau of the first movement. The second fugal exposition of the finale (Example 1.15), however, shares key and character with the second theme in the slow movement: basic triadic descent, soft dynamic level, and longer durations (especially in the fugue, in relation to earlier sixteenth-note passages). Thus, the moment of relief that the second exposition provides might also be interpreted as a motivated spiritual insight akin to the positively resigned acceptance of the second theme in the previous movement. In the finale, when the second subject is com-

Example 1.15. Beethoven, *Hammerklavier*, fourth movement, mm. 250–53.

bined with the first for a double-fugal closing section, *integration* is completed not only within the movement, but with respect to a significant expressive goal of the previous movement. The integration of fugue subjects entails a corresponding semantic interaction, or *troping*, of meaning that tempers the heroic first subject with a spirituality born of the more serene second subject's reference to spiritual resignation.

If the interpretive journey has been convincing to this point, one reason is that all the outstanding or salient structural events have been related to an overarching hypothesis, the *expressive genre* "tragic-to-transcendent." In turn, local oppositions that are exploited in the movement have been analyzed for *stylistic* correlations that they exploit, and the *strategic* (work-specific) intepretations which their contextual use suggests. Later analytical chapters will uncover other instances of the stylistic *types* found in the *Hammerklavier* movement and provide further evidence for the interpretation given here.[17] It is time to turn to the problem of reconstructing oppositions in a style, and the theory of markedness which underlies correlations between structural and expressive oppositions.

II

Correlation, Interpretation, and the Markedness of Oppositions

The Structure of the Theory

There are two competencies involved in musical understanding, the stylistic and the strategic (Figure 2.1). These correspond respectively to the
general principles and constraints of a style, and the individual choices
and exceptions occasioned by a work. In the sense that styles and works
are different ontological categories, there will always be an irreducible
and productive interaction between the two in terms of their reconstruction by the theorist/historian. I call the interaction a "methodological dialectic" (Hatten, 1982: 100). It reflects a similar constructive

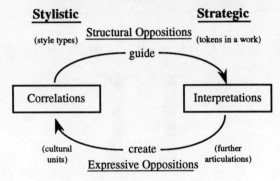

Figure 2.1. Basic model of the interaction between stylistic correlations and strategic interpretations, with respect to expressive meaning in music.

dialectic by a listener who learns a style in terms of generalizations from works, and whose strategic interpretation of works is in turn guided by an emerging stylistic competency.[1]

For expressive meaning, I have illustrated the dialectic between stylistic and strategic competencies by means of the interactive arrows linking stylistic *correlations* and strategic *interpretations* in Figure 2.1. Correlations and interpretations are conceived as mappings of expressive oppositions onto oppositions in musical structures. Correlations typically involve general *cultural units* (D. Schneider, 1968: 2, cited by Umberto Eco, 1976: 67) or expressive states defined by basic semantic oppositions in a culture (sad vs. happy; tragic vs. nontragic). These cultural units are mapped onto general stylistic types, as oppositionally defined by traditional or other theories (minor vs. major). Interpretations, on the other hand, further specify or contextualize expressive states as they relate to *entities*—structures or processes—actually manifested in musical works (i.e., *tokens* of their stylistic types).

Tokens have a range of allowable variation, constrained to the extent that such variation does not obscure the identification of their type. Thus, contextual *interpretation* of variation in a token can lead to more individuated and less general expressive meanings than are offered by the expressive *correlation* of its type. Despite the constraint of remaining "true to type," tokens allow for growth of meaning, and may lead to the creation of new types in the style.

The model I have outlined is somewhat misleading in its presumably hierarchichal derivation of interpretations through a process of further *articulation* or subdivision of general correlations. I will consider several alternatives to such a strict derivation in Chapter 7, where I examine the roles of troping, irony, and levels of discourse as less predictable means of achieving, or creating, meaning. Furthermore, a simple diagram cannot convey the subtleties of context as they affect tokens in a work, and contextual relationships are often more important than any variation within the token itself as a guide to interpretation. Larger contexts involving what I call *expressive genres* (Chapter 3) and *thematic discourse* (Chapter 5) highlight those structural features that require further interpretation.

Faced with the complex overlapping of many features in any given musical excerpt, one might accede to Roger Scruton's (1983: 50–52) pessimistic view that expression cannot be captured by rules because of the unpredictability of contextual effects. My purpose is not to predict the effects of unique contexts, nor to formulate rules of expression, but rather to provide, by means of correlations, starting points for further interpretations that will take account of a particular context.

For Scruton, another problem associated with theories of expression is that they are often "intransitive"[2] because "we are reluctant to identify the content independently of its form" (1983: 54, 98). In other words, if the expressive content is unique and can only be identified with reference to a particular musical passage, then it is problematic to assume a separation of form and content in the first place. Although I agree that unique forms in musical works should have correspondingly unique expressive contents, that is not to say that the more basic structures underlying them cannot be understood in terms of more-general correlations that in turn constrain the interpretation of those unique surface structures.

In his concern for establishing the intransitive nature of musical expression, Roger Scruton dismisses "the currently fashionable 'semantic' and 'semiotic' theories of musical meaning" (1983: 35), referring in particular to studies by Deryck Cooke (1959) and Jean-Jacques Nattiez (1975). The semiotic enterprise is seen as a rather trivial exercise, lacking a solid foundation in musical understanding (*Verstehen*):

> Anybody who is ingenious enough can interpret music as a language, or a code, or a system of signs; for example, by taking individual parts, struc-

tures, motifs and connections, and then correlating them with the objects, feelings and attitudes that they are supposed to symbolize. All that is required for this exercise is that the music should display syntactic structure (i.e., separately meaningful "elements" which can be combined into meaningful wholes), and a "field of reference" with which it can be conjoined. To express would then be to signify or stand for some item in the field of reference, according to rules of musical semantics. [1983: 35]

In my view, Scruton's charge applies only to what I have called the correlation stage, and it would be a valid argument only if that stage were not continually being enriched by the hermeneutic process of interpretation leading to new types (and thus more highly refined correlational networks). The musical examples to come should help counter the charge that a semiotic theory of music can offer only a simplistic decoding according to semantic rules.

The division of labor between stylistic and strategic competencies, I would argue, allows a musical semiotic theory to escape what would be a rather damning criticism put forth by Scruton:

It seems to me a singular defect of those theories of musical meaning which proceed by giving conditions for the application of emotion terms to music [is] that they solve the critical question ["when is it right to hear music in terms of some 'content' "] too *easily*. They enable us to say what a passage expresses, only by reducing the experience of expression to a recognitional capacity, and so removing its importance. [1983: 99]

But the *interactive* levels of understanding I have modeled here—the stylistic level of types and their correlations, and the strategic level of individual tokens and their interpretations in actual works—involve far more than mere recognition. The following list illustrates the variety of processes a listener must attempt, and a theorist reconstruct, in pursuing aspects of that elusive totality known as musical understanding (or *Verstehen*):

1. Identification of the structural *types* that exist in the *style* and their *correlation* with expressive types (cultural units);
2. Identification of *tokens* in works, and their potential correlations as tokens of stylistic types;
3. Interpretation of the contextual relationship among tokens in terms of their strategic usage;
4. Generalization of those features insofar as they define new *types*;

5. Incorporation of some of the new types (and their correlations) in one's *stylistic* competency for interpreting later works in the style (style *growth*[3]), as opposed to those that remain piece-specific;
6. Speculation about how to interpret the unique features of a work that are not (as yet) generalizable.

Another means of describing the fundamental dialectic between stylistic and strategic competencies is analogous to that of understanding an utterance in a language: first, one *decodes* according to the code (Scruton's "recognition") and second, one *interprets* according to the context. Linguists dispute the degree to which these two stages are autonomous in our processing of language, and even here a dialectic is at work. Although phonology is understood as a relatively closed system (defined by the analysis of distinctive features), it is faced with the range of (acoustical and articulatory) variation in phonemes as a result of their contextual placement in words. Other aspects complicating the phonological system, such as stress and intonation (the so-called suprasegmental aspects), are structurally dependent on input from higher (semantic and pragmatic) levels. Thus, even the most systematic level of language cannot insulate a competent listener from the demands of interpretive acts, and these interpretive acts can never be reduced to the simple decoding one might have assumed for this stage.

Philip Lieberman (1985) has hypothesized that listeners do not even need to process (or decode) every phoneme, but are able to understand with the aid of guesses based on their knowledge of larger units (words, syntactic constructions, semantic relationships, and pragmatic contexts).[4] Michael Silverstein (1976) argues that one cannot understand semantics without pragmatics. He cites the case of indexical lexemes (such as pronouns) that require a context to acquire their full significance.

The lesson from linguistics is that decoding (correlations) and interpreting (interpretations) need not be completely separable stages even when language is at its most systematic. By analogy, we should not expect the identification of style types and the interpretation of strategic types—similar to style analysis and critical analysis in Leonard Meyer's (1973) terminology—to be clearly autonomous stages, either for competent listeners or the theorists who reconstruct those competencies.

Another analogy one might draw from linguistics is that a commitment to meaning, however elusive, is the only check on the reality of formal categories. Such considerations are especially important for more remote styles, especially when theorists might be tempted to determine formal categories by mechanical segmentation or Gestalt-based perceptual groupings alone. The cognitive organization of music must be assumed to be richer than such rudimentary slicings could begin to predict or discover.[5]

But *markedness* is perhaps the most productive concept linguistic theory has to offer music theory. A concept generalized by Michael Shapiro (1983) for semiotic systems besides language, markedness can be applied to music in a way that helps explain the peculiar organization and fundamental role of musical oppositions in both specifying and creating expressive meanings.

The Concept of Markedness

Markedness as a theoretical concept can be defined quite simply as the valuation given to difference. Wherever one finds differentiation, there are inevitably oppositions.[6] The terms of such oppositions are weighted with respect to some feature that is distinctive for the opposition. Thus, the two terms of an opposition will have an unequal value or asymmetry, of marked versus unmarked, that has consequences for the meaning of each term.

As understood in linguistics, "[a] *marked* term asserts the presence of a particular feature, and an unmarked term negates that assertion" (Battistella 1990: 2). The marked term specifies phonological, grammatical, or conceptual information which is not made specific by the more general, unmarked term; thus, the unmarked term may be used either when the opposition does not matter or when the exclusion of marked information is required.

For example, when we use the unmarked term "cow," we may not need to distinguish the sex of the animal; when we use the marked term "bull," we specify male, and in that context, the use of cow would be more likely to cue the oppositional meaning of female. Thus, "bull" is marked for the distinction of gender, whereas "cow" is unmarked.

A *privative opposition* (presence of A vs. absence of A) functions in this manner; the unmarked term can be used either when A is not relevant or when A is expressly excluded. *Equipollent oppositions* (A vs. B, where A = not B, and B = not A), on the other hand, "assert the presence of contrary features rather than the presence or absence of a single feature" (Battistella 1990: 2). "Man/woman" is clearly a privative opposition (at least until current reforms affecting English usage are more generally accepted), since "man" (unmarked) can be used to refer generally to all humankind, whereas "woman" (marked) invariably specifies gender (just the opposite of the "bull-cow" example). On the other hand, the opposition "male/female" is equipollent.[7]

Another example may be helpful. In English and in other languages the difference between present and past tense does not, as one might think, have the meaning "presentness" vs. "pastness" in a symmetrical, equipollent, or mutually exclusive opposition. Rather, the opposition is privative and yields a corresponding asymmetry of content with respect to presentness and pastness. The marked tense in this opposition, the past tense, consistently carries the conceptual content of pastness; the unmarked present tense, on the other hand, can and often does convey presentness or pastness. Consider the sentence "He works late." Employing the unmarked present tense, the sentence can mean either that the person is working late now, or that he did and currently does work late. Past instances are inferrable from such uses of the present tense. On the other hand, "He worked late" can never refer to a present state of working. Indeed, the narrower range of meaning, restricted to past events, suggests a marked opposition with respect to the unmarked present tense.

Singular vs. plural also illustrates privative opposition, with singular being the unmarked category. Battistella gives the following examples of the use of singular nouns in their broader or more general usage that includes the plural:

The *beaver* builds dams. [beaver*s* build dams]
When I came to, I saw that *everyone* was staring at me and I smiled up at them. [*all* were staring]
The *team* is putting on their uniforms. [the *teammates* are putting on their uniforms]
Both Ford and Carter were *president* during difficult times. [Ford and Carter were both president*s*]
[Battistella, 1990: 4; bracketed glosses added]

Although markedness values are language-particular, certain universal tendencies do emerge. As Battistella observes, "singular number in nouns . . . seems to be universally unmarked with respect to the plural and dual; present tense is usually unmarked with respect to past" (1990: 24). Indeed, the suggestive relationship of marked/unmarked to atypical/prototypical, figure/ground, or foreground/background "suggests that markedness may be a useful concept for describing the organization of society, culture, and the arts" (Battistella, 1990: 5). I turn now to such considerations with respect to music.

Markedness and Music

A familiar opposition for music is that between major and minor modes in the Classical style. Minor has a narrower range of meaning than major, in that minor rather consistently conveys the tragic, whereas major is not simply the opposite (comic), but must be characterized more generally as nontragic—encompassing more widely ranging modes of expression such as the heroic, the pastoral, and the genuinely comic, or *buffa*. Although apparently equipollent, the opposition is actually asymmetrical because of the wider range of potential expressive states that correlate with the major mode. Indeed, one might argue that the opposition is also privative, in that major is occasionally used for expression of the tragic (Gluck's famous "Che farò senza Euridice") or poignant (the *Cavatina* movement from Beethoven's String Quartet in B♭, Op. 130, analyzed in Chapter 8).[8] The minor mode, on the other hand, is not likely to be used nontragically in Classical works, and modal mixture (the use of minor inflections in a major mode work) always indicates a tragic or poignant perspective.

One kind of evidence for the stylistic encoding of a marked opposition is that the distribution of terms often reflects the asymmetry of their opposition—in other words, the marked term will occur less frequently than the unmarked. This is true for minor vs. major in the Classical style, but not in the early Baroque, where minor does not consistently invoke expressive states within the realm of the tragic.[9]

Another kind of evidence for the markedness of the minor mode comes from the reception history of Classical works. If minor correlates with a narrower range of meaning than major, then works in minor should tend to provoke more-specific expressive interpretations than works in major (except for those major works that are themselves marked with oppositions enabling interpretation as heroic, pastoral, *buffa*, etc.). Indeed, if one considers some of the early- and middle-period Beethoven piano sonatas, one finds that the minor mode movements of Op. 2, no. 1; Op. 10, no. 1; and the *Pathétique*, *Moonlight*, *Tempest*, and *Appassionata* are the focus of much greater attention, and more specific expressive interpretation, than the major mode move-

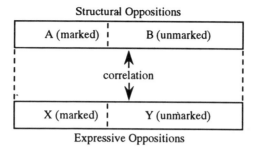

Figure 2.2. Markedness as the
asymmetrical organizational structure
underlying correlations between structural
and expressive oppositions.

ments of Op. 2, no. 3; Op. 10, no. 3; Op. 14, no. 2; Op. 31, no. 1; or
the *Waldstein*. Appellations such as the *Tempest*, whether sanctioned by
the composer or not, also reflect markedness. The major mode movements of sonatas that have received expressive titles—the *Pastoral* and
Les Adieux—are either characteristic in the case of the former, or
programmmatic in the case of the latter, thus illustrating markedness
with respect to oppositions other than mode.

Obviously, reception history can only roughly indicate tendencies. I
do not claim that works like the *Waldstein* cannot be interpreted in ways
further specifying the nontragic—there are clearly heroic and hymnlike
topical elements in the first movement, for example—but that to go
beyond "nontragic," one must invoke oppositions other than major vs.
minor mode.[10]

Assuming that the above analysis is correct, what is the function of
markedness values? Figure 2.2 illustrates how marked oppositions
organize the correlational mapping between structural and expressive
oppositional pairs (within the larger scheme of Figure 2.1). The marked
terms "line up" with each other and encompass a smaller area, since
they each reflect both a narrower range of (expressive) meaning and a
less-frequent usage (or better, a more-constrained distribution of places
where they can be used) than their unmarked counterparts. This "congruence" between the markedness of *signifier* and *signified* is considered
basic to markedness in language, and according to Battistella, it is
related to a fundamental principle known as *markedness assimilation*:
"marked elements tend to occur in marked contexts while unmarked
elements occur in unmarked contexts" (Battistella, 1990: 7).[11]

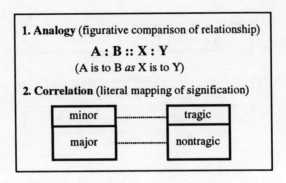

Figure 2.3. How correlation differs from analogy.

Analogous markedness is not, of course, the only relationship required to *motivate* the original association between oppositional pairs; other historical arguments are required, as Scruton's arguments would suggest. I have relied largely on a general consensus about the expressive meaning of the minor-major opposition for the Classical style, since probing historical motivations would take us too far afield. Markedness relationships can, however, reflect the coherence underlying correlations even when their original motivations have been lost. Motivations tend to break away when the correlation becomes *conventional*, or *symbolic*, as opposed to relying on an immediate *iconism* of properties shared by A and X, or B and Y. Thus, in one important construal, markedness may be understood as a *systematic motivation* in that it establishes the way stylistic meanings are encoded. Furthermore, as will be seen, markedness helps coordinate the growth of meanings in a style.

Correlations should not be equated with analogies, despite their obvious similarities. Analogies help motivate correlations, but correlations have a different structure (Figure 2.3). An *analogy* is a relationship arising from a comparison of relationships: A is to B as X is to Y, where "as" implies a figural meaning illuminating the nature of one relational pair in terms of another. A *correlation* is a more literal mapping of meaning (literal for a given style) coordinated by the analogous markedness values of the two pairs of oppositions. It is in this sense that A can "mean" X. "A is to B as X is to Y" does not imply that A means X, but that it relates to B in some way (similarity, contiguity, part-for-whole, etc.) comparable to the way X relates to Y. Often, that "way" requires the creativity of metaphor to interpret. Analogy can best be understood as one of the *motivations* underlying the mapping of a correlation (see Chapter 10).

Growth and Change of Markedness Values

In language, markedness values can change. As mentioned above, "man/woman" is, or at least has been, a privative opposition in that "woman" was marked for female but "man" was unmarked and could be used either specifically for male or generically for human (as in "mankind"). On the other hand, "male nurse" is an instance of a marked term, since nurse, the unmarked term, is culturally conceptualized as female.[12] Such "local reversals" indicate the relative status of markedness values and their "contextual as well as general nature" (Battistella 1990: 24–25).

We can observe similar cases of markedness growth in music. Consider the familiar opposition between major and minor triads exemplified by the use of a Picardy third to end a movement in a minor key (as in the slow movement of the *Hammerklavier*; see Example 1.14). In such cases, an opposition is activated between the (prevailing) minor tonic triad and (a final shift to) the major form. Both its limited distribution (it may occur only at the end of a movement, understood as including codettas and codas) and its special "effect" (a salience due to the striking shift in expected chord quality) can be considered as evidence for assignment of markedness to the Picardy-third tonic.

The asymmetrical relation characteristic of markedness evaluation suggests a special meaning for the Picardy-third tonic, a meaning more specific or narrower in range than would be associated with the use of a minor tonic triad in the same place. Formulations of that special meaning might range from the more syntactic (perfect closure, since more "consonant") to the more poetic ("light at the end of the tunnel," since reversing from tragic to nontragic in Classical and Romantic styles).[13] Regardless of how one attempts to characterize the new meaning, its particularity relative to an unmarked minor triad should be apparent. Indeed, conferring a label such as "Picardy third" in itself reflects the greater specificity of a marked term.

The important consequence of the stylistic closural markedness achieved by Picardy-third endings is that any movement in minor mode which ends on a minor tonic can now produce a new effect, one that would not have been possible before the Picardy third was established as a strong convention in the style. A new opposition has been created between the "might-have-been" background of an expected Picardy third and the now-unexpected appearance of the minor third in the final tonic. Since it is marked with respect to the potential Picardy-third

Example 2.1. Chopin, Prelude in F# minor, Op. 28, no. 8, mm. 31–end.

tonic, the meaning of the minor tonic is now more specific, no longer merely unmarked or neutral with respect to its chord quality. The meaning of the ending minor triad is specified by its opposition to the major tonic, leading to such interpretations as "denial of positive ending." This option is stronger if it actually denies a Picardy-third ending, as occurs at the end of Chopin's Prelude in F# minor Op. 28, no. 8 (Example 2.1).

The new opposition between the minor close and an expected major close, while requiring an initial, creative interpretation on the part of the listener, may be *encoded* as a systematic, stable part of the style. Indeed, the new opposition is already so well motivated by an established opposition in the style that *usage* (its instantiation in several pieces) need hardly be argued as a criterion for *encoding*. The importance of this point for artistic styles, where a crucial event may nevertheless be unique (as opposed to language grammars, where unique utterances are not focal) should be evident. If a clear oppositional derivation can be made, the resulting interpretation of musical meaning can rest on a foundation of stylistic competence even if the actual event is unique.

Style is a semiotic competency subject to growth and change, as the above examples suggest. Composers of musical works play with, or

Example 2.2. Bach, Prelude in E♭ minor, WTC I, mm. 36–end.

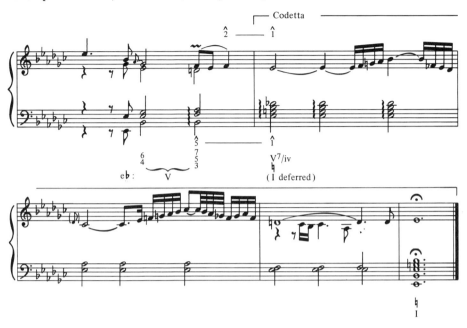

against, the oppositions encoded in the style. Of the many motivations for such play, associations by *analogy* are basic to human semiotic growth in any code or language.[14] The substitution just described can apply analogously to other cases where an effect can be achieved by substituting an opposing term for an expected entity. Indeed, oppositional substitutions may lead to a more general principle, such as "denial of implication" (Leonard Meyer, 1973), which may be fundamental to a stylistic, interpretive competency even though individual instances of it remain unique, unpredictable, or only retrospectively understood by a listener.

To return to closural situations, codettas or closing sections may reveal instances of *growth* that stem from the oppositions between major and minor tonic. At the end of the Prelude in E♭ minor from WTC I (Example 2.2), Bach exploits a similarity between the Picardy third and the dominant of the subdominant (compare Beethoven's related use of this device at the expected final cadence in the coda to the slow movement of the *Hammerklavier*; Example 1.14, m. 174). In the Bach example, the presumed final cadence elides with a codetta launched by V[7]/iv. The aural equivalence between the major tonic (I) and V/iv (despite

Minor Key (Presumed) Final Cadence	Markedness
(1.) V $\longrightarrow$ I$^{\#}$	Marked, Picardy third in opposition to expected i.
(2.) V $\longrightarrow$ i	Originally unmarked; now, after establishment of (1.), marked with respect to the expectation of a Picardy third.
(3.) V $\longrightarrow$ V^7/iv	Marked, as in (2.), but also as in (1.), since hints at Picardy third with raised $\hat{3}$, and predicts its arrival at the next cadence.

Figure 2.4. Strategic growth of markedness.

different functional interpretations) allows for their merging at the point of resolution of the structural dominant. To avoid interpretation as a Picardy-third tonic, however, the seventh is added to specify V^7/iv. This addition undermines the stability of "final" sonority in an elision that is both closural and initiatory: closural in that the crucial outer-voice resolutions of $\hat{5}$–$\hat{1}$ in the bass and $\hat{2}$–$\hat{1}$ in the soprano define, contrapuntally, the point of final cadence; initiatory in that the codetta (an expansion of the close) begins with a clear harmonic implication. Furthermore, because of the raised third ($\hat{3}$), the eventual Picardy-third tonic close is effectively foreshadowed.

Now it is the V^7/iv that is marked with respect to its oppositional usage against the expected tonic (whether major or minor) in this context. Its effect (and thus potential meaning) is more specific than we would find with a straightforward resolution to a tonic or with other, unmarked uses of V^7/iv.

In this case, and in the case of an (unexpected) ending on a minor triad, one can observe that the Picardy-third ending has become the unmarked term in two new oppositional contexts (Figure 2.4). This process involves strategic markedness that may well lead to style growth, or encoding as stylistic markedness.

Has the Picardy-third ending lost its original markedness? No, because markedness values adhere to oppositions whether or not those oppositions are foregrounded or implemented in a strategy. In other words, while salient events will tend to be marked, markedness must not be equated with salience. In this case the Picardy third is still marked with respect to any earlier minor triads, but the composer has created a new environment where it is possible for another chord to be used in place of the Picardy third (in this case, motivated by similarity, the $V^7/$ iv; in the earlier case, by opposition, the minor tonic). The growth of markedness can then be incorporated into the style—perhaps surviving in a later style, as its use by Beethoven suggests.

The further specification or articulation of meaning offered by a growth case (minor ending, $V^{(7)}/$iv) alters the relative sense of the Picardy third's range of content. Though still narrow with respect to minor tonics elsewhere in the piece, the effect of the ending major tonic now seems rather broad in relation to the "substitution" of a minor ending or a $V^7/$iv. If this observation is correct, then it would appear that the growth of style could be viewed from the perspective of efforts to further articulate the realms of meaning associable with musical events. Explaining expressive intentions as *motivations* for unusual syntactic or formal events (strategies) is obviously as important to their interpretation as analyzing the coherence of those unusual events in terms of their relation to (derivation from) normative voice leading, as in Schenkerian analysis.

Markedness of Key Relations

With experience in the style, one learns that Picardy thirds are confined to the ending of a movement (including its coda or codetta). Any earlier "major tonics" must be interpreted as dominants of the subdominant, as in the same Bach prelude exemplified above (m. 7, $V^6/$iv).

The final temporal location in a piece is marked, even in the most primitive styles, by the (at least retrospective) understanding of that temporal location as the last one. Western styles tend to anticipate and enhance the experience of ending a movement or a work by the use of material that cues a stylistic closural function. In the Classical style, reference to the subdominant is one such cue, suggesting another marked opposition, between moves to the dominant and moves to the subdominant. This opposition appears to be equipollent, in that a move to the dominant (whether by applied dominant or full modulation) is forward-looking, dynamic, dissonant, and nonclosural. The move to the subdominant, on the other hand, is backward-directed, static, stable, and closural. Rosen (1972: 23–27) generalizes the opposition to include any modulations to the sharp (dominant) side vs. the flat (subdominant) side as mapped by the circle of fifths for any given tonic key. This opposition dates back to Rameau, and it "eventually became the dominant factor in the conception of key qualities" (Steblin, 1983: 103).

The circle of fifths is also useful for mapping the relative distance of a modulation from the home key or between any two keys. As suggested by the *Hammerklavier* analysis in Chapter 1, the opposition between extremity (regardless of affect) and normalcy is based on the relative distance of keys.

Putting oppositions of direction and distance from tonic together with opposition of mode, we can interpret correlations of keys in the slow movement of the *Hammerklavier* still further: F♯ minor suggests an extreme (distant key), "dissonant" (dominant side), and tragic (minor mode) state in the context of a B♭ major work; and G major a correspondingly extreme (distant key), consonant (subdominant side), and nontragic (major mode) state, which can be further interpreted as serene (simplicity) and transcendent (higher register, half-step higher tonic as opposed to F♯ minor).

It is by exploring systematic and contextual oppositions, not by claiming absolute key characteristics, that one can avoid the inconsistencies of associations attributable to expressive pieces in those keys.[15] Correlations are based on the mapping of oppositions in expressive meaning to oppositions among keys, not upon one-to-one correspondences based on the presumed properties of a given key.

Types and Tokens

Another criterion for markedness has to do with divergence from the prototypical. In language, "front" vs. "back" can be evaluated according to the prototypical presentation of individuals from the front (the face is in the front, etc.). Thus, front is unmarked and back is marked as different from the norm (Battistella, 1990: 42; see also Lakoff, 1987: 60–61, cited by Battistella, 1990: 41). In considering the home key as normative and modulation as marked, I have made a similar distinction. Now I would like to extend this notion to the (privative) opposition between *type* and *token*, where the type is to be understood as unmarked and the token marked.

The philosopher and scientist Charles Sanders Peirce (1839–1914) was the first to introduce the terminology of types and tokens to distinguish entities at two different levels of reality. A type is an ideal or conceptual category defined by features or a range of qualities that are essential to its identity. A type is understood or conceived as an inference at the level of cognition; it does not exist at the level of perception, though acts of perception are fundamental to its inference. A token, on the other hand, is the perceptible entity that embodies or manifests the features or qualities of the type. Generally, those features and qualities are not the only ones which the token possesses; they are merely the ones which are relevant to its being understood as a token of the type. Thus, type and token exist at two fundamentally different levels, but their relationship allows us to pass smoothly from one to the other. For Peirce, symbolic signs designate types; for my theory, music structural types correlate with cultural units as types of expression, not necessarily with perceived or experienced emotions (although such reactions are not denied by my approach).

Type-token distinctions are common to any theory. In the broadest sense, the style as a whole could be considered a type, and works in that style would be tokens. The problem with such labeling is that it is too general to be of much use. Furthermore, if style is conceived as a competency, then its characterization merely in terms of oppositions with other styles would not be adequate to our understanding of its coherent organization. A more practical level for the study of types is that of more determinable entities in a style. These then enter into the larger competency of style, interacting with a strategic competency that can interpret the token as it goes beyond type identification.

A type—for example, "tonic triad"—is usually defined in terms of certain features. More sophisticated theories (such as Schenker's) include or imply an account of the range of variation permissible and the relevant context for identity as a tonic triad. Not every C–E–G sonority in the key of C is a functional tonic triad, and a tonic triad may be identified as such even if the third or the fifth is not represented. The fundamental assumption of any harmonic theory is that the listener can distinguish harmonic entities in pieces as tokens of their respective functional types. Even typical progressions (or *syntagmatic* relationships) may be categorized as types.

Interestingly, these "building blocks" of musical styles can have expressive associations in and of themselves—associations beyond the formal relationships implied by their functional definitions. The qualities (sonorities) of triads—major, minor, diminished, and augmented—have accrued associations based on their inherent tension or dissonance value in a given style. And many obvious syntagmatic examples—a major chord mutating to minor in a Schubert song, or a dominant moving to an augmented triad that suggests anxiety in a Wagnerian evaded cadence—are based on *paradigmatic* relationships, such as the substitution of one triad for another in a given context.

Markedness, however, is dependent not solely on distinctive features of the type itself (obvious candidates for opposition), but also on the oppositional positioning of the type in a larger paradigm of types (such as a functional system of chord relationships). The tonic, dominant, and subdominant triads in a major key are all equally major triads and thus lack oppositional distinctiveness when each is considered in terms of sonority. The operative distinctions in this case are provided by scale-degree placement—that is, the location of triads within the major diatonic system. The rare intervals which contribute to one's understanding of orientation and implication in a diatonic system, namely, the tritone and minor seconds (Babbitt, 1972; Browne, 1982), are not physically present in the triads themselves; rather, these relationships must be inferred from the context.

Markedness can also be invoked to explain the functional development of the dominant seventh, a chord type which possesses the rare interval of the tritone and which is the only major-minor seventh chord found among the diatonic seventh chords in major. When one considers the fact that its resolution involves the other two rare intervals of the diatonic set, the minor seconds, one understands the powerful systematic features that support a functional role for the dominant seventh chord.

The dominant seventh's narrower range of meaning, however, seems concentrated at the syntactic level, as illustrated by its powerful tendency to resolve to the tonic rather than progress to other chords. Perhaps because of its primarily syntactic role, the dominant seventh needs the influence of other features (textural, etc.) to claim an expressive content as specific as that accorded the diminished-seventh sonority.

It is rare, but not without precedent in Beethoven, that the Mm^7 sonority is used not simply as a functional V^7 but for its particular richness as a sonority type. For example, in the second movement of Beethoven's String Quartet, Op. 95 (see Example 2.3, mm. 149–50), an expanded C Mm^7 (major triad with minor seventh) has dominant orientation with respect to its neighboring F major six-four, but it is used here more for the effect of its sonority. That effect is emphasized by the *forte* dynamic level, the two-bar stasis of repetition, and the chromatic relation (as V^7/III) to the key of D minor that governs the phrase. Indeed, the C^7 helps create a moment of insight (like an epiphany) by its

Example 2.3. Beethoven, String Quartet in F minor, Op. 95, second movement, mm. 145–53.

momentary, glowing harmonic reversal of the fugato's tragic minor and chromatic subject. It also anticipates (or contributes to) the expressive character that the home-key functional dominant seventh will possess when it arrives with equivalent textural emphasis (Example 2.4, mm. 165, 168). The true dominant seventh does not merely participate in

Correlation, Interpretation, and the Markedness of Oppositions | 47

Example 2.4. Beethoven, String Quartet in F minor, Op. 95, second movement, mm. 164–70.

Example 2.5. Maximal oppositions of pitch and sonority in typical Landini under-third cadences.

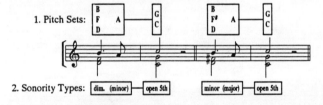

syntactic closure; it signals a more positive expressive closure for the coda through a clear affirmation of its own, reinforcing the positive ending in D major. These interpretive considerations leap beyond the current discussion, however, and will be pursued in later chapters.[16]

The historical development of harmonic cadences offers an illuminating example of markedness in the development of stylistic types. The "vii°⁶–I" and "vii⁶–I" three-voice cadences of Machaut and Landini, shown in Example 2.5, were originally conceived intervallically as pairs of voices against the lowest voice. A more complex sonority (diminished or minor) is juxtaposed to the simple sonority of the open fifth/octave "perfection" of the final sonority. The under-third cadence ($\hat{7}$–$\hat{6}$–$\hat{1}$ in the upper voice) maximizes the differentiation of actual pitches by adding a fourth, nontonic pitch to the pretonic sonority. Thus, stepwise voice leading, the return to tonic, and the move to a closural "perfection" are intensified by a maximal differentiation (sonority type and pitch collection) between the two cadential entities.

Note an interesting difference between this case and that of the major I, IV, and V triads. In the earlier cadences, specificity of syntactic function is earned without benefit of a comparable underlying harmonic system, but rather by means of locally maximized differentiation. Of course, any progression could become a formula with sufficient usage to "grind in" the habit of recognition; however, the locally systematic motivation of maximal differentiation has greater explanatory force in accounting for the success of this particular "habit."[17]

Structural distinctions cannot in themselves tell us what expressive correlations they may take. For that, a clearer notion of available cultural units (semantic oppositions) is required, along with a careful hermeneutic effort to correlate those semantic distinctions with the structural or formal distinctions available in the style.

Determining such correlations could become a flawed enterprise if one attempted to create a vocabulary of expressive types that had relatively fixed and overly precise meanings (as in Deryck Cooke, 1959). On the other hand, one can find general (type) correlations that are well established for certain sonorities—correlations that may apply even when the sonority is encountered in a minimally defined context.

One such example is the diminished-seventh sonority, mentioned earlier. The opening of Beethoven's String Quartet in C, Op. 59, no. 3, features a diminished seventh chord that conveys more than a sense of syntactic ambiguity.[18] There is also the straightforward expressive association between the diminished-seventh sound and a sense of "tension," or more specifically, human *angst*, that has a long history of rhetorical usage going back to early Baroque recitative. The strength of this association, which can be considered a (stylistic) correlation, is due to a markedness valuation based on the uniqueness of the sonority in the minor mode. In other words, there is systematic, and not simply habitual, justification for the consistency of this correlation. And, like the Medieval cadence, the uniqueness of a diminished-seventh sonority enables a strong correlation to be fixed in advance of the stabilization of the functional harmonic system of the later Baroque.

The potential syntactic ambiguity of the diminished-seventh sonority (based on its symmetrical acoustical interval structure, which allows any of its pitches to be understood enharmonically as a leading tone) is

Example 2.6. Beethoven, String Quartet in F major,
Op. 59, no. 1, third movement, mm. 1–2.

certainly part of the significance of its use by Beethoven, but a tendency to focus exclusively on that aspect may lead one to neglect the expressive correlation of the sonority type itself. And the ambiguous use of the type can in turn suggest a more distinctive expressive interpretation than one would give to a diminished seventh chord unambiguously preceded by its tonic triad.[19]

Types and Tokens in Beethoven's Triad Doublings

Let us assume that we have a proper description of "tonic triad." A description of this type in the style of Beethoven would no doubt include such properties as scale-degree membership and other relationships that would serve to distinguish the functional tonic triad from passing chords and the cadential six-four. A complete description of *invariant* features would have to make allowance for common exceptions involving a missing third or fifth of the tonic triad, omissions which are not sufficient to destroy its identity. Indeed, a category such as tonic triad, which we tend to take for granted in theory pedagogy, is rather tricky to characterize exhaustively when one considers the wide range of variation in accepted tokens of the functional type.

One class of variation among tonic triad tokens that does not affect the functional type is doubling (as opposed to inversion, where the six-

Example 2.7. Beethoven, String Quartet in F minor, Op. 95, second movement, mm. 182–end.

four position creates a different functional interpretation). Related to the question of omitting the chordal third or fifth is the doubling of roots, thirds, and fifths within a given tonic triad token. Interestingly, two clusters of variation in tonic triad tokens are those that emphasize root and fifth (excluding the third), and those that emphasize root and third (excluding the fifth). Indeed, cases of each can be found to support an expressive content which is far more specific than that found in cases of more normal doublings.

Example 2.6 shows the opening of the third movement of Beetho-

Example 2.8. Beethoven, String Quartet in C♯ minor, Op. 131, second movement, mm. 189–end.

ven's String Quartet in F major, Op. 59, no. 1. In m. 1 the open fifth token of the F minor tonic triad is clearly emphasized. Compare the starkness and stern quality of this example with Example 2.7, the ending of the second movement of the String Quartet in F minor, Op. 95, which concludes in mm. 189–90 with a tonic triad possessing two roots, two thirds, and no fifth. The latter example has a warmer, sweeter, more-consoling expressive quality, precisely the quality appropriate for an interpretation of the movement as moving to a state of grace after the

Example 2.9. Beethoven, String Quartet in F, Op. 135, third movement, mm. 52–end.

tortuous, ricercar-like, minor fugato in the middle of the movement. Further instances of this marked type occur at the final tonic close of two other string quartet movements—Op. 131, II, and Op. 135, III (see Examples 2.8 and 2.9). Such consistent usage provides strong evidence that the doubled third in this context was a stylistic type for Beethoven.

These tokens may be generalized as a new *type* since they exploit what previously were only free variants (doubling or omission of third or fifth). The tokens have now become *marked* with respect to the range of doubling variation. By carving out their own new *invariants*, they can be understood as having become new types, stable enough to govern their own range of *tokens*.[20] In the process, normal doubling is understood now as unmarked, in opposition to the marked types. Figure 2.5 summarizes this growth process.

Though strategically earned types may be generalized from one or two pieces, the survivability of these types necessarily depends on subsequent use. Usage may not be a sufficient condition, however. The new opposition must also fit with those already in the style, and the richer its web of relationships with other oppositions, the more likely it is to survive in the style after its other motivations have worn out or been lost.

Correlation, Interpretation, and the Markedness of Oppositions | 53

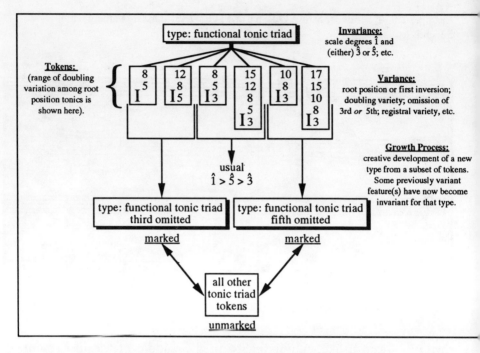

Figure 2.5. Growth of types for triad doublings.

Open-fifth tonic triads have other associations, most notably, the intertextual link with Renaissance style by way of the *stile antico* of Classical church music (recall the ending of the Mozart *Requiem*). But the deletion of the fifth and the balancing of thirds and roots becomes an original and identifiable type with Beethoven, and it takes, perhaps by analogy with the Picardy third, the positive expressive correlation argued for above.

Remarkably, the starkness of the open-fifth type can be supported by reference to an example of further variation in the token. An extremely dissonant passage, amounting to a shriek of sorts, occurs in the last movement of Beethoven's String Quartet in A minor, Op. 132 (see Example 2.10, mm. 35 and 39). Here, the dissonant F is placed a minor sixteenth (minor ninth plus an octave) above the upper fifth of the A minor triad. The minor triad, again, has no third and in this case only one root representative. Because the doubled fifth is part of a larger compositional design emphasizing a pedal $\hat{5}$, this example of the open-fifth type is not as prototypical as the other examples. But the importance of a similar expressive effect is underlined when one considers the

Example 2.10. Beethoven, String Quartet in A minor, Op. 132, fifth movement, mm. 34–39.

violation of a common rule of dissonance treatment—the doubling of E, the tone of resolution for the unprepared dissonant F. The putative violation[21] is compensated by the expressive effect it earns—furthering the starkness of the open-fifth tonic triad with the juxtaposition of the harshest possible dissonance (the minor ninth). In other words, one can understand a seeming anomaly in the style as, instead, an atypical but understandable expressive strategy. The markedness of the unusual dissonance treatment assimilates itself to the marked open-fifth triad type, further specifying the expressive content of the musical event. We are guided by the *correlation* of starkness to an *interpretation* of the dissonance as a heightening of that expressive meaning.

Interpretation need not be limited to further articulation of the content of the correlation. Other factors enter into the individual chains of interpretants[22] that are possible avenues for competent listeners. Assuming that the quartet movement is a personal utterance (of a fictive *persona*, to avoid the intentional fallacy), one might interpret the event as akin to a primal shriek. Such an interpretation is supported by comparisons with other works of Beethoven. For example, the open-fifth and pedal dominants are reminiscent of the opening of the Ninth Symphony and share something of the primal, or primordial, significance of that generative interval. The harsh F–E dissonance serves not only as a concatenation of the larger-scale lowered $\hat{6}$ to $\hat{5}$ gestures, with their tragic associations (Deryck Cooke, 1959), but as reminiscent of the grinding crux (expressive focus) of frustrated tension that helps create the climax in the development of the first movement of the *Eroica*. Many commentators have noted the particular half-step relationship between $\hat{6}$ and $\hat{5}$ in minor as thematic to the Op. 132 quartet, and part of a four-note set of half-step pairs ($\hat{7}-\hat{1}$ and lowered $\hat{6}-\hat{5}$) thematic to several of the late quartets (as in the opening of Op. 131, analyzed in Chapter 6). These relationships constitute an *intertextual*[23] dimension of motivation (or evidence) for more-specific interpretations.

It is the relationship between *correlation* (in the *style*) and ongoing *interpretation* (demanded by the unique strategies of a work) that is crucial to a hermeneutic understanding of music. The dissatisfaction by musicologists and theorists with attempts to explain expression in music may have to do with a limiting focus on either overly general (and thus trivial) correlations, or overly specific (and thus subjective or impressionistic) interpretations. The next section illustrates how the two must work hand in hand, as part of the methodological dialectic mentioned earlier, in order to advance knowledge of both generalized stylistic meaning and unique significance in a work.

Hermeneutic Interpretation: Moving From "Yielding" and "Negation" to "Willed Resignation" and "Abnegation"

One of the most basic oppositions in music is that between up and down. Another is that between the realization of an implication and its denial, deflection, or deferral (Meyer, 1956, 1973). The innumerable associations one might construe for these oppositions are, of course, too varied and general to be much of a guide in interpreting the significance of a complex musical passage. Part of the hermeneutic effort involved in interpreting a particular passage comes from the other direction, working from one's expressive intuitions toward culturally appropriate meanings. When arrayed oppositionally, these cultural meanings (or *types* of expressive states) may be mapped onto the structural oppositions that in turn serve to keep them distinct.

Two concepts key to Romanticism are "yearning" and "resignation." A reading of Goethe, with whom Beethoven was quite familiar (especially *Wilhelm Meisters Lehrjahre*; see the Appendix), provides evidence that these concepts are not only culturally appropriate but a part of

Beethoven's understanding of his culture. Thus, it is not unreasonable to suggest them as potential correlations for certain expressive musical events.

One can easily imagine how "yearning" might correlate with "upward" motions, since upward motions are iconic with "reaching," and "reaching" relates to yearning through metaphors such as "reaching for a higher existence." "Resignation" could then attach to "descending" motions, through a similar derivation (as in "lapsing" from an implied ascent), or simply by being considered oppositional to "yearning." In the song "Resignation" (WoO 149), discussed in Chapter 1, Beethoven uses a descending-third motive to set the words "Lisch aus." But the resignation appears "unearned" (no prior ascent or yearning was implied), and thus we are not likely to take the song as seriously in terms of its emotional stake.

Interestingly, yearning (*Sehnsucht*) has its negative aspects, in the sense that it is usually unfulfilled, as in most love songs. On the other hand, resignation might be viewed in a more positive light as acceptance—or in the case of abnegation, a positive spiritual surrender to a higher power. Thus, Beethoven's songs entitled "Sehnsucht" are typically in the minor mode, but "Resignation" is set in major, perhaps reflecting the detachment that the text indicates is desirable ("du musst nun los dich binden").[24]

But the interpretation of expression must take into account more than texted works, with their referential cues, or parameters such as register, dynamics, and tempo, with their rather obvious iconic associations. If markedness theory is any indicator, a highly developed harmonic and tonal structuring (or "syntax") provides a rich network of potentially marked oppositions that can further articulate the "semantic space" (Eco, 1976: 125) of expression.

For example, the difference between the progressions, V–I and V–V$_2^4$–I^6 (see Example 2.11) involves a deferral of implication and the change from a strongly closural bass leap to a descending stepwise bass. The stepwise "lapsing" can begin to suggest "resignation" by way of "yielding." The bass descent also involves a clear reversal of implication—strength of closure is "yielded" by the imperfect authentic move as the strong root "yields" its place to the seventh of the V^7.

Compare the use of V–V$_2^4$–I^6 in the first movement of Op. 101 (Example 2.12). In this contextually enhanced usage, a "yearning" upward arpeggiation is answered twice by a "yielding" or "resignational" V–V$_2^4$–I^6. The varied repetition of this opposition suggests its

Example 2.11. Authentic closes.

a. Perfect   b. Imperfect

Example 2.12. Beethoven, Piano Sonata in A, Op. 101, first movement, mm. 19–25.

Example 2.13. Resolutions of V$^6_5$/V to V$^4_2$.

a. Normal   b. Elided

dramatization as dialogical[25]—perhaps between two sides of the same persona. One side appears to reach longingly for something beyond, while the other counsels moderation or acceptance. The dynamics seem to substantiate the basic correlations of yearning and yielding, with the latter undercutting the former. In Chapter 4 similar undercuttings will be seen as *thematic* for the first movement of Op. 101, serving to sustain a pastoral *expressive genre*, as well.

Another progression that exhibits both upward yearning and downward yielding is given in Example 2.13a. The chromatic raising of tension and expectation (V$^6_5$/V) is here fulfilled with the arrival of the V, but the V is undercut by V$^4_2$ before it can resolve to I. Once again, there is a balance of yearning (this time, realized) and yielding in the complete musical event.

Example 2.14. Beethoven, Piano Sonata in E♭, Op. 7, second movement, mm. 1–8.

Example 2.13b has the same progression elided to link V⁶₅/V directly with V⁴₂. Now the yearning is not realized (as F♯–G); instead, a reversal (F♯–F♮) displaces the goal and creates a denial, or *negation*, of the implication of the bass F♯.[26] The combination of yielding and denial of implication is a powerful pair, creating a sense of resignation that is more actively involved in its reversal of yearning. This "willed" resignation is more than a passive yielding, and may suggest the more refined concept of *abnegation*. Abnegation implies not only a conscious choice, but a positive spiritual outcome resulting from acceptance of a less than pleasant situation.

Example 2.14 shows the elided progression as it appears in the slow movement of Beethoven's Piano Sonata in E♭, Op. 7. The context of a hymnlike topic (slow, chordal texture) supports the spiritual interpretation implied by the concept of abnegation. The local details associated with the progression in m. 4, namely the *sf* and the appoggiatura, serve to mark the event as expressively focal. I call it the crux (expressive focal point) of the phrase, to distinguish it from the apex (highest pitch) in m. 6. Ratner considers the apex as the climax of the phrase (1980: 39); my analysis considers the reversal in m. 4 as the expressive climax, and inter-

Example 2.15. Beethoven, Op. 7, second movement, mm. 37–43.

prets the expressively focal (7–6 suspension) but less strategically marked apex as a reaction to the reversal (interpretable as gently poignant "acceptance" of the more powerful, willed resignation). Note that the chords on the third beat of m. 5 and the first two of m. 6 restore a diatonic version of m. 3, where chromaticism first intruded, producing the effect of a single phrase expanded by an expressive interpolation (compare Example 8.3).

The emphatic way in which Beethoven *thematizes* the progression F♯–F♮ points to its function in the dramatic structure of the movement as a whole.[27] Indeed, the move occurs at two other expressively focal locations, the crux of the development and the crux of the final codetta.

In the first case (Example 2.15), the F♮ in m. 41 provides a reversal of the expected move to a G dominant pedal preparation for the return. This time, F♮ is not the seventh of V but the root of a new V⁷, that of B♭ major. The extreme register and dynamics strategically mark this moment as focal. When a return of the principal theme occurs in a higher octave in B♭, the impression is not of a witty "false recapitulation," but rather of an epiphany that is also transcendent (the importance of high register for correlations of grace or transcendence was noted earlier in the *Hammerklavier* analysis). If my interpretation is

Example 2.16. Beethoven, Op. 7, second movement, mm. 86–end.

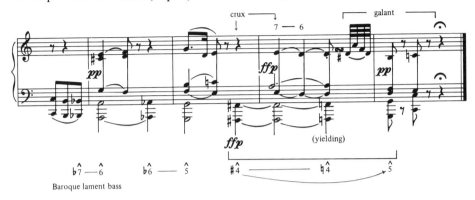

granted, then the thematic relationship of this passage with a pitch sequence previously interpreted in the context of abnegation reinforces the expressive power of the epiphany.

The final appearance of the F♯ to F♮ move (Example 2.16) could easily be dismissed as a coincidental result of the extended chromatic descent, were it not for the context. Now, the dynamic marking is at the other extreme, and the F♯ receives the stress. The *lamentoso* bass line triggers a Baroque-style tragic affect; the 7–6 suspension and starkly open spacing and doubling reinforce the topical use of the high tragic style. But the F♮ serves to disperse the tension generated by this sudden irruption and yields or resigns graciously to an embellishing turn figure. That figure then cues the *galant* style for a somewhat tenuously positive ending, one undermined by recent exposure of the tragic tensions lurking beneath an otherwise optimistic surface.

Thus, the F♯ to F♮ reversal, though no longer functioning as part of the original progression, maintains its generic significance throughout. In each later appearance, the basic "yielding" correlation holds true; but specific interpretations are sensitive to the context of each stage in the unfolding thematic drama.

It is this kind of method that I have called *hermeneutic*: working back and forth between stylistic knowledge and interpretative speculations; grounding those speculations in hypothetical stylistic oppositions; and then moving beyond established correlations of the style to a contextual and thematically strategic accounting of the unique significance of musical events.

It remains to consider the markedness values of the oppositions hypothesized in the foregoing analysis. If the correlations are motivated as part of the style by the various *hermeneutic* interpretations that have been made, how are they systematically motivated, or encoded, in terms of their markedness values (what is their *structuralist* explanation)? According to the prototypicality criterion, and considering the standard arch contour of a phrase as a prototype, ascending to the apex of a phrase would be unmarked (although the particular ascent may well be strategically marked in other ways, and the apex is marked in terms of register); descending to the cadence would also be unmarked. Thus, with respect to this opposition, a descent in the first part or an ascent in the second part of a phrase would be marked. According to the criterion of salience, any reversal or denial of implication would also be marked (strategically); thus, undercutting an ascent by reversal of direction would be marked.

It is more difficult to specify the markedness of up vs. down in general. In English, if one asks "How tall are you?" the word "tall" is unmarked, since there is no assumption that the person is either tall or short relative to the general population. But in asking "How short are you?" there is an implication that the person is indeed short; thus, "short" is the marked, or more specific, term of the opposition (Battistella 1990: 3). Culturally, this might suggest that ascents are unmarked with respect to descents in music. But high and low are both marked with respect to middle, and ascents and descents are both marked with respect to stasis (although a pedal point can be marked by its extreme stasis, in the context of a style that presumes ongoing harmonic motion).

Why, then, might yearning be unmarked when in opposition to resignation? Perhaps because yearning implies a wider range as far as the object of desire (and we tend to think of Romantic yearning as characteristically unfocused), whereas resignation is more focused, with its acceptance in the face of a particular frustrated desire. Although an attitude one might call "Romantic resignation" may also be adopted (as, for example, by Brahms), with a more diffuse and wider-ranging application akin to a world-view (e.g., *Weltschmerz*), one might also consider less-focused resignation as contributing to still another cultural unit, namely, melancholy. Beethoven's *Malinconia* movement, functioning as a slow introduction to the last movement of the String Quartet in Bb, Op. 18, no. 6, would qualify. It begins with static repetition before a stepwise ascent, and the second phrase repeats three of four bars exactly, down an octave, before a reversal in m. 8. The sudden reversals throughout are also much less rational, and more like disturbances, than productive of states such as abnegation.[28]

Summary

In pursuing both structuralist and hermeneutic investigations of more local examples, I have attempted to illustrate in greater detail the components of a semiotic theory of musical meaning. On the structuralist side, markedness has been defined and illustrated both in terms of its growth in a theorized historical sequence (*diachronically*) and in terms of a given point in style history (*synchronically*). On the hermeneutic side, a harmonic progression has been examined for its contribution to the interpretation of abnegation, supporting my claim for its role in the slow movement of the *Hammerklavier*.

I have given only limited historical evidence for my hypothesized correlations and interpretations, since my intent is primarily to establish the theoretical possibilities of such interpretation. Claims of historical plausibility require further investigation, critique, and refinement of speculative hypotheses, but at the same time further historical investigation may be more productive if framed within the theoretical constructs and models illustrated here.

Since the theory of markedness is probably the newest and most problematic for the reader, the following may be helpful in summarizing the principles of markedness as I have applied them. Although markedness was first described in relation to language, its generality as a principle of human cognition should allay fears of a "reduction" of music to language, or music theory to linguistics.

1. Markedness evaluates any difference understood as oppositional.
2. The evaluation is asymmetrical, in that one term of the opposition is marked, the other unmarked.
3. Some consequences of asymmetry in markedness valuation are: that the marked entity of an opposition has a narrower range of meaning with respect to the unmarked one; that the marked entity tends to appear less frequently than the unmarked one; and that the marked entity has a narrower distribution than its unmarked counterpart.
4. If a marked opposition in structure correlates with a marked opposition in meaning, the markedness values also correspond (see also 10., below).

5. Markedness may originate from a unique or salient event which the competent listener understands as creating or implementing a new opposition. This new opposition may then become a part of the style, as an instance of style *growth*.

6. Although markedness may originate in this way, the markedness value of an opposition, once accepted into the style, is not lost when the opposition is no longer salient. The theoretical concept of markedness, then, must not be confused or equated with salience.

7. Salience, on the other hand, is basic to the perception of expressive focal points, and such crucial events will be strategically marked, even as tokens of stylistically unmarked types. (See Chapter 5 for the consequences of strategic, or thematic, markedness.)

8. A particular novelty or departure may be *motivated* by many kinds of associations (similarity, analogy, contiguity, synecdoche; see Chapter 10) from any imaginable domain (including other musical works or styles as well as other cultural codes). But its *systematic encoding* as part of a stylistic competency depends on its coherence as an opposition—presumably with some already established entity (structure or process)—and the resulting establishment of its markedness within that opposition.

9. An entity (*type* or *token*) may be a member of several different oppositional pairs; its markedness can differ in those different contexts, and its evaluation must be clarified in each case with reference to the particular aspect governing each opposition.

10. Marked values from different oppositions tend to cluster in a given entity or location, creating or reinforcing larger marked entities. This principle is called *markedness assimilation*.

We can gauge the appropriateness of a provisional markedness assignment based on intuitions about the relative specificity of meaning in any given opposition. Conversely, given a markedness assignment derived from the novelty of one member of the pair, we are led to ponder what that more-specific meaning might be. This circularity of method is typical of an investigation that is *hermeneutic* as opposed to scientific. As Michael Shapiro claims with respect to linguistics,

the mutual dependency of the elements of the solution [to a linguistic problem] . . . all cohere as an ensemble of conditions informing the phenomena in question. [Thus, the investigation of many linguistic phenomena] hinges on the admission of circularity into the coherence of structure and the concomitant methodological devaluation of "independent motivation." [1983: 87]

A theory of style competency, even though it constrains interpretation of new events that the style affords, cannot be a complete explanation for musical works in that style. One also needs a complementary "theory of practice"[29] that can explain novel strategies in terms of their relation to and departure from the style. The interpretation of a work leads to an appropriate level of complexity through the strategic interpretation of new categories (*types*) and their unique instances (*tokens*).

Markedness plays a role in the *interpretation* of a work's strategies beyond the encoded oppositions of style, as well. This strategic markedness, however, may or may not survive in the style, but certainly exists in the "systems" (thematic and other) the work creates for itself.

Commentary

These basic tenets leave several issues to be resolved. Again, a listing may be helpful:

1. It is unclear to what extent markedness applies in a given musical style (how much, and on what levels, does it explain), or the extent of its applicability to a variety of musical styles. I focus principally on Beethoven in this study, where I believe a case can be made.
2. Because this book is not essentially concerned with style *change*, little will be conjectured about how markedness values themselves might change, but only how new values might emerge through a process of *growth* (see Chapter 10).
3. Scholars are not always sure, or in agreement, about how to express in words the significance or meaning of a musical passage. This problem, especially severe in the case of music as opposed to literature or representational art, makes it difficult to define or defend a "narrower range" of content for the marked term of an opposition. Markedness, however, allows one to probe the relative range or specificity of that content, even if it can only be expressed in oppositional terms.
4. Finally, I have only suggested why some oppositions and not oth-

ers become a part of the style—namely, that there is a systematic coherence based on a logical growth process of oppositions.

In many cases, a temporal sequence of development for some musical entities may provisionally be assumed, based on a commonsense judgment of the relative newness of one entity (for example, a chromatic move as opposed to a diatonic move). The historical dangers of this approach are obvious, and the reader should remember that relative newness is only one kind of evidence for the assignment of markedness values.

Circular argument is inescapable in determining temporal development by surface novelty, and at the same time claiming novelty by reference to chronological sequence; or in determining markedness value by (range of) meaning, and determining that meaning by markedness value. But this circularity is offset to some degree when one considers that successful semiotic styles share a characteristic capacity for multiple interpretations and the flexibility to create contexts in which old structures take on new meanings. Thus, the strategic range of many styles far exceeds that which can be determined systematically. Interpretation proceeds from, but is never exhausted by, systematic categorization. Instead, other evidence must be sought to support each interpretive claim. But if sufficient evidence is lacking—perhaps because a crucial structure was either too obvious or too complex for contemporaneous commentary—then the theorist must have recourse to a larger construct in which coherence within the whole work can support the provisional status of an individual interpretation.

This argument illuminates the importance of such larger constructs as Schenker's hierarchical theory of voice leading or Schoenberg's *Idea* and its embodiment in the *Grundgestalt* and developing variation. The systems of these theorists and their disciples, however, have dealt with "purely musical" relationships almost exclusively. What is proposed by a semiotic theory of markedness is the grounding of musical relationships in the cultural universes of their conception, in order to address the expressive significance of formal structures in a richer way.

III

From Topic to Expressive Genre

The concept of an overarching expressive genre guided the interpretation in Chapter 1 of expressive topics and dramatic events within the slow movement of the *Hammerklavier*. This chapter considers the concept of genre from the perspective of literary theory as well as music theory, and develops a general theory of expressive genres for Beethoven. Expressive genres cut across the distinctions between formal genres. They are based on, and move through, broad expressive states oppositionally defined as topics in the Classical style. Mapping the structural oppositions that articulate a fundamental topical universe in Beethoven's music offers a theoretical refinement of Leonard Ratner's (1980: 3–27) account of topics and styles as documented by historical sources.[1]

Formal and Expressive Genres

Western literature has a long history of genre classification based on formal features alone. Aristotle distinguished epic from tragedy not in terms of content but in terms of overall length and particular verse type (*Poetics*, ca. 350 B.C., section 24). Music theorists have also tended to classify genres in technical terms. For Classical music we have formal genres such as string quartet, symphony, and piano sonata (or looser families of forms such as the *divertimenti*); and formal schemes such as sonata form, theme and variations, and rondo. Textbook definitions and charts focus on the typical formal features that define the sequence of movements and their tonal/thematic schemes.

The construal of form in terms of style, including expressive features of the style, is a striking feature of Charles Rosen's *The Classical Style* (1972). Rosen characterizes sonata "style" in terms of the dramatic action of modulation, the emotional range of thematic and textural contrast, and the coordination and symmetrical resolution of tonal and thematic forces. In this sense, the style was "so powerful that it [could] apply almost equally well to any genre" (1972: 47). When expressive considerations are brought to bear, the misleading separations implied by generic or formal classifications can be overcome:

> Old forms, like the fugue and the theme and variations, were still used, thoroughly transformed; some forms like the concerto, the overture, the aria, and the rondo, contain vestiges of older forms buried within them; and there are dances, mostly minuets, Ländler, and polonaises. Everything else is sonata: that is to say, plain music. [1972: 53]

Expressive considerations often enter into discussions of formal genres when the same form (e.g., binary) is used with a range of styles (e.g., the dances of a Baroque suite). Even then, the differentiation is made primarily in terms of tempo, meter, and characteristic rhythmic design. But as Allanbrook (1983) has shown for Mozart, the oppositions of rhythmic gesture have expressive consequences; dance types are arrayed among high, middle, and low styles, with consequences for the representation of social status among characters in Mozart opera.

On the other hand, the Fantasy as a genre may be defined by its lack of adherence to sonata style expectations:[2] "[I]n the rare cases where the material implied either a markedly asymmetrical resolution, or a form . . . that is relatively unarticulated, the result was a Fantasy" (Rosen, 1972: 91).

Another characteristic genre that more radically avoids the penetration of sonata style is the Romance, described by Rousseau in terms that highlight its expressive features. Owen Jander (1983) has explained the unusual structure of the second movement of Beethoven's Violin Concerto in D Major, Op. 61, as largely due to the influence of this genre. Rousseau's definition of the Romance is worth citing because of its fluent blending of structural and expressive observations, as opposed to a strict or even sufficient formal accounting:

> An air to which one sings a little poem of the same name, divided into strophes, the subject of which is ordinarily some amorous, and often tragic, story. Since the romance should be written in a style that is simple, affecting, and in a somewhat antique taste, the air should respond to the character of the words: not at all ornamented, devoid of mannerisms, a melody that is sweet, natural, and pastoral, and which produces its effect all by itself, independent of the manner of the singer. It is not necessary that the song be lively; it suffices that it be naive, and that it in no way obscure the text, which it should allow to be clearly heard, and that it not employ a large vocal range. A well-made romance, having nothing striking about it, does not move one right at the outset. But each strophe adds something to the effect of the preceding ones, and the interest grows imperceptibly; and the listener finds himself moved to tears without being able to say where the charm lies that has produced this effect. [Rousseau, *Dictionnaire de Musique*, 1768; cited by Jander, 1983: 162]

The clear inference to be made from this characterization of the Romance is that its genre is more expressively than formally motivated.

In terms of markedness, one might observe that the more marked the genre, the more narrowly its range of (expressive) content can be described. But even a technically defined form need not be considered as an inviolable mold into which expressive material is poured; rather, the negotiation between the constraints of the form and the demands of the material can lead to unique form-tokens of a formal type or types (as in Newcomb, 1983, 1984a, and 1987; and Dreyfus, 1987).

Expressive genres such as the tragic-to-transcendent are, in one sense, the largest types encountered in a style. As is the case for forms such as sonata, they also function as schemata, but at a more archetypal level.[3] As schemata, they direct a wide range of different events and their interpretations, without specifying precise outcomes in terms of formal design.

Thus, in addition to correlations for the topics they invoke (tragic, transcendent), there will also be further interpretations guided by dramatic or expressive schemata (the nature, pacing, and placement of the changes from tragic to transcendent, for example). Indeed, a distinctive scenario results from the interaction between a work's thematic (topical) strategies and the larger expectations of its expressive genre.

What this implies for stylistic competency is an adeptness at both typological identification of topics and temporal or processive interpretation of these and other events in terms of the overarching expressive genre—all in negotiation with the relevant formal genre (sonata, variation, fugue, etc.).[4]

Expressive genres are tenacious, despite a necessary looseness in their definition. Since they could be viewed as archetypes that are invariant across a number of styles, I shall not attempt here to recover the original motivations behind their emergence or the rationales for their modification. Instead, in what follows, I shall present a framework for understanding some of the more important expressive genres as used by Beethoven.

One candidate, the pastoral, has already been examined as a topic; its extensive history has been documented by Herman Jung (1980).[5] Traditionally, the pastoral in music has not been understood as governing a sequence of events in a dramatic scenario—unless from the standpoint of drama, as in pastoral opera, or the case of a storm providing the dramatic outburst in a "characteristic" symphony. The tragic-to-transcendent genre, on the other hand, offers a more readily understood dramatic model, since a change of state is encompassed by its label. But even the pastoral can acquire the status of expressive genre, and I shall demonstrate how the pastoral not only evokes its topical affect but more impressively guides the listener through an interpretation of succeeding events as part of a coherent dramatic scenario. In the next chapter an analysis of Beethoven's Piano Sonata in A major, Op. 101, will further exemplify the pastoral as an expressive genre.

When framing expressive genres for Beethoven, one must consider how genre is characterized or distinguished by oppositions in the style. I shall illustrate how markedness governs those oppositions and provides an explanation for the narrower expressive range of one genre as opposed to another. In turn, my account of expressive genres in relation to formal types will suggest their increasing kinship in Beethoven's later works, leading to the idea of expressive associations for formal types or procedures such as variation and fugue.

But before proceeding with these investigations, I offer a small sampling of historical and theoretical concepts of genre in literature, in order to anticipate the problems and possibilities of generic classification for music.

Genre as a Literary Type

In literary theory it has been neither possible nor even at times desirable to construct a system of genres based solely on form or expression. Genres may be understood in more than one sense, and they may be organized along different lines of classification. A perusal of Paul Hernadi's (1972) broad study of the concept, or Barbara Lewalski's (1985) more specific categorizations in Milton's *Paradise Lost*, reinforces the historical importance of genres but undermines any illusions one might have held about the possibility of a theoretically precise classification scheme.

Hernadi's survey of generic classifications throughout literary theory is rich in its own meta-classifications of possible approaches to a rather old problem. Hernadi distinguishes four orientations among literary theorists, differing by their focus on the author (expressive), the reader (pragmatic), the verbal medium (structural), or the evoked world (mimetic). Each has its pitfalls; the extreme positions possible with each focus would yield respectively the intentional fallacy, the affective fallacy, dogmatic formalism, and a "preoccupation with 'message' and subject matter" (Hernardi 1972: 7). Each orientation is capable of producing innumerable classifications and subclassifications, as well.

Lewalski, on the other hand, considers her highest classification—that of narrative, dramatic, and lyric—as involving *"literary categories* or *strategies of presentation,* not genres" (1985: 9). Her successively embedded levels are generic class, genre, subgenre, and mode. Generic class is based on poetic meter, structure, and purpose. It is derived from the Alexandrian *Canons* and the works of Horace, Cicero, and Quintilian; and it includes such classes as epic, elegy, tragedy, comedy, history, and oratory. Genre is then based on formal and thematic elements, conventions, and topoi as encountered in actual historical genres, such as epic, tragedy, sonnet, funeral elegy, hymn, and epigram. Subgenre involves subdivisions based on subject matter and motifs. Finally, mode is a cross-cutting category "identified chiefly by subject matter, attitude, tonality, and topoi" (Lewalski, 1985: 10); modes are represented by the pastoral, satiric, comedic, heroic, elegiac, and tragic.[6] Actual works exploit topoi and generic paradigms, the latter both structural and thematic. These are "reinforced by verbal, thematic, and structural allusions to specific works or episodes," suggesting an intertextual strategy "common among epic poets" (Lewalski, 1985: 20).

Lewalski's classification is certainly pluralistic, if not somewhat bewildering. With its hierarchical overlaps it reflects the flux of both historical practice and contemporaneous theoretical classification. One can make more sense out of the resulting contradictions by realizing that two kinds of ordering or classification are being used: the familiar hierarchical taxonomy, progressing from generic class to genre, subgenre, paradigm, and topos; and the characterization of genres by adjectival forms, such as pastoral, heroic, tragic (as opposed to a pastorale, an epic, a tragedy). The characterizing strategy is useful in that it helps one account for the mixing of genres or generic classes (a dramatic lyric, or a lyrical epic).

Paul Hernadi (1972: 24, 58) cites the work of Emil Staiger (1946) and Albert Guérard (1940) in regard to such adjectival characterizations. Staiger distinguishes degrees of characterization (pointing out, for example, that not all dramas are dramatic), and in general he differentiates the adjectival form from the noun form with regard to such terms as lyric(al), epic(al), and drama(tic). His preference is for adjectival characterizations that emphasize generic styles as opposed to a typology of genres.

Guérard, on the other hand, exploits both characterizing and classifying formulations, creating a network of spirit and form respectively. Guérard's network and his examples (1940: 197ff.) may be extracted from Hernadi's summary and arranged as in Figure 3.1, where a strategic matrix of characterization and classification illustrates the possibilities of mixing among pure generic types.

In terms of markedness, the "lyrical lyric," "epic narrative," and "dramatic drama" are clearly unmarked with respect to the mixing of genre; the other possibilities involving mixture are marked with respect to the "spirit" conveyed by the adjective.

One may be disturbed by the reliance on simple categories and the fusing of epic and narrative. Hernadi criticizes the scheme by observing that still other categories are neglected by such traditional three-part classifications; these categories include proverbs, maxims, precepts, popular saws, descriptive and philosophical poems, essays, etc. (Hernadi, 1972: 59). Obviously, no such broad, tripartite schemes can pretend to be exhaustive.

Form

	Lyric	Narrative	Drama
Lyrical	Lyrical lyric: Goethe's "Wanderer's Nachtlied"	Lyrical narrative: Byron's "Don Juan"	Lyrical drama: Shakespeare's "The Tempest"
Epic	Epic (narrative) lyric: "Ballad of Sir Patrick Spence"	Epic narrative: "Iliad"	Epic drama: Shelley's "Prometheus Unbound"
Dramatic	Dramatic lyric: R. Browning's dramatic monologues	Dramatic epic: Dickens' A Tale of Two Cities	Dramatic drama: Molière's plays, many of Shakespeare's plays

(left margin label: **Spirit**)

Figure 3.1. Matrix of literary character and class (adapted from Guérard [1940: 197ff.] and Hernadi [1972: 58]).

Northrop Frye takes a slightly different approach to the issue of classi-fication in his *Anatomy of Criticism* (1957: 162) by setting up four narrative categories of literature viewed as "logically prior to literary genres": romance (a desirable world), irony and satire (a defective world), tragedy (a move from innocence to catastrophe), and comedy (a move from the world of experience or threat to a "post-dated inno-cence"). Again, an oppositional structure is created which can in turn support the coherent identification of these categories in actual works.

Eric Bentley, in *The Life of the Drama* (1964), adds to these classifica-tions the important category of tragicomedy (echoed by Karl Guthke, 1966). The two types of tragicomedy he presents are strongly suggestive of my interpretation of expressive genres in Beethoven. Hernadi sum-marizes the two types as "works in which genuine tragedy is encoun-tered and transcended rather than simply averted [as in Op. 106, III], and works in which the penetrating eye of comedy refuses 'to look the other way' " (1972: 111) (compare the tragic elements intruding into the nontragic sphere of the pastoral in the first movement of Op. 101). The literary examples that Hernadi gives are interesting in that they were available to Beethoven, from Shakespeare's *Measure for Measure* to Kleist's *Prinz von Homburg* and Goethe's *Iphigenie* and *Faust*.[7]

This brief survey of literary theories demonstrates how a flexible generic conceptualization may be preferable to narrowly fixed types, but the danger in that flexibility is a proliferation of categories, as in Lewal-ski. What might be considered the result of a mixed genre (e.g., the pastoral with tragic irruptions) may develop into a genre in its own right (as in Bentley's tragicomic types). Indeed, the tragicomic is recognized as a new genre in literature as early as 1601, in Battista Guarini's celebrated preface to a later edition of his pastoral verse drama *Il Pastor fido* (1580–84).[8]

Such mixed genres are suggestive for Beethoven, since we rarely find a tragic expressive genre, such as the last movement of the *Appassionata*. Furthermore, dramatic contrast is often achieved by the use of conflicting topics or styles, which in turn may imply a mixed genre. Chapter 7 discusses a kind of musical troping as one means by which incompatible or unexpected entities are brought together to provoke a fresh interpretation from their interaction. For expressive genres, the subtlety of the tragicomic may well illustrate the potential of generic troping. Another way of conceiving contrast, however, is in terms of an ongoing, dramatic "working out" of oppositional forces, and it is this characterization that underlies change-of-state expressive genres. Thus, the tragic is relieved by transcendence, but only after a struggle between the two. However, one of the expressive meanings that emerges from that struggle, *abnegation*, suggests a genuine trope because it fuses the conflicting negative and positive aspects of resignation (yielding, yet transcending at the same time).

The proliferation of musical expressive genres may be controlled by maintaining a distinction between the stylistic level of basic types and the strategic level of their creative mixing, as illustrated for literary genres in Figure 3.1, above.

Understanding Expressive Genres in Music

For historical classifications of musical topics, Leonard Ratner's *Classic Music: Expression, Form and Style* (1980: 3–27) provides a rich source based on a thorough study of contemporaneous treatises. The following outline displays the rough hierarchy implied by Ratner's presentation:[9]

   I. Codes of feelings and passions, linked to:
     A. pace, movement, tempo
     B. intervals
     C. motives used to symbolize affect
  II. Styles, based on:
     A. locale/occasion/situation

1. ecclesiastical/church style
2. chamber style (*galanterie*)
3. theatrical/operatic style (relative to chamber style)
    B. degree of dignity
        1. high style
        2. middle style
        3. low style
III. Topics, either:
    A. types (fully worked-out pieces), such as dances (minuet, contredanse, etc.) in high, middle, or low styles, or
    B. styles (figures and progressions within a piece)
        1. military, hunt
        2. singing style
        3. French overture
        4. musette, pastorale
        5. Turkish music
        6. Storm and stress
        7. sensibility, *Empfindsamkeit*
        8. strict, learned style (vs. *galant*, or free style)
        9. fantasia style
IV. Pictorialism, word painting, and imitation of sounds in nature.

As with Lewalski's literary categorizations (1985), Ratner's scheme involves the overlapping use of terms, such as style, and the mixing of categories, such as the French overture "style" as distinct from the formal implications of the overture itself. Each of these approaches, however, provides valuable orientation with respect to the inevitably messy categories provided by theorists of the time.

Obviously, one cannot expect historical practice or contemporaneous terminology to be neatly systematic or critical in the use of categorizing terms. That is in fact one justification for a structural analysis of important oppositions—they reveal patterns that may not have been observed or commented on by theorists or practitioners of the time, but that influenced musical practice nonetheless.

The broadest level of musically relevant oppositions occurs between styles considered as a whole, such as sacred vs. secular, or historical vs. current styles. As indicated in category II.B., above, the Classical style also embraces the contrast between high, middle, and low (*buffa*) styles. Interestingly, the sacred or ecclesiastical style, because of its slower style growth, eventually takes on the character of a historical style. By anal-

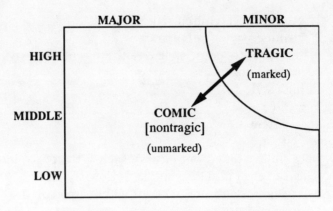

Figure 3.2. Expressive oppositional field as defined by a matrix of structural oppositions for the classical style.

ogy, any conservative style (e.g., the fugal style of the Baroque) will take on a higher valuation because of the dignity inherent in the conservative sacred style. Thus, the correlations and interpretations for the high style might include not only religious sentiment but also dignity, majesty, or "authoritativeness," as reflected by adherence to an older compositional creed.

Another fundamental musical opposition that can help differentiate genres is that already noted between major and minor mode. The correlations of happy and sad were already clearly a part of Beethoven's early stylistic competency, as humorously illustrated by an early *Klavierstück* (WoO 54, 1798), whose two sections are subtitled *Lustig* (C major) and *Traurig* (C minor). The opposition is best interpreted by the comparable dramatic opposition of comic and tragic genres.

The matrix of categories created by the oppositions between major and minor, on the one hand, and high, middle, and low styles, on the other, is constructed in Figure 3.2. Remarkably, these two sets of oppositions are sufficient to situate the different expressive genres in the Classical style, even though other oppositions also help keep the genres distinct and contribute to their systematic coherence. The redundancy of mutually supportive oppositions (markedness assimilation) ensures a higher degree of interpretive consistency.

If we consider the matrix more loosely as a field, then implied boundaries give way to the notion of polarities within a continuum. Oppositions are still potent, but fixing each genre in a bounded corner is impossible, as will be seen.

The two most general or fundamental genres for Classical music are the tragic and the comic. Traditionally, a tragic dramatic genre deals with characters from the higher classes and demands the highest (serious, elevated) verse. Likewise, a tragic musical genre exploits the higher end of the style continuum and uses the affectual associations of minor mode. The comic genre in Classical music stems from the *buffa* tradition, thus suggesting a lower, popular style; it takes the nontragic affect of the major mode (as shown in Figure 3.2). Indeed, because of the narrowed range of the tragic (predictable from the markedness of minor mode) and the variety of genres possible in the comic arena (*buffa*, pastoral, high comic), the unmarked comic is more appropriately labeled "nontragic."[10]

Rosen (1972: 96) claims that the Classical style originated as "basically a comic one." That perspective accords well with the notion of the comic genre as the unmarked category opposing the tragic genre; therefore, I have placed the comic more centrally in the generic field.[11] But the Classical style emerged as a style of balance and symmetrical resolution as well, and the comic is more central because (theatrically, at least) comedy typically achieves balance and proportion after its upsets, whereas tragedy forces one beyond the balance of ordinary life to the imbalance of a catastrophic final outcome. The tragic, when relying on the seriousness of more conservative styles, also implements an opposition at the most fundamental level of style; thus, it is highly marked generically.

The relative rarity of the high style also suggests that it is marked with respect to the common *buffa* style, but perhaps both are marked with respect to an increasingly important "middle" style characterized more by balance and proportion than by simple symmetry, and more by wit and irony than by obvious humor. This central, unmarked style is labeled the *galant* and occupies the middle of the generic field in Figure 3.3. An unmarked assessment is supported by a historical survey of the use of the term *galant* in the eighteenth century (Sheldon 1989). Sheldon concludes that "the concept of a *galant* or free style was used to moderate between stylistic extremes, whether between old vs. new, strict vs. free or, in Scheibe's terms, high vs. low" (97).

The *buffa* style is one possibility within the comic orbit, directly oppositional to the tragic. With the *galant* as the unmarked center of the comic field, the *buffa* style may now be considered as marked within the realm of the comic, and situated within a narrower range of expressive humor, wit, or high spirits.

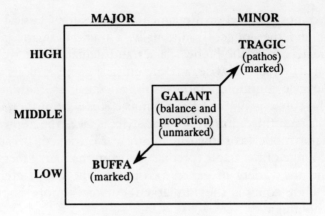

Figure 3.3. Galant as the unmarked mean
between expressive extremes.

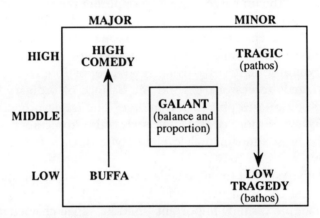

Figure 3.4. Effect of contextual revaluation
(shift in "stylistic register").

The arrows in Figure 3.4 indicate how these genres can be raised or lowered by contextual revaluation. Such contextual revaluation suggests the possible influence of *irony*. In Mozart's *Don Giovanni*, for example, the high style of Baroque seriousness is used for Donna Elvira's complaints, but in such a context as to create not a pathetic, but a *bathetic* effect (Allanbrook, 1983: 233–38). The "low tragedy" of bathos is clearly comic, and thus the potential tragic correlation of the high style is reduced to at most a poignant remainder.

Irony may be less clear in cases of high comedy. Here, the irony is more like Friedrich Schlegel's concept of *Romantic irony*, but operative

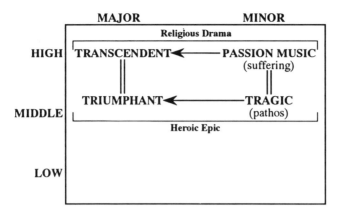

Figure 3.5. Archetypal expressive genres and their
relative stylistic registers.

at the level of a cultural phenomenon.[12] The comic style developed by
Haydn and others for *opera buffa* became the basis for a style compre-
hending a far greater range of experience beyond the *buffa*, as Rosen
(1972) and others have shown. This is the sense of "high comedy" as it
appears in Figure 3.4.[13]

Among the possibilities for expressive generic schemata is the dramatic progression tragic-to-triumphant, which Beethoven exploits at
the level of the sonata cycle itself in such exemplary works as the Fifth
Symphony. This generic progression, or a comparable one beginning
with heroic stability and dealing with increasingly tragic conflicts (the
first movement of the *Hammerklavier*, Op. 106), could be characterized as "heroic epic" (as in Figure 3.5). In Beethoven's third period the
tragic-to-triumphant genre appears to be interpretable in terms comparable to the theatrical category of religious drama—namely, tragedy that
is transcended through sacrifice at a spiritual level. The pathos of the
tragic may be understood as stemming from a kind of Passion music,
depicting a personal, spiritual struggle; and the "triumph" is no longer
a publicly heroic "victory" but a transcendence or acceptance that goes
beyond the conflicts of the work (after having fully faced them).[14] Certainly, the slow movement of the *Hammerklavier* fits this description.

The pastoral as genre needs further explanation. A primary opposition
that distinguishes pastoral genres within the broader comic field is that
of simplicity versus complexity. In terms of the oppositional field in
Figure 3.6, greater simplicity may be understood as greater consonance
or diatonicism, and thus the pastoral is placed on the extreme left of the

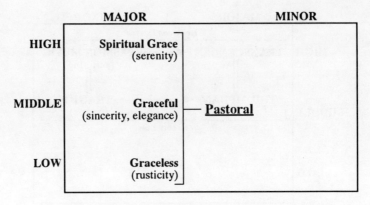

Figure 3.6. The pastoral as interpreted in high, middle, and low styles.

continuum from major (implying greater consonance) to minor (implying greater dissonance). Other "simple" oppositions could be applied, as well, highlighting such characteristic features as slow harmonic rhythm (pedal point and drone fifth), simple harmonization (parallel thirds), and rhythmic or textural suggestions of placid stasis.

In terms of high, middle, and low styles, the pastoral straddles all three "registers" (to borrow a term from sociolinguistics). This phenomenon may be explained by a gradual (historical) growth process in which the pastoral is raised in significance from rustic simplicity[15] or gracelessness; through the revaluation of simplicity as elegant and graceful, perhaps even correlating with sincerity itself; leading to the elevation of simplicity to sublimity, suggesting spiritual grace, serenity, or transcendence.

Herman Jung (1980) discusses instances in Bach and Handel where the pastoral has a more spiritual context, but these are clearly derived from conventions of Christmas shepherd music or applications of the pastoral to support the figure of Christ as the Good Shepherd. Nevertheless, it is striking that Bach takes the arias and ensembles from his *Shepherd Cantata*, BWV 249a, and incorporates them with new texts in his *Easter Cantata*, BWV 249. An especially relevant metaphorical extension in terms of the enrichment of the pastoral is the relation Jung points out (1980: 217) between the "Hirten-Wiegenlied" and the "Gedanken des Petrus am Östermorgen" through the bridging of "Wiegen—Schlaf—Todesschlummer." Since for Peter on Easter morning, Death has been transformed into a mere sleep before eternal life, he sings a shepherd's lullaby to the tomb in order to enrich the "himmlischen Pastorale" with an image of "christlichen Paradies" (Jung, 1980: 218). Beethoven, then, had quite an extensive tradition to draw from in further extending the connotative range of the pastoral to the sublime.[16]

The opposition simple versus complex can also be articulated for the pastoral with reference to tempo; broadly speaking, the pastoral is slower paced in comparison to the *buffa*. An interesting example is provided by the history of the siciliano, originally a fast-paced cousin of the gigue before it broke away and settled into a slower-paced pastoral dance (Jung, 1980).

Over the course of pre-Classical to Classical style history, one can observe a revaluation of the simple as opposed to the complex in the realm of ornamentation, as well. Perhaps the change signals a recognition of the limits of ornamentation or the manneristic growth process by which ornaments had begun to proliferate. There is a reversal in the value of the Rococo style, from its height as the epitome of French elegance to its perception as superficial or stuffy.[17] The simpler singing style, with its more direct melodic outlines, displaces the ornamental Rococo style with a different kind of elegance; and in the process, a more "natural" simplicity is raised in cultural value.

Allanbrook (1983: 31–70) has classified the principal Classical dances in terms of high, middle, and low style, and in terms of their characteristic features. In her classification, in most cases, some combination of meter, tempo, and characteristic rhythmic figure distinguishes these kinetically derived but stylized dance types. Although it is possible to write a complete movement in such a type,[18] the dance types are of greater interest as topics within larger works. In order to avoid confusion with my concept of style, I will avoid Ratner's term "style" for the use of dance types as parts of other pieces, and simply retain the term *topic* for all such thematic uses.

Topics come laden with associations (the military associations of a march, for example), but more importantly for reconstructing correlations, these topics invoke a well-established oppositional network of meanings. Such correlational meanings do not exempt the theorist from further interpretation. For example, in the last movement of Beethoven's Ninth Symphony, the famous Turkish march is a topic few contemporaneous listeners would have failed to recognize. Its use was criticized because of the lamentable drop in stylistic register (from high to low) it occasioned. Many listeners were unable to reconcile its immediate stylistic connotations with its new context. Indeed, without the elevation of the topic and a corresponding revaluation of this seeming parody of the "Freude" theme, one would scarcely be able to comprehend an interpretation that both depends on and transcends the humble comic origins of the Turkish march. The evocation of the hero ("wie ein Held") obviously calls for a march topic. But what the "low" Turkish march achieves is a thematically appropriate universality by embracing the low style (democratically promoting the dignity of the common man) and reaching out across cultural boundaries (since "*alle* Menschen werden Brüder").[19]

The Pastoral as an Expressive Genre

As defined thus far, any movement in a major key with a relatively simple character would qualify as pastoral. The literary tradition offers other features that help to clarify the pastoral as a genre, even though they do not provide as clear a dramatic framework as that associated with the tragic-to-triumphant genre.[20] The following summary from *A Dictionary of Literary Terms* (1960) is helpful:

> Any writing having to do with shepherds may be called pastoral literature. Theocritus (third century B.C.), a Greek, wrote pastoral poems about Sicilian herdsmen, and some of his themes (e.g., a singing match between shepherds, a shepherd lamenting his mistress' coldness, an elegy for a dead shepherd) have been widely used by later poets, including Vergil, Spenser, and Milton. Pastorals are often set in Arcadia, a mountainous district of Greece, proverbial for its peaceful shepherds who lived a simple happy life. A pastoral poem can also be called a *bucolic* or an *idyll* or an *eclogue*. (Idyll sometimes refers to a miniature and picturesque epic, as Tennyson's *Idylls of the King*; an eclogue is commonly a dialogue between shepherds, yet sometimes it is any dialogue where some attention is also paid to setting.)
>
> In general, ancient poets after Theocritus depicted rural life as unsullied and therefore superior to urban life. Christian poets have sometimes fused the Graeco-Roman tradition with the Hebrew-Christian tradition of the shepherd as the holy man (cf. David, the shepherd who sang psalms, and Christ as the Good Shepherd), thus enlarging the form. . . . The georgic is a poem dealing with rural life, especially with farming; unlike the pastoral, it usually depicts a life of labor rather than of singing and dancing. [1960: 64]

From this concise dictionary account one can glean features of a larger pastoral mode—peaceful, simple, happy, picturesque, and unsullied—

and themes such as a singing match, a lament or elegy, a dance, or even the "workaday" world. Other possibilities found in musical works include a sunrise (Haydn), a storm (requiring the use of a nonpastoral topic, the *Sturm und Drang*), a representation of seasons (Vivaldi), or any appropriate pictorialism.

If the varieties of pastoral literature are defined by considerations of theme and verse structure, perhaps this genre in music could be defined by thematic and formal constraints as well. For example, the presentation of a stormlike scene in the development of the first movement of Beethoven's *Pastoral* Piano Sonata in D major, Op. 28, is a typical negotiation of formal and expressive generic concerns. The first movement of the Piano Sonata in F♯ major, Op. 78, might be interpreted as opening with a sunrise (the gradual ascent over a tonic pedal that acts as a horizon) and continuing with a "workaday" set of themes in the following Allegro, strongly suggestive of the georgic category in pastoral literature.[21]

But to reduce the pastoral to a thematic type or topic, or even to an elaborated group of such types, would be to miss an important aspect of its contribution to our sense of genre in those works where the topic becomes the central theme and premise. The pastoral as a topical field can serve as an interpretive frame for a movement or cycle of movements, prescribing an overall outcome (or perspective on that outcome) regardless of intervening events. The perspective of the pastoral is one of integrative, sturdily optimistic assurance, perhaps originating from earlier pastoral associations between nature and the harmonious natural order. For a Classical composer the natural order could be captured metaphorically by balance and proportion in the realm of the passions. For Beethoven, who worshipped nature as a source of inspiration, and who admired the pantheistic message of the Austrian preacher Christoph Christian Sturm (Crabbe, 1982: 105–107), the association with nature resonates with even deeper spiritual symbolism.

As an illustration of the way a pastoral perspective frames and organizes the significance of a complete sonata cycle, Beethoven's Piano Sonata in A major, Op. 101, is the focus of the following analytical chapter. Although I intepret the pastoral as the expressive genre for the sonata, its use of the tragic may also suggest the tragicomic category of Bentley and Guthke, mentioned at the beginning of this chapter.[22]

The pastoral has a tendency toward milder expressivity, typically achieved by greater consonance, simpler harmonies, pedal points, more-flowing melodic lines, and so forth. All may not be present, but some

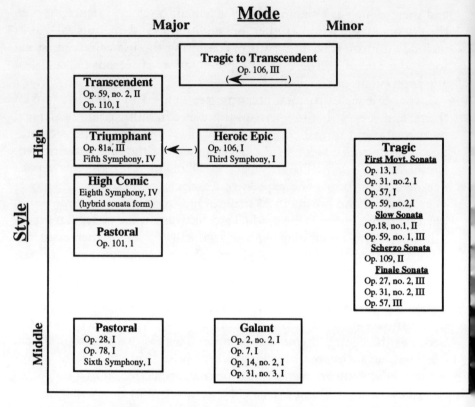

Figure 3.7. Placement of Beethoven sonata-form movements according to expressive genres and styles.

combination of these characteristics is typical.[23] In the case of the first movement of Op. 101, as will be seen, the consistency with which expressive gestures and climaxes are undercut suggests one strategic means Beethoven employs to maintain a pastoral sensibility even while exploiting various tragic turns.

Genres and Formal Types

If the concept of expressive genre is to be considered as independent of form (sonata, binary, rondo, variation, etc.) or texture (fugue, dance types), then it should be possible to find representatives of various expressive genres among the tokens of a single formal type. Given their

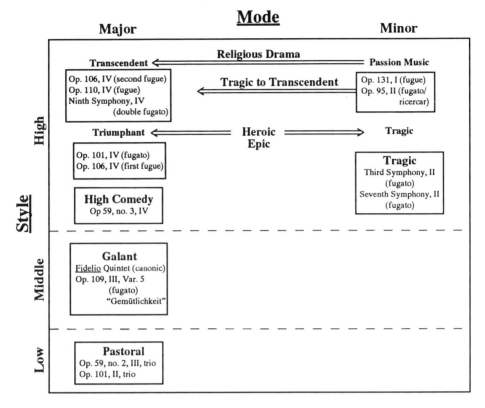

Figure 3.8. Placement of Beethoven fugal or contrapuntal movements or sections according to expressive genres.

ubiquity, examples are not hard to find for sonata form or for fugal procedure. Figures 3.7 and 3.8 indicate how these movements could be located within the topical fields constructed earlier.

Tragic sonata movements or fugal movements are works in minor that maintain the darker affect of the minor key, as in the finales of the *Tempest* and the *Appassionata* piano sonatas. Beethoven's commitment to this generic view is reflected in his use of the minor dominant as the second key area of the exposition (in the first movement of the *Tempest*, as well) and his featuring of the subdominant region in the development. Besides the dominant, the subdominant of a minor tonic is the only other closely related key that is also minor in mode; thus, its use sustains the tragic intensity of the movement. Interestingly, another feature that adds to the interpretation of obsessiveness is the perpetual motion in both finales.[24]

That the same form can accommodate different expressive genres should come as no surprise. Even a purely formalistic perspective accounts for the use of sonata form in other movements of the sonata cycle—for example, the slow movement of the *Hammerklavier* and the scherzo-like middle movement of the Piano Sonata in E major, Op. 109. The openings of these two movements, both in minor keys, explore the tragic genre, although the differences in tempo and other features individuate the two openings. The third movement of Op. 106, as analyzed in Chapter 1, moves toward a transcendent state of acceptance by means of positive resignation (abnegation), and thus constitutes a genre that is characterized by a change of state, modeled here as a movement through the oppositional topical field. Although similar to the tragic-to-triumphant genre, the tragic-to-transcendent is elevated in style because of its spiritual associations. The second movement of Op. 109, on the other hand, is relentless in its tragic character. That relentlessness is indicated by the closing passage in E minor, capping a nearly perpetual rhythmic intensity. Although the middle section is characterized by quieter pleading, it is brutally undercut by the sudden jolt of an unprepared recapitulation in E minor following a "false" dominant preparation for B minor.

Just as some sonata movements are tragic, others may be triumphant or transcendent. For the former, the last movement of the Fifth Symphony comes to mind; for the latter, the second movement of the String Quartet in E minor, Op. 59, no. 2, fulfills the condition of transcendence as its basic premise.[25] William Kinderman (1985) offers insights into spiritual transcendence in the *Missa solemnis* and the Ninth Symphony, mentioning as well the variation movement of the String Quartet in E♭ major, Op. 127. His concern is with referential sonorities as musical symbols for the deity or the heavens. Beethoven's remark about the second movement of Op. 59, no. 2, tying it to a meditative contemplation of the stars, suggests the Kantian moral overtones of his later conversation book entry cited by Kinderman (102): "'das Moralische Gesez [*sic.*] in uns, u. der gestirnte Himmel über uns' Kant!!!"[26]

The tragic-to-triumphant/transcendent genres are often extended over more than one movement. In the Fifth Symphony, a tragic first movement is answered by a triumphant last movement (this pattern has been dubbed a "Victory Symphony" by Ratner 1980: 155). In the *Eroica*, the tragedy hinted by the first movement is completed in the funeral march, but overcome in Promethean fashion by the last movement. The Piano Sonata in A♭ major, Op. 110, begins with a modestly transcendent first movement, and the final movement alternates between tragic arioso and an increasingly transcendent and triumphant fugue.[27] A contrasting pattern characterizes both the *Tempest* and the *Appassionata* sonata cycles. Their moments of transcendent serenity occur in their respective slow movements, but these offer only a respite between relentlessly tragic outer movements.

Since fugues and fugatos appear both as independent movements and as parts of movements, and since the only thematic formal prescription constraining a fugue has to do with the initial exposition of all its voices, the fugue seems to offer fewer structural possibilities for negotiation with an expressive genre than does the sonata, with its archetypal dramatic shape. Actually, fugal technique has an important correlation in the Classical style. Ratner (1980: 260–71) points out the association of fugal writing with those forms that were carried over from the Baroque, particularly those that were prominent in the more conservative music of the Church. Once again, an immediate association with sacred music can be misleading. As noted earlier, the use of fugal textures acquires a general sense of "authoritativeness" as a stylistic correlation from its association with earlier or current Church styles. The "authoritative" correlation is then subject to further interpretation in terms of the particular affect involved in the movement. In the hectic fugal finale of the String Quartet in C major, Op. 59, no. 3, it is ecstatic joy authoritatively (that is, absolutely) affirmed. In the first movement of the String Quartet in C♯ minor, Op. 131, it is tragic grief authoritatively (that is, implacably) faced in all its dimensions (see Chapter 6). The sense of exploration is effectively correlated with the "seeking out" of a ricercar-like fugue. Figure 3.8 places these and other fugal movements in the style/mode matrix.

Although not every fugue is "profound" in the sense of being serious or tragic, many fugues carry the stylistic markedness of continuous texture, as opposed to the articulation of texture most typical of Classical style. One correlation for continuous texture, as may be recalled from the perpetual motion movements, is "obsessiveness." Again, this correlation, like the "authoritative" one, may co-exist with more than one affect.

Some other examples of fugal or imitative movements may be helpful in providing a sense of expressive range. Along with the triumphantly transcendent fugal ending of Op. 110, the finale of the Ninth Symphony reflects, in its double fugal treatment of themes, an integrative triumph of "joy" ("Freude") and transcendence of boundaries ("Seid umschlungen, Millionen''). The *Fidelio* quintet, canonic in its entries, is a good example of an imitative work in the *galant* style. The third movement of the String Quartet in E minor, Op. 59, no. 2, exploits the humor of a "low style" folk tune in a fast-paced fugato that works up to a hurdy-gurdy climax. And in the third movement of Op. 109, the *gemütlichkeit* of the fugal fifth variation is a perfect foil for the elevated return of the theme in the final section, where the technique of character variation gives way to progressive diminutions, and where transcendence is achieved by an increasing atomization (diminution) of the rhythmic texture.

The last example leads to the role of variation movements in Beethoven's strategic exploitation of genres. Obviously, movements based on character variation have great potential for conveying a multitude of emotional states, or affects, and thus a more widely ranging series of dramatic stages; what they may lose is a sense of coherence if the variations wander too far from the theme or from its guiding generic implications. Diminutional variations, such as those in the middle movement of the *Appassionata*, maintain a stronger sense of connectedness because of the progressive subdivision of the beat. The brevity of the *Appassionata* movement is due to its quick exhaustion of a strategy of registral ascent for successive variations, rounded by a return to normative register.

What is fascinating about Beethoven's variations in his later sonata cycles is the consistency with which they are used for expressing transcendence in a larger generic structure. The stasis of variation sets can be highlighted by the use of diminutional variations and emphasized by slow tempos. When hymnlike textures and soft dynamic levels are also chosen, variations support interpretation in terms of the contemplative and the meditative—a transcendent serenity. Figure 3.9 illustrates the preponderance of late variation movements (chosen from the symphonies, string quartets, piano trios, and piano sonatas) that occupy this place in the topical field.

Even when the movement is not a variation set, use of variation techniques for thematic exposition in a sonata movement can be one way of supporting a similar correlation of transcendence. Consider, for example, the variational presentation of the opening theme in the second movement of Op. 59, no. 2,[28] or the variational returns of the hymnlike A section in the third movement of the String Quartet in A minor, Op. 132.

It appears from the foregoing survey that in late-style variation movements, Beethoven often employs the extremes of soft dynamics, slow tempo, and hymnlike texture to create an atmosphere of serene contem-

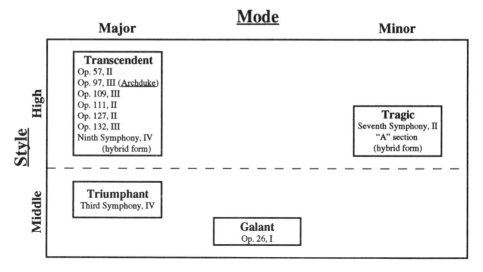

Figure 3.9. Placement of Beethoven variation movements according to expressive genres.

plation or transcendence. The additive nature of variation form (especially diminutional variations such as those in the second movement of the *Appassionata* and the finale of the Piano Sonata in C minor, Op. 111) supports the more static quality of serene contemplation. But these movements also encompass points of dramatic climax in extreme registers.

Summary

Expressive genres serve to place interpretive activity in the proper realm. They are cued by basic oppositional features such as mode, high/middle/low style, texture, tempo, and thematic exploitation of familiar topics. In Beethoven's late style, even formal types such as variation and fugue may associate with certain expressive genres. Once a genre is recognized or provisionally invoked, it guides the listener in the interpretation of particular features (such as the abnegation or resignation progression) that can help flesh out a dramatic or expressive scenario.

The more clearly a work encompasses an expressive genre, the more one is able to specify its expressive significance. In this sense, expressive genres are marked in opposition to purely formal genres. Furthermore, those works whose expressive genres are marked by minor mode, extremes of high or low style, or some other salient set of characteristics (such as the pastoral) are likely to attract more fully articulated expressive interpretations.

The simple matrix created from cross-referencing two kinds of oppositions is intended to illustrate how even a few basic distinctions lend coherence to a system of expressive genres. Other oppositions, such as that between slow and fast (which help differentiate, for example, *Empfindsamkeit* from *Sturm und Drang*), could be cross-referenced in more sophisticated arrays or simply in a series of matrixes.[29]

What markedness reveals is the asymmetry of those oppositions, in that the tragic can be more narrowly interpreted than the wider range of unmarked, nontragic genres one might loosely label comic. When a label or term seems unsatisfactory because of this kind of looseness, it may be an indicator that the entity is unmarked and thus systematically less articulated in its expressive correlation. Other oppositions may articulate the unmarked entity, but only by further dividing its field of meaning into asymmetrical parts.

The foregoing survey of expressive genres in Beethoven's music is in no way exhaustive, and can only provide a background for interpreting play with or against the expectations of a genre. Figures 4.7 through 4.9 display some of the relatively unambiguous candidates for each of the expressive genres, but the oppositional categories of style are only as a starting point for the analysis of subtler strategies.

The Pastoral Expressive Genre

The Four Movements of Op. 101

Although expressive genres may involve a progression from one topical state to another, it is also possible, as suggested by the example of the *Appassionata* finale, for an expressive genre to remain within a single topical state chosen from among the expressive fields mapped in the previous chapter. The *Appassionata* sonata cycle as a whole moves from a tragic first movement to a transcendent second movement before returning (with the *attacca* diminished sevenths as cue) to the tragic for an obsessive finale. Thus, the tragic frames and governs the expressive genre of the complete work.

The pastoral expressive genre can be understood in this way, as well. A movement or a multimovement work need not remain exclusively in the pastoral; but if the pastoral acts as a frame, it can be said to govern

the expressive genre as a whole. How, then, does the pastoral as overarching genre penetrate to the details of a work and permeate the character of an individual movement? These questions will direct the
interpretation of Beethoven's Piano Sonata in A, Op. 101, with special
attention to the first movement.

The Pastoral Premise in the First Movement of Op. 101

The first movement of Beethoven's late Piano Sonata in A major, Op.
101, is remarkable in its formal condensation and elliptical tonal style.
Although critics have explained a great deal in syntactic or formal terms,
the role of topic and expressive genre has largely been overlooked.[1] But
expressive motivations help explain the function and the coherence of
unusual compositional choices by showing how their expressive effects
support a plausible dramatic form.

Many writers have commented on the unusual formal features of the
movement, and at least one writer has offered a thoroughgoing expressive account of the whole work (Wilfred Mellers, 1983), but no one to
my knowledge has recognized the pastoral as the fundamental topical
premise coordinating formal features and expression. Pastoral conventions, cued in emblematic fashion by the first two measures, account for
many local features—the undercutting of climaxes and resolutions, and
the use of pedal points. But the pastoral as expressive genre does more,
providing an expressive context that guides further interpretation of the
movement and the cycle as a whole.

The pastoral as a topic suggests no clear dramatic pattern, with the
exception of disruptive storms that soon pass, as in characteristic works
like the Sixth (*Pastoral*) Symphony.[2] Rather, the function of the pastoral
intuitively appears to be the evocation of a mood, or the premising of a
topic. In the works of Beethoven, however, the pastoral also involves the
poetic conceit of feelings inspired by Nature, either in the secular sense
of a grounding in the "natural" (Rousseau) or in the pantheistic sense
of God in Nature.[3]

The topical contrast of the pastoral with the tragic, then, creates a
typical dramatic structure. In the first movement of Op. 101 (reproduced in full as Example 4.1), tragic irruptions create dramatic
moments of crisis. The pastoral exerts its control over these outbursts,
and the movement ends with a serenity that, in its registral extremes,
invokes transcendence or spiritual grace. In other words, the mixing of

Example 4.1. Beethoven, Piano Sonata in A, Op. 101, first movement complete.

Example 4.1. (Continued)

Example 4.1. (Continued)

tragic elements endows the pastoral with greater seriousness and the elevation of style in turn supports the interpretation of the pastoral as a poetic conceit for a spiritual state of innocence (or serenity) subject to the disturbances of tragic experience (or remembrance).

The primary tragic climaxes in the drama of the movement occur in the middle of the development (mm. 50–51) and the transition to the coda (mm. 85–87). These tragic events are reinforced by the greatest dynamic surges of the movement, but forceful projections are undercut each time—by *subito piano* in m. 52 and by decaying dynamics in mm. 87–88—before attaining their climactic goals.

Two reversals of chromatic voice leading are tied to the thematic argument of the work in a way that maximizes their expressive potential. In the first case, the reversal hinges on the A♯ in the bass, which resolves correctly in m. 47 but is pulled chromatically in the opposite direction in m. 49, just when the sequence is compressed to a half measure. The chromatic reversal may be understood to trigger both the acceleration and the tragic outburst that follow.

The pull of chromatic reversal is anticipated in the second theme (m. 17). Interestingly, the same pitches—A♯ to A♮—occur there as $\sharp\hat{4}$ to $\natural\hat{4}$, suggesting the resignation progression analyzed in Chapters 1 and 2. Depending on their contexts, such "yielding" progressions can provoke differing "responses" from subsequent music events. In the *Hammerklavier* example poignant resignation in the exposition was transformed to glowing spiritual acceptance in the recapitulation. Here, poignant (even questioning) reversal in m. 17 is transformed to frustrated reversal, in a turbulent context (syncopated accents) leading to outrage in mm. 50–51.

An even earlier appearance of chromatic reversal (raised $\hat{7}$ to $\natural\hat{7}$) results from a passing tone in the first measure. Although less focal since it serves as part of a contrary-motion "wedge" unfolding the pastoral theme, its inflection may nevertheless be construed as a reversal: the D♮ undermines our initial interpretation of the key as E major by strongly suggesting tonal motion from tonic E major to its subdominant, A major. Thus, when the listener understands the actual home tonic to be A, that key has received an appropriately pastoral "subdominant coloring."

This chromatic move (m. 1) suggests at best the more general correlation of "yielding" (in the context of "gracious unfolding") rather than in the more specific interpretation of "resignation," because of its less focal reversal. The more marked reversal in m. 17 calls forth a correlation of resignation, though perhaps less powerfully than the reversal in Op. 7, II

(m. 4). But in mm. 48–49, resignation takes on a negative connotation of frustration, whereas in the developmental epiphany of Op. 7, II, the reversal triggers a far more positive interpretation.

The potential for abnegation, however, is not neglected in Op. 101. After the second disturbance (mm. 85–87), the undercutting of a tragic climax is achieved not merely by dynamic withdrawal, but by the chromatic pull of $\sharp\hat{6}$ to $\natural\hat{6}$ and its resolution to an "arrival" six-four that invites an eventual cadence. Arriving in this manner, the six-four correlates nicely with the achievement of "grace"; the move from the German augmented sixth chord involves a minor-to-major transformation of $\hat{3}$, thereby inheriting the Picardy-third correlation. Indeed, this technique of arrival on a major six-four, whereby a complete theme is then presented on a dominant pedal as a kind of "elevation," is often exploited by Liszt (as the "salvation six-four" mentioned in Chapter 1) to suggest an apotheosis. In the Beethoven movement, the six-four suggests the arrival of a "saving grace," or positive spiritual insight.

Turning now to the tragic reversal beginning in m. 85, one can observe that it functions not as an evasion but as a departure, since it launches from a harmonically, if not metrically, stable tonic. The descent in the upper voice may be understood locally in terms of modal mixture; lowered $\hat{7}$ and $\hat{6}$ recall the sadness of the transition to the recapitulation, also in minor (mm. 55–56). The resolution in the upper voice of D$\sharp$ to E (mm. 89–90) relates thematically to previous chromatic reversals. This otherwise stylistically unmarked resolution is now marked as "a reversal of a reversal." Another relationship, already mentioned, is the positive outcome of the raised-to-lowered $\hat{6}$ in the bass, as it "resolves" into the six-four, uniting the resignation of the bass with the positive, Picardy-like six-four to produce a resolution combining abnegation with spiritual grace.

The brief coda has other thematic events that support this expressive interpretation. These events will be discussed below, in the course of a more-detailed examination of the movement.

Returning to the opening of the movement, one can observe that the first two measures, although tonally open, present a complete expressive package of typically pastoral features:

1. Six-eight meter. Pastoral movements are often in compound meters.

2. Pedal on $\hat{5}$. Pedal points, along with drone fifths, are typical cues for the pastoral.

3. Harmonic stasis achieved by the V^7 arpeggiation. Although partly a consequence of the dominant pedal, consonant diatonic harmony and slower harmonic rhythm are typical of the simplicity of the pastoral.

4. Relatively simple melodic contour. Besides being the kernel of a complete expressive contour (moving stepwise with a "climactic" leap to an appoggiatura that resolves downward and falls away), the simplicity of the upper line also supports a pastoral interpretation.

5. Contrary motion creating a "wedge" shape. The texture suggests an unfolding or flowering. Leonard Meyer has commented on the importance of such wedge shapes for Romantic music.[4] This movement has also been considered reminiscent of Schumann's style.[5]

6. Rocking accompaniment. The alto voice creates a rocking or perhaps wavelike accompaniment, with a hint of the syncopation to come. Later, wavelike syncopated chords (mm. 29ff.) may suggest a "waterlike" image, or at least a sense of stasis like that of waves lapping against the shore (compare the barcarolle topic and its pastoral flavoring in the second movement of Beethoven's Piano Sonata, Op. 79). Although a structural rationale could be given for the rhythmic syncopations—namely, that they are simply a means of sustaining rhythmic activity to create a linkage between sections—the flavor of such imagery need not be neglected. The rhythmically unstable harmonic stasis creates a sense of expectancy which invites contrast.

7. Parallel thirds. The alto creates fairly consistent thirds with the soprano. Melodic parallel thirds are a "sweetener" akin to the doublings of root and third discussed in Chapter 2. They are often encountered in pastoral movements from the Baroque, not only for their sweetness, but because of the simplicity they suggest (as opposed to a more contrapuntal relationship of voices), and perhaps because of their image of a duet between two singers in complete accord.

8. Consonant appoggiatura. The soprano leaps toward a metric location where an appoggiatura would be expressively appropriate (the downbeat of m. 2), but the "crunch" is undercut since it is consonant with the pedal bass. Schenker ([1920] 1972: 16) notes this subtle effect by analyzing the soprano E as an appoggiatura to the chord-tone seventh of V^7, the melody unfolding an arpeggiation (G$\sharp$–B–D) of V^7.

9. Elaborated resolution of dissonance. The 4–3 suspension in the alto is undercut in intensity since it does not create a sharper dissonance (such as a second with an adjacent voice, rather than the perfect fourth with the bass), and since it is elaborated as an escape tone in the decorated resolution. It also provides the first hint of the syncopation to come

in the next phrase, which transforms the already weak syncope of the suspension to an accompanimental pattern.

10. Major mode, quiet dynamics. Obviously, these are typical features of the pastoral topic, but they do not fully distinguish the pastoral from other topics or styles that may exploit quiet dynamics and the major mode—for example, the hymn topic with its spiritual connotations. Combined with a hymnlike texture, however, the pastoral topic can acquire deep spiritual significance.

Although the features enumerated above do not have the same exclusivity in defining the pastoral, they contribute to a theme that is overwhelmingly pastoral in its effect. There is a surface of graceful and gentle expressivity, and the events that occur can be associated with the pastoral genre either directly or through practiced interpretations.

In Beethoven, genres such as the pastoral and the tragic constitute a flexible but systematic network of oppositions, provisionally organized by the matrix of mode and style in Chapter 3. Thematic discourse, to be investigated further in terms of strategic markedness in Chapter 5, can be understood here as building expressive coherence through the manipulation of topical material within the framework of a genre. Thematic relationships, to which the analysis now turns, are not simply conformant pitch or rhythmic patterns, but may also involve relationships that cannot be notated: for example, analogies among processes (such as various implementations of the process of undercutting).[6] In this construal, the analysis of the thematic is taken beyond motivic minutiae (Rudolph Reti, 1951), or even the more substantial relationships favored by theories of the *Grundgestalt* or developing variation (Schoenberg, [1950] 1975). These earlier theories are often restricted to pitch or rhythmic relationships, and limited to that which is amenable to representation in musical notation. But the *Grundgestalt* may involve a more general idea that requires verbal formulation rather than a notational "kernel."[7]

The notion of undercutting, applicable to a climax or a cadence, is a good example of such a verbalized concept. Expressively appropriate to the pastoral genre, undercutting may be understood initially as creating a graceful, continuous flow across boundaries and past implied climaxes. As Beethoven exploits such undercuttings, however, they take on further expressive significance and become thematic to the movement in a richer sense.

Another general concept (though more specifically expressive than undercutting) is that of yearning. It is conveyed in this movement through two kinds of processes: extended rising lines or step progressions (note the stepwise ascent through a whole octave, the most extended line thus far, in mm. 7–9); and immediate upward chromatic moves (including the chromatic intensification of the deceptive cadence in m. 6). These yearnings, if allowed to reach a climax or resolve to a goal, might either upset the self-established propriety of the movement or too decisively break its continuity. They are counterbalanced by undercuttings that gain expressive significance by being understood as opposing (reversing, negating) that which they prevent. Thus, yearning gives way to resignation.

The various structural vehicles of this thematic undercutting include:

1. evasions of authentic cadences:
   a. (weak beat) half cadences (mm. 2 and 4)
   b. (weak and strong beat) deceptive cadences (mm. 6 and 16)
2. "eludings" of climax:
   a. harmonic stasis and "consonant appoggiatura" (m. 2)
   b. deceptive move (m. 9), including an elaborated (hence delayed) and weak-beat resolution of the leading tone in the soprano, followed by an immediate leap downward (further denying strength of resolution)
   c. the upper voices' descent against the intensifications of the bass ascent (mm. 9–11), leading to prolonged stasis on V_3^4 of E (mm. 12–13)
   d. weak-beat resolution of the ongoing bass ascent to E (m. 15)

A further interpretive step, from undercutting of yearning to tragic reversal, is achieved by the two outbursts discussed earlier. It is also prefigured by the construction of the second theme, beginning in m. 16. The potential stepwise move to the A♯ (m. 17) is undercut by octave displacement; its resolution is then reversed by the thematic pull to A♮. Thus, potential yearning is reversed to yielding. When the second voice answers imitatively in inversion, it splits into two voices that simultaneously achieve chromatic and registral reversal on the downbeat of m. 18, thereby heightening the tension between yearning and yielding. Next, the difference between yearning and actual resignation is made explicit with the intercutting of an upward-arpeggiated figure (mm. 19, 21, and 23–24) and a responding V_2^4–I^6 move (as analyzed in Chapter 2). With the third arpeggiation, the gesture of yearning is permitted to climax and achieve completion, as confirmed by the first perfect authentic cadence of the movement. Consistent with a thematic strategy of undercutting, this otherwise strong cadence is undercut dynamically by means of a *subito piano*.

The development section (mm. 35–57) emerges out of the restlessly syncopated background into which the exposition fades. After fragmentary echoes of the opening two-bar theme, a move to F♯ minor heralds the tragic outburst to come. The latter half of the two-bar opening phrase is now extracted, and the appoggiatura is made to bear a greater poignancy (of yearning) by expanding the leap from a third to a fourth and then a fifth, and by realizing the dissonant potential of the appoggiatura figure. The dissonance, like the expansion, is graded, reaching its peak in mm. 47–48 with the minor ninth of G♮ against F♯ (a lowered $\hat{6}$ vs. $\hat{5}$ collision like that discussed in Example 2.10, from the last movement of Op. 132). At this point the reversal (negation or denial of the yearning) is triggered by the bass move from A♯ to A♮ (mm. 48–49).

The reversal is also marked by the sudden shift in phrasing of the melodic fragment. The compression from a four-note pattern in mm. 43–47 to an overlapping three-note expressive kernel (F♯–B♯–C♯, C♯–E♯–F♯) in mm. 48–49 features an inversion of the half-step appoggiatura resolution. Although the half step sounds like (and functions as) an inversion of the appoggiatura, it is actually derived from the half-step link between units of the previous sequence (C♯–D in m. 47). Thus, what was unmarked is raised, strategically, to the status of marked (an important process which is discussed further in Chapter 5). The fourth note of the original fragment is changed to a dissonant B♯ (m. 48) and treated as an appoggiatura resolving upward. Its resolution, already on a weak beat, is then heavily syncopated by means of a *sforzando*, creating the overlapping group C♯–E♯–F♯. These melodic inversions are analogous to the bass negation (A♯ to A♮) in that each constitutes a reversal supporting a tragic interpretation. The mechanics of motivic manipulation are guided by the drama of an evolving expressive genre.

Direction is again reversed in the stepwise descent of mm. 50–51, and the climactic contrary motion between hands is in turn undercut by a *subito piano* in m. 52. If the two-measure expansion of V^7 in C♯ minor (mm. 50–51) recalls the first denied climax (m. 9, also in C♯ minor), then the stasis of the *subito piano* V^6_5 (m. 52) is reminiscent of the sustained V^4_3 in mm. 12–13, where poised stasis on an inverted Mm^7 sonority was first marked as significant. But instead of the graciousness and ease of mm. 12–13, the inverted Mm^7 in m. 52 is more like a stunned pause after an outburst, or a repression of the outburst altogether. By undercutting the violence of the outburst, providing a return to the original dynamic level, and sustaining that moment by means of the fermata, this chord could be interpreted not only as an evasion of a cadence in C# minor, but also as a questioning interruption of an anguished outburst. Note how the sudden reversal of contrary motion contributes to the interrogatory effect at the fermata.

Upward-resolving appoggiaturas over a contrapuntal 5–6–5–6 (mm. 53–54) give the two-note motive a plaintive character, expressively transformed from outright anguish in the preceding measures.[8] The two-note plea may now be understood as implicit in the stepwise motion of the main theme, and its poignance reinforces the sense of loss conveyed by the theme's return in the minor mode (m. 55).

The recapitulation in major is delayed until m. 58. It condenses the already brief first group and returns the second group fairly literally, leading to the threatening chords that mark the coda. In spite of this tragic reminder, the end of the movement returns to much the same state as the beginning, but with an exaltation deriving from extreme registers and a closural fade. In this context, the transcendent image of the resolution to a cadential six-four in m. 90 must be recalled. The emblematic nature of that passage is partly due to the fact that it occurs after both the formal close of the recapitulation in m. 77 and the codetta on a tonic pedal in mm. 81–85. Thus, while it can be construed structurally as a more definitive, less undercut resolution to tonic than has yet occurred, it also absorbs the closural digression of the diminished sevenths in mm. 85–87. But codas in Beethoven are concerned with more than tonal closure.[9] Even if the cadence in mm. 90–92 is justified structurally as a more strongly weighted cadence than that of m. 77, its closural function is best understood as thematic, and therefore as expressive.

Although the expressive effects of the linear and tonal arrival at the cadential six-four were discussed earlier in this chapter, the role of the second theme's motive in the bass line (second beat of m. 88 through m. 90) remains to be considered. Octave displacement in the bass occurs simultaneously with a vii°6/V (only implied in m. 17), which leads by way of an augmented sixth chord to a dominant-functioning cadential six-four. The octave displacement, and its questioning effect, are eventually resolved as well, but not until the very last measure.

In mm. 92 (second beat)–94, an augmentation in the upper voice of the initial three notes (derived from the fragment immediately preceding it at the beginning of m. 92) leaps to E (m. 94), reversing the direction and size of the octave displacement, but not resolving it by step in the same register. Instead, the leap of a third is reminiscent of the opening theme's appoggiatura, suggesting an integration of the first and second themes.[10] Such mediation between contrasting themes helps create thematic closure. Meanwhile, the lower voices in mm. 92–94 offer an epigrammatic summation of earlier chromatic reversals, first from F♯ to F♮, and then from D♯ to D♮ to underline the climactic leap in the soprano. The harmonic progression from vii°$^4_3$/V to V$^6_5$ conveys resignation, as though this one poignant phrase might summarize, reflectively, an essential insight of the whole movement.

The remainder of the coda contributes further to thematic closure. A final wedge motion in mm. 100–102 helps resolve the octave displacement of the second-theme motive by providing the missing step in the same register (mm. 101–102, E–F♯–G♯–A), but with a weak-beat delay of tonic in the upper voices. The delay of a weak-beat cadence is a well-worn *galant* technique, but here the suspended chord takes on a thematic poignancy as it casts its associative net back to the upward-resolving appoggiaturas of mm. 52 (second beat)–54. In addition, the left hand alludes to syncopation on a pedal E in mm. 101–102, recalling the pastoral role of this element.

With all the thematic logic in support of an expressive scenario for the movement, why is the recapitulation so literal? The stylistic pressure of sonata form on the recapitulation might be argued as stronger than the strategic pressure of thematic and expressive arguments. Another possibility is that a regular return avoids further complication in an already freer adaptation of the schema, to provide a compensatory stability for such an elliptical movement. Indeed, symmetrical resolution is such a basic premise of the form, stylistically understood, that the nearly literal return from the rewritten transition through the codetta is hardly surprising. But two changes in the recapitulation, one large and one small, show concern for the expressive logic of thematic discourse. At m. 59 five measures are omitted, making for an even more elliptical first theme. The omission isolates (and supports as emblematic) the opening two-measure representative of the first theme as a sufficient return before the transition begins. The smaller change is an adjustment for register in the upper voice of mm. 75–76, but the removal of the sixteenth-note acceleration (compare m. 25) also serves to lessen the excitement of impending completion, or resolution, of the yearning motive.

In view of Beethoven's inheritance from Haydn, reinterpretation in the recapitulation is not surprising. The analysis of the slow movement

Example 4.2. Beethoven, Piano Sonata in A, Op. 101, second movement, mm. 1–8.

of Op. 106 documented reinterpretations of the main thematic material and of a progression in the transition section that could be understood as a turning point in the drama of the movement. But in both movements from Op. 101 and Op. 106, the coda was shown to have greater responsibility for summing up thematic ideas and achieving the dramatic closure appropriate to each expressive genre.

From March to Finale

Though the pastoral frames and organizes the whole of Op. 101, the cycle offers a range of topics. The second movement, although topically a march (and in a march-trio-march form), also displays the pastoral characteristic of prominent pedal points (Example 4.2, mm. 4–6). Its trio (Example 4.3) is largely canonic, in a primitive (simplistic) texture that at times exploits *Stimmtausch* (mm. 58–59, immediate voice exchange of motives) as well as pedal point (mm. 55–58, 76–78). It begins with a dronelike motive and takes full advantage of parallel tenths and sixths (increasing the perception of consonance) in the measures that follow. The dominant pedal is used to highlight the rounded-binary

Example 4.3. Beethoven, Op. 101, second movement, mm. 55–64.

returns in both the march and the trio, as well as the *da capo* return to the march proper. The pedal is given a lowered $\hat{6}$–$\hat{5}$ heightening each time; in the march lowered $\hat{6}$ is expanded to a brief region of ♭VI, a subdominant-side coloration that further supports the pastoral. Finally, the key relationships themselves are pastoral in their subdominant orientation: F major in the context of a sonata in A major, and its subdominant, B♭ major, for the rustic trio.

These pastoral relationships may be overlooked if one does not understand and interpret the mixing of topics involved. The concept of a pastoral march may seem strange, and a learned yet rustic trio may strike one as fanciful.[11] An interpretation that selects the energetic or heroic connotations of the march may suppress a military connotation, especially in view of the softening pastoral elements. And an interpretation of the trio in terms of the pastoral may well understand the canon as less learned and more primitive—akin to the rustic echo of a single pipe or a simple round involving two pipers. In the same way that the pastoral can be elevated, the learned style can be deflated, perhaps with gentle irony. Alternatively, one can construe the motivation for the imitation as having nothing to do with the learned in the first place, but rather as representation of a peasant round or a natural echo.

With the Adagio movement (Example 4.4), the tragic element is placed on center stage as the principal topic. Minor mode, characteristic 7–6 suspension (m. 3), Neapolitan (m. 3), modal change at the half

Example 4.4. Beethoven, Op. 101, third movement, mm. 1–20.

cadence (m. 4), chromatic descent in the bass (mm. 12–17), and diminished seventh chords (mm. 14–16) all contribute to a tragic expressive focus. Formally, the movement has hardly established itself before it lands on a dominant (mm. 17–20) for a cadenza transition to the Finale. The movement may be understood retrospectively as part of an extended slow introduction to the last movement, even though it suggests a more autonomous interlude, akin to the middle movement of the Piano Sonata in E♭, Op. 81a (*Les Adieux*), or the third movement of the Cello Sonata in A, Op. 69. Clearly, however, a sense of transformation is part of the dramatic intent of the transition, with its surprise return of the opening measures from the first movement (Example 4.5, mm. 21–24), fragmented and sequenced to a cadential flourish on the dominant (mm. 28–32). Pastoral elements need not have occurred in the third movement, since it obviously serves as a foil to the optimism restored by the Finale, in A major.

The quotation of the quintessentially pastoral opening measures (mm. 21–24) restores the topical field that governs the expressive genre of the sonata as a whole. The Finale commences with a heroic/learned topic that conveys triumphant resolution in the opening measures (1–4). The consequent phrase (mm. 5–8) features a pastoral pedal point, syncopation, and musette-like sixteenth figuration. There is also the canonic simplicity of echo imitations, used both linearly and with upper and lower pedal effects (Example 4.6, mm. 29–32 and 33–37 respectively). A folk element is evident in the closing theme, with its traditional jump-bass accompaniment for the overlapping melodic imitation (Example 4.7, mm. 59–62). Thus, the pastoral clearly inflects what might otherwise have been interpreted as a straightforwardly heroic/triumphant finale.

Modal change (reminiscent of the mutation in m. 4 of the third movement, Example 4.4) launches the development proper, a fugato in four voices, where the authoritative connotation of high style is clearly appropriate.[12] Even with the somewhat tragic disputation of the fugato, the outcome is, from a generic point of view, never in doubt. A less tense arrival in the region of C major ushers in the pastoral with a texture reminiscent of the echolike effects in mm. 33–37. The tragic fugato closes with a stretto that leads to a climactic augmented entry between dominant pedals in the left hand, and the recapitulation is a triumphant capping of this energy.

The first change in the recapitulation involves a greater emphasis on pastoral-oriented material, with pedal and overlapping entries displacing

Example 4.5. Beethoven, Op. 101, transition to fourth movement, mm. 21–31, and opening theme of fourth movement, mm. 1–8.

the heroic material. The next significant event in this trajectory occurs when the coda arrives (Example 4.8); here, the modal change that launched the development proper is deflected to a subdominant-oriented F major. Besides reminiscences of earlier pastoral material, one finds cuckoo-like effects (mm. 308–14)[13] followed by a pedal trill with dominant pedal "bells" tolling in mm. 318 and 322. The section sums up the drone effects so important to this movement and the trio of the march. A poetic fading is disrupted at the last moment by topical reaffirmation of the heroic, with a *subito fortissimo* tonic punctuation (mm. 327–29). The insistence on a single tonic harmony is in keeping with the underlying simplicity of the pastoral genre, while its repetition sug-

Example 4.6. Beethoven, Op. 101, fourth movement, mm. 29–37.

Example 4.7. Beethoven, Op. 101, fourth movement, mm. 59–63.

gests the monumental texture discussed in Example 1.2. Here the effect is one of primal triumph.

This brief survey of the Finale illustrates the importance of pastoral elements in conditioning the heroic and guiding a more spiritual interpretation of its triumphant outcome. Chapter 7 reconsiders the integration of heroic and pastoral topics in this movement and provides a further, tropological interpretation of their significance.

Commentary

The concept of the *thematic* has been expanded in several fruitful senses:

1. Any element, or relationship, or analogy among relationships (for which notation may not be adequate and some verbal label or character-

Example 4.8. Beethoven, Op. 101, fourth movement, mm. 305–end.

ization is required) may be strategically exploited as thematic for a given movement. Thus, key structure may be understood as thematic when it goes beyond a stylistic formal scheme, and local tonal events may be treated strategically as thematic.

2. That which is strategic, or thematic, to a movement is intimately linked to the expressive intent of the movement, serving as a vehicle for correlation and further interpretation. The thematic, in this sense, is what the work is about. As expressively salient (by necessity, since we must be able to hear an event prominently and usually more than once to gauge its significance), thematization results in strategic markedness. Salience is not to be measured in purely psychological terms, but rather in terms of semiotic (or cognitive) expectations as provided by the *style*.

3. Traditional mechanics of thematic development (inversion, fragmentation, etc.) may bring previously unmarked or potential features to the level of thematic markedness. The manipulation of motivic material is not simply a play among purely musical forms, but rather is motivated by the interpretations those forms may suggest in the unfolding expressive discourse of the movement.

CHAPTER

*The Thematic Level and the Markedness
of Classical Material*

The thematic level, understood as including tonal and harmonic as well as melodic and rhythmic events, is what I consider the strategic level of a work. Beethoven, drawing on the example of Haydn, gives high priority to thematic discourse: the presentation, generative development, and reconceived return/resolution of ideas that are clearly foregrounded and often strikingly configured (even developmental, in the sense to be outlined below). Any consistent use (repetition, variation, development, return) of a musical idea helps to define its thematic status as a subject of discourse. But the significance of an idea emerges to some degree from foregrounding, or salience in and of itself; and salience, as we have seen,

implies markedness. Thus, that which is thematic in a work is by definition strategically marked, above and beyond whatever stylistic markedness (or unmarkedness) its constituents may possess.

The opposition between thematic (foreground) and nonthematic
(background) is of course too general in itself to specify an expressive
interpretation. The narrower range of meaning attributable to strategic
markedness requires an ongoing thematic discourse, a progressive
"interpretation" that emerges from more than what has traditionally
been treated as motivic development. Thus, in the first movement of
Op. 101, expressive reversal and undercutting were as important as
means of development as the more familiar techniques of fragmentation
and sequence.

In the nineteenth century thematic discourse, or the presentation and
development of significant material, was understood as central to poetic
interpretation, often to the neglect of generative tonal processes basic to
Classical forms. In the past few decades, in part because of the enormous
influence of Heinrich Schenker, overemphasis on thematic discourse in the
traditional sense was corrected by a deeper concern for the tonal organization of Classical works. Tonal structure became, for Schenker, the true
content (*Inhalt*) of music, in place of unsupported or impressionistic programs.[1] His reaction, while healthy in terms of its deeper penetration into
voice leading processes at various levels, may also have been an over-
reaction, in that the role of thematic discourse was subsumed into the
"discourse" of voice-leading and purely tonal processes.[2]

Recent exceptions to an overemphasis on tonal structure and voice
leading are found in studies by David Epstein and Kofi Agawu, with
their concern for a balance between thematic and voice-leading analyses.[3] David Epstein (1979) contributes a fresh construal of Schoenberg's
concept of the *Grundgestalt*, or "basic shape," and a concern for the
thematic in terms of the basic premise for a movement. Kofi Agawu
(1991) applies Ratner's (1980) topics and a notion of beginning-middle-end structure to the analysis of Classical music.

Agawu (1991: 113) insightfully reveals the error in relegating the
thematic dimension to the function of "design," as Rothgeb (1977)
appears to imply in assuming that thematic or motivic material is laid
out primarily to help reveal the basic voice-leading structure. Although
Rothgeb's concept of design is helpful as a guide to voice leading in
monotextural Baroque works (e.g., the Prelude in C major from Bach's
WTC I), it cannot adequately convey the rich interaction of theme,
topic, and tonality in the Classical style.

This chapter puts forth a more broadly conceived definition of the *thematic*, not limited to motivic or melodic material alone, but including everything that is strategically marked as significant for the musical discourse. To the extent that a particular melodic or rhythmic motive, a novel texture, an unusual instrumental combination, or a striking tonal event is thematically foregrounded, it may function either as an initial premise (Epstein, 1979), or as a part of the ongoing expressive discourse. It should be clear that tonal processes have not been excluded from thematization, based on the previous analyses. In the first movement of Op. 101, tonal processes contributed to the quintessentially pastoral premise of the movement. In the slow movement of the *Hammerklavier*, a tonal progression supported abnegation as a thematic hinge in the expressive genre of the movement.

Tonal structure in the Schenkerian sense could be said to provide the underlying coherence of musical motion, expressively conceived as tension and release (dissonance and consonance; instability and resolution; expectation, denial or deferral, and realization), and formally conceived in terms of the hierarchy of closures (Meyer, 1973: 89) that any extended discourse requires. In exploring another aspect of musical meaning, I do not exclude any of these crucial functions of tonality, but rather suggest that they should also serve the thematic level of interpretation. Thematic interpretation of tonal events may in turn feature those very "nonstructural" pitches that disappear in a reduction to an underlying contrapuntal framework. But Schenker's principles of voice leading are clearly relevant to interpretation of the expressive significance of nonstructural pitches, and I have drawn on them both explicitly (Schenker's analysis of the consonant appoggiatura in the second measure of Op. 101, I, cited in Chapter 4) and implicitly (the reversal of the implied voice-leading resolution in the *Hammerklavier* movement; see also the analyses of phrase expansion in Examples 8.3ff.).

In this chapter, markedness at the thematic or strategic level is investigated from several angles. To begin with, three basic *types* of musical material in the Classical style are mapped in terms of a series of marked oppositions in the style. Next, a matrix of material function cross-referenced with locational function is used to illustrate the varieties of mixing and matching by which Beethoven strategically plays with the "pure" stylistic categories of musical material. In addition to considering "developmental" themes that exploit pitch instabilities, I demonstrate how the strategic markedness of unusual phrase structure can help individuate stylistically unmarked musical material, as in the opening theme of the first movement of Op. 18, no. 6. Finally, I introduce another level of consideration, that of the intentionally unmarked theme (as opposed to a generative theme more central to the musical discourse), in order to account for the unexpected expressive designs of certain second-theme groups in first-movement sonata expositions.

Analyses of two complete movements in Chapter 6 provide further applications of these ideas. The opposition of two themes and their progressive integration is a compositional strategy that helps explain the unusual formal design of the first movement of Beethoven's String Quartet in B♭, Op. 130. And the opposition of marked and unmarked entities from both stylistic and strategic perspectives helps account for fluctuating perspectives on the tragic in the first movement of Beethoven's String Quartet in C♯ minor, Op. 131.

Markedness of Classical Textures

In terms of formal function, there are three basic kinds of material in the Classical style: thematic/presentational, transitional/developmental, and cadential/closural.[4] These materials are defined in terms of several different oppositions, as illustrated by Figure 5.1. The three kinds of material, familiar from taxonomic classifications such as Jan LaRue's *Guidelines for Style Analysis* (1970), are oversimplifications of more complex material actually found in sophisticated Classical music. Nevertheless, these basic *types* are fundamental to our understanding of the subtle mixtures actually employed.[5]

As shown in Figure 5.1, thematic or presentational material is characterized by broader periodicity of phrase structure (typically four bars), relative tonal stability, and (less specifically) a distinctive topic, idea, melody, etc., presented straightforwardly. Developmental or transitional material is distinguished by aperiodicity, tonal instability, and greater complexity or ambiguity of design in the treatment of distinctive material. Cadential or closural material is characterized by shorter, extremely regular periodicity (typically 2 + 2 rather than 4 + 4 measures), extremely stable tonality (with formulaic progressions), and a tendency toward clear presentation of conventional material (scales, arpeggiation, trills, brilliant figuration).

Since each opposition can distinguish two but not three kinds of material, each column in Figure 5.1 includes a further, related opposi-

Material	Defining Oppositions		
Unmarked Categories:	Periodic	Tonally Stable	Conventional Material
Marked Oppositions:	Aperiodic	Tonally Unstable	Distinctive Material
Thematic/Presentational	Periodic (longer)	Stable (relatively)	Distinctive (clear)
Transitional/Developmental	Aperiodic	Unstable	Distinctive (complex)
Cadential/Closural	Periodic (shorter)	Stable (extremely)	Conventional

Figure 5.1. Stylistic oppositions defining three basic categories of Classical material.

tion—longer vs. shorter periodicity, for example. Note that the most extreme oppositions are found between (marked) developmental and (unmarked) closural material.

The status of thematic/presentational material—standing, as it were, between the extremes of complexity and stability, or novelty and rigid tradition—may appear problematic. On the one hand, given its important presentational role, it is cognitively important that thematic material be balanced between what is new and old, or daring and familiar, in a given style. Thematic material, in this construal, should create interest and have a distinctive character, while (for initial themes) establishing key, meter, and tempo—those structures that require some degree of regularity at the beginning in order to be intelligible. The most interesting features of a theme, then, are the special, if not spectacular, configurations that create a memorable, but coherent, musical idea.

On the other hand, there is a problem in reconciling the intermediate position of thematic material with respect to markedness. Thematic material falls between marked and unmarked extremes, yet by its intrinsic salience (or thematic interest) it deserves to be marked at some level. One solution was proposed earlier: to consider the possibility of thematic markedness, stemming from the functional role, or arising from the individual treatment, of thematic material as *thematic* (i.e., significant, in the strategic sense defined earlier). Thematization alone can mark what might otherwise be merely unmarked stylistic material. Framing within a thematic location, as determined by formal genres, may also accomplish this goal.

Developmental material that derives from such thematic material will have, appropriately, both the strategic markedness of thematic foregrounding and the stylistic markedness of those aspects of instability that define a separate species of material (aperiodicity, tonal instability).

It may be worth restating this point from a slightly different perspective, since there is a crucial distinction between stylistic and strategic markedness. Thematization is achieved when the work makes certain material the explicit focus of its formal and expressive argument. The result of this process is a foregrounding or salience of the (thematic) material so endowed, which otherwise might have been construed as unmarked with respect to the extremes of cadential and developmental material. Foregrounding or salience yields a markedness at the level of strategy for material that may not have been marked at the level of style. Obviously, and to the degree presentational intelligibility can be preserved, there will be an evolutionary pressure toward incorporating more stylistically marked material as well, and composers such as Beethoven do find more daring

ways to achieve salience in their important themes. The featuring of instabilities, leading to more developmental themes, is just one instance of the
mixing and matching of categories resulting from strategic play.

But whether a theme is a unique combination of otherwise unmarked
stylistic features, or whether some novel feature is present, thematic
material is strategically marked by the very fact of its thematization.
Strategic (thematic) markedness goes beyond the markedness of style in
just this sense—any material can be thematically foregrounded by
becoming a subject, or even the premise, for a musical discourse.

The implications of strategic markedness will inform any analysis of
individual works. At this stage of inquiry the focus has been on the stylistic
markedness of general types of materials. The three types of material have
been defined by basic stylistic oppositions whose markedness values must
now be defended. Since cadential material is conventional and expressively
"worn out" (according to this somewhat idealized modeling), and since
its significance relative to thematic or transitional/developmental material
is so general as to permit substitution of whole patches of cadential scales,
trills and arpeggios from one piece to the next, it appears to be unmarked
material *par excellence*. By this inference, and in line with markedness in
language, its defining features are equally unmarked with respect to their
opposites. Thus, aperiodic, unstable, unclearly presented material (characteristic of transitional and developmental material) is marked with respect
to all three features.

Interestingly, such coordination of markedness values is typical of
semiotic systems, and is also suggested by the principle of *markedness
assimilation* (Andersen, 1968: 175, 1972: 44–45; Shapiro, 1983: 84),
described in Chapter 2. According to the principle of markedness assimilation, "the normally unmarked value for a given feature occurs in an
unmarked (simultaneous or sequential) context, and the normally
marked value in the marked context" (Shapiro, 1983: 84).

Markedness assimilation offers another explanation for Beethoven's
tendency to move thematic material toward the developmental pole. By
flirting with one or more instabilities, his themes acquire the additional
salience that comes from stylistically marked oppositions. In turn, that
increased markedness creates a greater specificity of content, which
enhances the expressive force of such themes. Nevertheless, sufficient
stability, periodicity, or clarity of presentation will be preserved to maintain the distinction between thematic statements and even thematically
derived transitional or developmental materials. In that way, stylistic
coherence is not threatened.

To the extent that "expressivity" depends on salience, and strategic markedness provides that salience, composers wishing to enhance the expressivity of their themes may exploit two marked oppositions—namely, tonal instability and irregular phrasing. Since Beethoven was concerned with the immediacy with which his themes could convey expressive content and the specificity with which they "spoke," it is reasonable to assume that tonal instabilities or phrasing irregularities would be used to mark significant themes. Note that this argument for more focally expressive themes does not exclude the explanation of other instabilities as generative premises for compositional working-out.

Formal Location as Functionally Marked

The "sensitizing" of location within a formal scheme may reinforce the particular function of material in that location. To the degree that we recognize a "thematic" slot, we are more likely to accept whatever material appears there as "the theme," even if the material would otherwise be understood as closural or developmental.

The section-building module basic to Classical style is one of statement–elaboration–closure, corresponding to the three types of material (thematic, developmental, cadential). In this module a theme is presented, possibly elaborated or continued through developmental means, and cadenced, possibly with a few measures of cadential material.

This model occurs at a larger level as the design of the tripartite sonata exposition used by Haydn in his early piano sonatas (e.g., the Piano Sonata in C minor of 1770). The same modules can be found as expansions of the sections of an exposition, including those with a second theme group. The following scheme, adapting LaRue's (1970) symbols, is illustrative:

Section	P	T	S	K
Module	P D K	(P) T K	S D K	(SK D) K
Tonality	I	V/V	V	

Note that I have reserved T in the smaller modules for the actual modulation within the transition section, and substituted D when the intent is developmental extension or elaboration of a theme. The transition section may start with a counterstatement of the first theme (P), or a new theme (Op. 10, no. 3, first movement), and its cadential section will be a dominant prolongation to prepare the arrival of the new key. The closing section may start with a closing theme (SK) and it may feature an elaboration or brief digression (D) before the final cadence. Interestingly, this suggests a hierarchy of formal design, based on the order of material types in sections, that is as important as the hierarchy of tonality for the definition of form.

If it appears that any of the three material types can be found hierarchically nested within any of the three location types, note that there is still a constraint on the order of their use.[6] Furthermore, it is not likely that a theme appearing within a cadential section (K) will be purely thematic—rather, it will implement at least one of the relevant oppositions distinguishing cadential material, to guarantee its interpretation as a closing theme. Otherwise, the listener might assume another second theme had been introduced (an expansion of the form).

In the first movement of Beethoven's *Pathétique* Sonata, Op. 13, the appearance in m. 51 of the second theme in E♭ minor is clear. Despite certain tonal instabilities—modal mixture, dominant pedal, brief tonicization—the theme has a clear four-bar periodicity, and the location has been defined as thematic. The preceding transition section has reached a clear dominant of the new key (E♭) and confirmed this with cadential material; thus, the articulation between sections is dramatically clear. Although this articulation of the exposition might differ from a strictly Schenkerian articulation, which would be based on the later drop of the dominant pedal to the E♭ major tonic, the noncongruence (Meyer, 1973: 85) between thematic and tonal perspectives (which need not be analyzed away in favor of a single "solution") is fundamental to understanding the strategically marked expressiveness of the second theme, in E♭ minor.

Coupled with the multiplicity of oppositions used to differentiate kinds of material, this sensitizing of formal locations in terms of material functions enables a composer to achieve strategic markedness by the use of material presumably inappropriate for the location—beginning with a "cadential" theme, for example.[7]

The impact that location has on material, inflecting it sufficiently to have at least one of the defining characteristics of the material most closely associated with that location, supports the strategic mixing of material types. A second matrix (Figure 5.2) illustrates the range of possible interactions between locational and material functions. The cross-referencing of material and location yields six marked categories of mixture and three

Locational Function

	Presentational Section	Developmental or Transitional Section	Closing Section, Codetta
Thematic	unmarked	(new) theme in development section; or transition theme (3)	closing theme (5)
Developmental/ Transitional	"developmental" unstable theme (1)	unmarked	closural digression, or developmental coda (6)
Cadential/ Closural	theme featuring closural gesture or (overly) conventional material (2)	closural gesture in an unstable development (4)	unmarked

Material Function (left vertical label)

Figure 5.2. Strategic growth by cross-matching of material and locational functions.

unmarked categories of congruence. The six new categories illustrate a logical (systematic) growth process[8] motivated by an interest in enhanced expressivity and achieved by strategic markedness.

Examples of each of these marked categories may be found in Beethoven:

1. the typically Beethovenian developmental opening theme, with its seed of instability (*Eroica* Symphony, I);
2. the closural opening theme (Op. 135, I);
3. the new theme in the development (Op. 10, no. 1, I) or transition theme (Op. 10, no. 3, I);
4. the use of closural material (thematized) in a development (Example 6.4: Op. 130, I);[9]
5. the cadential (closing) theme (Op. 13, I); and
6. the *closural digression* (Op. 106, I, coda).

In the *Eroica* example location is not in question. The tonal stability of the opening chords, along with the stability of the first phrase of the theme, is sufficient to prepare for the instability of the crucial chromatic gesture in the second phrase. Furthermore, Beethoven justifies the apparent aperiodicity triggered by the surprising chromatic gesture by restoring periodicity at a higher level.[10] This is but one example of a larger principle, *compensation*, which permits a composer license in a given parameter or level as long as it is "made up for" in another parameter or level. As an incentive for growth and strategic markedness that nevertheless preserves the coherence of the style, compensation is an important principle in the Classical style.

In the Op. 18 string quartets, Beethoven is concerned with another kind of thematic markedness, that which is achieved by unusual phrase construction.[11] This technique enhances opening themes that might otherwise be either too unmarked or too overtly conventional (worn-out) in their expressive rhetoric. Op. 18, no. 6 begins with the least promising (unmarked) thematic material of any of the six quartets (Example 5.1). The theme is extended to eighteen bars and then reinforced by a counterstatement, helping to solidify its otherwise unremarkable status as thematic material.[12] In Op. 18, no. 5 (Example 5.2) a conventional opening turns out not to be the theme proper, but an unconventional tonic anacrusis to the structural downbeat at m. 5. The opening theme of Op. 18, no. 4 (Example 5.3) is close to a typical *Satz* [2 + 2] + [{1+1} + 2] and exhibits the stylistic markedness of minor-key rhetoric, but that rhetoric is rather trite (cf. Kerman 1966: 67–68). The theme receives greater weight by its extension to thirteen measures (based on the expanded varied repetition of mm. 5–8). Op. 18, no. 3 (Example 5.4) plays a game of noncongruence between melody and accompanying texture; the latter is clearly and rationally eight bars (mm. 3–10), whereas the former starts two bars earlier with a poetic minor-seventh anacrusis that stretches the phrase to ten bars. The Haydn-like Op. 18, no. 2 (Example 5.5) presents an eight-bar opening theme filled with conventional gestures (also used, like the opening theme of Op. 135, I, to close the movement), yet it is not organized as a Satz. Instead, its discrete two-bar motives [a + b + c + c'] depend on harmony for their coherent integration. Finally, the opening theme of the first movement of Op. 18, no. 1 (Example 5.6) is clearly marked motivically, but Beethoven expands the parallel period (mm. 9–20) with a four-bar developmental interpolation that introduces another marked element, the thematically significant diminished seventh.

In these early quartets, Beethoven appears to be experimenting with strategies of markedness involving a variety of unusual phrase constructions for his opening themes, whereas in the middle period works, the strategy often involves tonal instability as well. The latter is more powerful, since it has richer potential as a thematic premise for a movement. But in either case, Beethoven enhances the distinctive thematic interest and potential of what might otherwise appear expressively conventional. We will see in Chapters 6 and 8 that the sketch history of two themes supports thematic markedness as a conscious compositional strategy on Beethoven's part.

Example 5.1. Beethoven, String Quartet in B♭, Op. 18, no. 6, mm. 1–20.

Example 5.1. (Continued)

Example 5.2. Beethoven, String Quartet in A, Op. 18, no. 5, mm. 1–11.

Example 5.3. Beethoven, String Quartet in C minor, Op. 18, no. 4, first movement, mm. 1–13.

Example 5.4. Beethoven, String Quartet in D, Op. 18, no. 3, first movement, mm. 1–10.

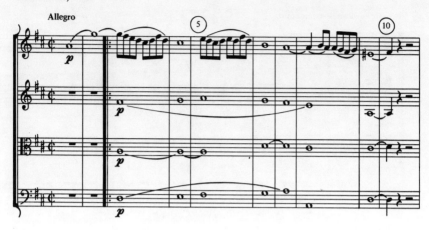

Example 5.5. Beethoven, String Quartet in G, Op. 18, no. 2, first movement, mm. 1–8.

The Unmarked Theme

Salient instabilities in an opening theme are chosen not merely to provoke a mechanical or formal working out in the remainder of the movement, but also to achieve the particular expressive character of a movement. The opposite case, in which a theme is intentionally con-

Example 5.6. Beethoven, String Quartet in F, Op. 18, no. 1, first movement, mm. 1–20.

structed to be stylistically unmarked, also occurs. Such unmarked themes simply do not play as significant a role in the thematic argument of the work, and indeed may function more as rhetorical place-markers than as generative themes.

An example of such a stylistically unmarked theme occurs in the first movement of Beethoven's String Quartet in E minor, Op. 59, no. 2 (Example 5.7). Here, the second key area is signaled by the extraction of the cello pedal and viola pedal trill, followed by the exchange of fragments in the cello and violin. The short-breathed "theme" arrives in m. 39, and although one could stretch a point and argue that it is marked with respect to its brevity (or even its derivation), the immediate, varied repetition it receives is enough to define but not expressively mark the brief theme. An interruption of the theme by $\flat\hat{6}$ (E♭) in the second violin in m. 42 is echoed by interruptions of the expected cadence in G at mm. 49 and 53, the latter triggering a move to the expressive climax of m. 55. Here, extremes of register support the ecstatic "arrival six-four" in G, but instead of fulfilling the twice-deferred perfect authentic cadence, Beethoven suspends time for one of the most extraordinarily expressive moments in music. The arrival six-four resolves the harmonic and rhythmic tension of the previous two measures (53–54), but the viola's octave leap energetically counters the sudden decrescendo. Both the first violin (in its transcendent register) and the viola then yield to the inwardness of the moment—the first violin by poignant mutation of the expected dominant with an F♮ that signals the descent, and the viola by a sudden sixteenth collapse that suggests an inward thrill of spiritual ecstasy. The next measure offers a sequential variation of the abnegation progression, with the bass line reversal (C♯ to C♮) in the second violin and the first violin paralleling the chromatic yielding in tenths. Here, the expressive context suggests a yielding of willful struggle (mm. 49–50, 53–54) to tender acquiescence, melting into acceptance. The harmonic result is a linear resolution to I^6, an imperfect authentic cadence that is immediately undercut by a varied repetition (mm. 57–58). The first violin continues to descend, accelerating to sixteenths in an expansion of the viola's melting descent in m. 55. The inner voices now echo the less-energetic octave leap (m. 57), which has migrated downward as well. Beginning in m. 58, a change of texture and metric instability obscure the symmetry of the varied repetition, and the next seven measures grope toward a definitive cadence. But the perfect authentic cadence never arrives; only a strong imperfect cadence with $\hat{5}$–$\hat{1}$ bass in mm. 64–65, accompanied by a shift to metrically stable cadential material, signals the actual close of this section.

Example 5.7. Beethoven, String Quartet in E minor, Op. 59, no. 2, first movement, mm. 36–59.

Example 5.7. (Continued)

Example 5.7. (Continued)

It is the evolution of the second theme that is expressively crucial, not the unmarked theme as it first appears. The original unmarked diatonic descent from G to B in mm. 39–40 is chromatically transformed in mm. 55–57, in a textural context that is expressively transported far from its conventional origins. Strikingly, the processive second theme group moves to its most salient, and thus most expressive, moment at the very spot where a typical stylistic scheme would have predicted the closural cadence. Yet this passage counts for far more than a formal characterization as an expanded cadence would convey.

The diminished role of an unmarked theme in the thematic argument of a work is further evidenced by the absence of the four-bar "second" theme from the development section or the coda. The movement is instead dominated by the principal theme, whose featured V^{m9} and Neapolitan harmonies recur thematically in the other movements, as well.

A deeper rationale for employing unmarked subsidiary themes, considering Beethoven's style, may be to avoid competing with the generative role of the initial theme. In the first movement of Beethoven's Piano Sonata in C minor, Op. 10, no. 1, the contrasting transition and the second theme pose no challenge to the hegemony of the first theme. Each is in fact derived from that theme, as Reti (1951) has observed. More direct reference to the first theme in the closing section rounds out this intensely unified exposition.

Beethoven's concern for maintaining intensity of affect as provided by a strong, minor-mode theme may be traced in the first movements of three piano sonatas: Op. 2, no. 1; Op. 13; and Op. 31, no. 2. In terms of minor affect, they illustrate in evolutionary sequence a strategy that results in *style growth*. In their respective expositions, Op. 2, no. 1, moves to a relative major colored with borrowings from the minor; Op. 13 begins the second group in E♭ minor before shifting to the traditional relative major; and Op. 31, no. 2, imposes a radical solution by moving to the minor dominant, thereby maintaining the minor mode throughout the exposition.[13]

Slow introductions that are thematically generative (Op. 13) or dialectical (Op. 31, no. 2) may displace the primary thematic contrast from that between the first and the second (contrasting key area) theme to that between a slow introduction and a fast first theme. The recall of introductory material at important formal junctures in both Op. 13 and Op. 31, no. 2, suggests a new role for the slow introduction. This consideration affects the analysis of the first movement of Beethoven's String Quartet, Op. 130, in the following chapter.

Thematic Markedness

The First Movements of Op. 130 and Op. 131

The first movements of Op. 130 and Op. 131 offer two perspectives on the role of strategic markedness, the former in realizing an unusual sonata form, the latter in generating a dramatic fugue. In the opening measures of each movement, thematic oppositions are foregrounded: as dramatic competition between themes in Op. 130, and as expressively differentiated halves of a fugue subject in Op. 131. And in each formal genre, the ways in which these oppositions evolve throughout the movement are fundamental to their expressive interpretation. The dialectics of thematic discourse involve more than the composing-out of basic tonal structures, and the significance of foregrounded features goes beyond their voice-leading derivations. Often it is the idiosyncratic that sparks hermeneutic insight into the expressive significance of a musical event.

Thematic Opposition in the First Movement of Op. 130

Markedness plays an extensive role in the oppositional contrast of opening themes in the String Quartet in B♭, Op. 130. This unusual movement departs from the idea of a slow introduction integrated into the thematic discourse of the movement (as mentioned earlier with respect to Op. 13 and Op. 31, no. 2). The opening Adagio theme, already more than introductory, is set in clear opposition to an Allegro theme. The consequences of this thematic dialectic are rich at both formal and expressive levels. Indeed, the conflict thus created and the strategies of integration and mediation that Beethoven explores in attempting to "resolve" the conflict are essential parts of the drama of the movement.[1]

Initially, contrasts seem to be carried to an extreme (Example 6.1). The opening theme is slow, in 3/4, soft, legato, and moves from octaves to a four-voiced hymn texture. The next theme (starting on the third beat of m. 14), is conversely fast, in four, loud, and nonlegato, and it features soloistic writing that Ratner (1980: 18–19) would characterize topically as "brilliant" (first violin) and "fanfare" (second violin). The earlier Adagio theme is slightly chromatic (with a subdominant inflection, A♭, in the opening gesture and a thrust toward the dominant in mm. 6–7), whereas the Allegro theme is plainly diatonic and sequences circularly within the home key of B♭.

Both themes are marked with salient features, and thus one cannot designate either as marked or unmarked in relation to the other. Instead, it is the opposition itself that becomes thematic, strategically marked as an idea, or premise, when the Adagio theme reappears in m. 20, on the dominant. The juxtaposition of themes is clearly an issue by this point: the Allegro theme now returns, in F major, with doublings that suggest a tutti after its earlier solo appearance. But F major has arrived too soon, and B♭ is quickly restored within the Allegro theme. After a cadence in B♭ (m. 37) the Allegro moves transitionally to the dominant, but the cadence in m. 51 does not hold. Instead, a chromatic scale ascends as if by fiat to D♭, which resolves as $\hat{5}$ of G♭ major, the subdominant-side key area for the second group.

The theme in G♭ appears to hark back to the Adagio theme because of its predominantly longer note values, softer dynamic marking, and legato, hymnlike texture. In fact, its motivic structure clearly recalls both themes (Example 6.2). This is the first instance of strategic integration as a mediation of the conflict between the slow and fast themes. By appearing in the subdominantly oriented key of G♭, this hybrid theme is

Example 6.1. Beethoven, String Quartet in B♭, Op. 130, first movement, mm. 1–19.

Example 6.1. (Continued)

Example 6.2. Beethoven, Op. 130, first movement, mm. 53–58.

in effect removed from the primal tonal argument of the form as stylistically conceived. The dialectical tension between the tonic and dominant has already been appropriated by the two generative themes of the movement. The hybrid theme is thus unmarked in that it has a less original identity and less stylistically typical role; nevertheless it is marked with respect to its striking integration of features from the generative themes. One might compare this theme with the unmarked second theme from the first movement of Op. 59, no. 2 (Example 5.7).

In spite of their apparently extreme oppositional characteristics, the Adagio and Allegro themes in Op. 130 share subtle features that will support further integration. These features include a *subito piano* undercutting of the goals of small gestures, and an initial metric ambiguity that is clarified by a reversal of downbeat-upbeat polarity. In the Adagio theme, the *subito* undercutting of crescendos is supported by weak-beat cadences that deny metric strength to the harmonic goal (Example 6.1, mm. 2 and 4). These moments are strategically marked by the unexpected change of dynamic level, and thus the two-note cadential slur motive is suitable for extraction and featured treatment, as happens in the development section.

Metrically, the first beat of each of the two main themes can initially be construed as a downbeat. Note how the crescendo marking in m. 4 supports this reading for the first theme by allowing a provisional interpretation in 4/4; and the dramatic change of dynamics and texture at the inception of the second theme suggests that the sixteenths are entering on a downbeat. This hypothesis is supported by the fact that most Allegros following slow introductions begin on a downbeat—indeed, usually on a large-scale structural downbeat.[2]

The hypothetical metric interpretation is also supported by the stylistic "tonal rhythm" (Schachter 1976: 313) implied by the opening scale degrees. The Adagio theme begins on $\hat{1}$ and moves to $\hat{7}$, which suggests, in the absence of conflicting evidence, strong-to-weak-beat motion. Similarly, the Allegro theme's quarter/eighth-note fanfare motive begins on $\hat{1}$ (m. 15), and in conjunction with a downbeat reading for the inception of the sixteenth notes, the tonic initiation may (provisionally) be construed as occurring on a strong beat. The notated meter for each theme is quickly clarified, but the brief confusion opens up the possibility that an opposition between downbeat and upbeat motivic inception might play a thematic role.

The development section begins with a compressed juxtaposition of the Adagio and Allegro themes, now reduced to motivic fragments that alternate in a tonal descent from Gb (= F♯) to D (Example 6.3). Both themes have been texturally inverted. The Adagio has also acquired a line in contrary motion (second violin, mm. 94–95) above a middle pedal, suggesting an unfolding or emergence. In the next statement (mm. 97–99), the pedal is on top, and its cadential drop of a fifth (mm. 98–99) sounds like a reversal of the upward leap of a fourth in the Allegro fanfare motive. When the Adagio recurs for the third time, the cadence figure from m. 99 is extracted. This weak-beat cadential resolution is transformed into an accompanimental figure, thus shifting from foreground to background in the thematic discourse to follow.

In the remarkable integrative passage that follows (Example 6.4, mm. 104–31), fragments from each theme are woven into a tapestry that, for all its hypnotic consistency of texture, remains highly unstable in terms of harmonically implied downbeats and their contradictory metrical placement.[3] The downbeat is often harmonically stable (m. 108), in a reversal of the weak-beat cadential expectation. The motives that are projected against this unstable background are highly marked themati-

Example 6.3. Beethoven, Op. 130, first movement, mm. 92b–103.

cally, as well as salient in a purely perceptual sense. A striking new motive seemingly derived from the integrative theme of the second key area (cello, mm. 106–107) is later linked explicitly with the fanfare figure (mm. 109–10), itself transformed by expansion of its leap to an octave and omission of its prefatory quarter notes (mm. 120–24). Throughout this section, traditional developmental procedures (fragmentation, modulation) meet stylistic expectations, but only extraordinary integrative strategies meet the challenge of the thematic premise.

Development, in the sense of dramatic motivic and harmonic action as well as in the sense of *Durchführung* ("leading through" tonal areas), spills across the putative boundary of the recapitulation (m. 132). Notable is the transformation of a new fanfare fragment, harmonized with a major-minor modal shift (Example 6.5, mm. 137–38). This transformation signals the tensions that follow: inversion and intensification of the fanfare leap in the cello, first with a diminished fourth (mm. 139–40) and then with a diminished fifth (mm. 141–42). The arrivals are harmonized respectively with (anxious) augmented and diminished-seventh sonorities.

Example 6.4. Beethoven, Op. 130, first movement, mm. 104–32.

Example 6.4. (Continued)

Beethoven escapes these familiar tragic portents with a subdominant key setting of the familiar resignation progression in mm. 142–43 (E♭: vii°⁷/V yields to V⁴₂ resolving to I⁶). The move to the subdominant (or one of its substitutes) occurs frequently in Mozart and Beethoven as part of a digression immediately following the recapitulation (Rosen, 1972: 79–80). Here, the subdominant key is strategic for this movement because it sustains a longer-range circle-of-fifths progression linking D major near the beginning of the development with D♭ major at the beginning of the second theme group in the recapitulation (compare Meyer, 1956: 127). This pattern is subsumed by a still larger-scale, and quite logical, key plan for the movement as a whole: an overall descent in thirds (Figure 6.1).

The coda (Example 6.6) presents juxtapositions reminiscent of the opening of the development, but with a difference. Now the Adagio theme receives a full four measures before the Allegro theme interjects, and the fanfare motive of the Allegro is suppressed. The motivic linkage is more explicit; the downbeat of m. 218 is at once a realization of implied downbeats for both the Adagio's cadential gesture (as already hinted in the development section's mosaic) and the Allegro's sixteenth-note initiation (as already hinted by reversals of polarity in mm. 138, 196ff., and 202ff.).

The Adagio segments that alternate from m. 219 on are minimal fragments of the cadential motive, each time resolving into the Allegro that follows, and supporting an upper-line ascent from B♭ (m. 218) chromatically to D (m. 223).[4] At that point an acceleration occurs. The Adagio motive's chromatic ascent resolves each chromatic inflection from Adagio to Allegro and creates the illusion of *thematic*

Example 6.5. Beethoven, Op. 130, first movement, mm. 136–45.

resolution of the Adagio theme (with its expressive content) into the Allegro. But the passage in mm. 223–28 goes one step further in providing a mediation of tempos between the Allegro sixteenths and the Adagio quarters. The first violin's eighths in mm. 227–28 sound like an augmentation of the sixteenth-note motive, whereas mm. 223–25 are clearly an acceleration of the chromatic ascent begun earlier, featuring the Adagio motive in each stepwise resolution of chromatic degree.

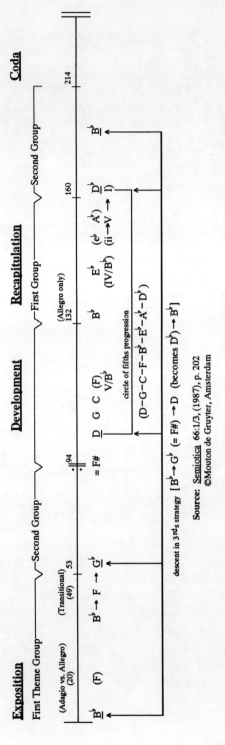

Figure 6.1. Diagram of key areas of Beethoven's String Quartet, Op. 130, first movement (compare Meyer [1956: 127]).

Example 6.6. Beethoven, Op. 130, first movement, mm. 214–end.

Example 6.6. (Continued)

After this extraordinary tempo mediation between, and metric resolution within, motives, the remainder of the coda returns the fanfare motive in an appropriately closural scale-degree sequence: 1̂–4̂ answered by 5̂–1̂. Once again, the sixteenths are downbeat-oriented. But as if in recognition of the remarkable melding of thematic affects in mm. 223–28, the final statement of the Allegro motive is pianissimo, with legato sixteenths.

In terms of expressive genre, the movement presents an interesting case. Because of its major-mode orientation and because its conflicts achieve at least provisional resolution in terms of the more positive Allegro theme, the movement would fall in the nontragic realm. The fanfare motive might suggest a highly stylized heroic element. But because of the significant chromatic and descending elements in the equally important Adagio theme, the expressive genre is mixed, along the lines of the tragicomic category.[5] Based on correlations appropriate to each theme, one might interpret a meditative, melancholy slow theme in contrast to a positive, brilliant Allegro theme, the latter suggesting the personal, heroic energy with which one might overcome the melancholy of reflection. The subtlety of the design indicates that no victory is achieved in a simplistic sense, but that understanding is gained through the clear acceptance of each state and the attempt to reconcile each within the realm of a single persona's experience. Therefore, "conflict" may perhaps be too strong a term for the contrasting themes and their implied states of being, since the attempt to reconcile admittedly unreconcilable states suggests a deeper sense of each state's value, and perhaps the contribution of each to a still higher, integrative state. It is the wisdom that grows from a Hegelian synthesis conceived not as a merging of opposites but as the emergence of a higher state generated from the productive tension of extremes. And it is the wisdom that in a Shakespearean sense reaches accommodation with life not through denial or presuming to conquer what is inherently tragic in the human situation, but through the unflinching and exhaustive exploration of the possibilities of mediation between juxtaposed and contrasting values.

Stylistic and Strategic Markedness in the Fugue of Op. 131

In the early nineteeth century completely fugal movements are rare and thus stylistically marked as a form (or formal procedure). Since the first movement of Op. 131 does not drift into a homophonic texture but remains committed to the polyphonic working out of its subject, the fugue is clearly marked at the level of style, as opposed to the mere topical use of fugal imitation.[6] The correlation of "authoritative" for the markedness of fugue or fugal style does not tell us what particular affect is involved. Recall the finale of Op. 59, no. 3, with its authoritative (= definitive) high spirits, interpretable as ecstatic delight. Op. 131 begins with an entirely different affect, and that affect appears to be influenced more by minor mode and slow tempo than by fugal style, when we compare the broadest oppositions in the movement.

The analysis that follows also explores thematic markedness and its role in the expressive organization of the movement. As with the first movement of Op. 101, the opening thematic material (here, the fugue subject) helps cue the expressive genre of the movement by exemplifying it in microcosm.

Upon cursory examination of the movement (reproduced in its entirety as Example 6.7), the slow tempo and minor key immediately bring to mind the seriousness of the tragic genre, and the fugal writing confirms the high style. But although the movement begins tragically, a Picardy-third ending on C♯ might suggest the tragic-to-transcendent as a possible expressive genre. In fact, an ambiguous Picardy third appears in Beethoven's earliest sketch, an overview of the entire quartet. In his book on the genesis of the quartet, Robert Winter observes:

There are relatively few occasions on which Beethoven concluded the first movement of a minor mode work in the tonic major (cf. Op. 5, no. 2; Op. 49, no. 1; Op. 111). . . . In the first overview [*Kullak*, folios 10r and 10v], the tonic major *Schluss* functions simultaneously as an orthodox tonic and as the dominant of the short recitative [in F♯ minor]. This dual function is commonplace in codas of sonata-allegro movements in Bee-

Example 6.7. Beethoven, String Quartet in C# minor, Op. 131, first movement complete.

Adagio, ma non troppo e molto espressivo

Example 6.7. (Continued)

Example 6.7. (Continued)

Example 6.7. (Continued)

Example 6.7. (Continued)

> thoven . . . but in these cases the subdominant tilt is preparatory and acts as a foil for the inevitable dominant-tonic resolution. This is not the case in Op. 131, either in the sketches or the finished work, where the potential ambiguity is both exploited and unresolved. [1982: 118]

From the report of a planned but rejected recitative link in F♯ minor, and with the striking move of the final version directly from the extracted C♯s to the Ds opening the second movement, one can infer that Beethoven has chosen to strategically mark an otherwise stylistically typical Picardy-third close.

The powerful transformation of C♯ from a tonic to a leading tone has a precedent in the String Quartet Op. 18, no. 3 (Example 6.8). In the first movement's linkage between development and recapitulation, a C♯ understood as $\hat{5}$ of F♯ minor is transformed into a C♯ functioning as $\hat{7}$ of D major, but the move to D is rationalized through the harmonization of C♯ as part of an incomplete V⁶₅ chord in D.[7] In Op. 131 the more powerful (since more abrupt) pitch class shift from C♯ to D may be related to a concern for submediant and Neapolitan relationships in the fugue itself.[8]

Interestingly, these concerns led to a revision of the exposition. In nearly all the sketches for this movement the answers in the exposition are at the dominant. But as Beethoven explored submediant and Neapolitan relationships, it appears that he realized the strategic potential for incorporating these relationships in the exposition itself. Thus, for the original dominant answer on D♯ Beethoven eventually substituted a subdominant answer featuring D♮ at the *sforzando* (m. 6). In that way, a Neapolitan lowered $\hat{2}$ answers the lowered $\hat{6}$ of the subject.[9]

Example 6.8. Beethoven, String Quartet in D, Op. 18, no. 3, first movement, mm. 152–60.

The subject also underwent an improvement from an initial sketch of rather unmarked material to a more expressively affective subject head. Example 6.9 presents both the sketch and the final form. Paul Mies (1929) attributes the "improvement" in the final version to Beethoven's avoiding an early apex. Once again, markedness considerations lead to a richer explanation.

Example 6.9. Earlier and final versions of the fugue subject head, String Quartet in C# minor, first movement, mm. 1–4 (Mies, 1929:10).

If one compares the opening themes of the second movements of Piano Sonatas Op. 7 and Op. 111 (Example 6.10), one discovers that a theme's apex (melodic high point) may or may not coincide with its expressive crux (point of expressive focus). In Op. 7, the apex and the crux occur at different points (see Example 2.14 and the accompanying analysis of this theme); in Op. 111, they coincide.

The structure of the Op. 131 subject exhibits noncoincidence between the apex (on C#) and a crux (*sf*, A♮) that immediately undermines the apex. Dynamic indications alone would suggest this interpretation, but an examination of the tonal events explains the effect even further. Just as the opening two measures of the first movement of Op. 101 are the perfect encapsulation of pastoral expressivity, so the head of the fugue subject captures the essence of the tragic with startling economy. The first three pitches, although insufficient to determine minor as opposed to major mode, are enough to establish C#. The presumed resolution of B# to C# as $\hat{7}$ to $\hat{1}$ is heightened with the sense of yearning created by placing B# as an appoggiatura on the strong beat. But the surprising intrusion of A♮ on the next downbeat undermines the strength of a positive resolution to C# while unequivocally confronting the listener with the minor mode. One may also hear the A retrospectively as having absorbed the C# as its third, thereby compressing the implied harmony of the opening progression from V–I–VI to a deceptive V–VI in C# minor. The deceptive move, when presented in four-voice texture, involves $\hat{5}$ moving up to $\hat{6}$ in the bass. In this four-note allusion to the move, the deceptive $\hat{6}$ is achieved through a melodic drop. Thus, not only is there harmonic reversal (of implied tonic), but melodic reversal (of direction).[10] It is not hard to imagine an interpretation of aspiration ($\hat{7}$–$\hat{1}$) suffering the reversal of a tragic drop (to $\hat{6}$, *sf*) as a brutal intrusion of tragic reality. Conceived in these terms, the structure of the four-note subject head is analogous to the dramatic scheme of tragedy.[11]

Example 6.10. Comparison of apex and crux in Beethoven. a. Op. 7, second movement, mm. 1–8; b. Op. 111, second movement, mm. 1–8.

Since the head of the subject is marked strategically for such specificity of expressive meaning, it is appropriate that the tail of the subject is unmarked, serving to absorb the shock created by the tragic drop.[12] The trailing quarter notes, primarily stepwise and without any dynamic direction, seem merely to elaborate in conventional fashion a structural descent from $\hat{5}$ (the immediate resolution of $\hat{6}$) to $\hat{3}$. This is a common underlying descent in fugue subjects.[13] Although the quarter notes move by step back to $\hat{5}$ to set up the answer (which otherwise would threaten a cross-relationship between E and E♯), there is a hint of sequence in the elaboration. Sequential extension of the tail is a conventional (and in that sense unmarked) process that occurs frequently in the fugue.

By reason of its stylistic unmarkedness, its deployment after the notably marked head and its inherent lack of expressive focus, the subject tail can be used as a kind of background, setting in relief the appearance of more expressive material. Sequential uses of the tail often involve more homogeneous rhythmic activity and less independence of voices than is found in the working out of the head. A good example occurs in mm. 15 and 17, where paired voices have parallel tenths and parallel thirds in simple contrary motion. Appropriately, this unmarked parallelism is employed with unmarked harmonic sequences in mm. 28–31 and 37–45, two passages that wind down from expressive cruxes in mm. 27 and 36.[14]

On the other hand, the tail may be marked strategically at a later point in the work in order to specify or narrow the range of its originally broad thematic correlation. That correlation is established as nontragic at its beginning because the tail is the unmarked opposition to the marked tragic head. The broad range of "nontragic" can be narrowed and the rather expressively neutral tail given a more expressive role by the acquisition of strategic markedness. For example, when in mm. 67–76 a fragment of the tail is used in stretto, in a high register, in major, and with a metric displacement (all devices which strategically mark the tail), its oppositional value with respect to the tragic head is enhanced in a manner appropriate to its "nontragic" correlation; that is, as a result of the local markedness it becomes less neutrally positive and more specifically peaceful or serene. Indeed, there is a further dramatic or emotional effect of extreme poignancy upon encountering such a vision within the relentlessly tragic atmosphere of this fugue.

Interestingly, it is the tail that embraces the Picardy third (mm. 114, 116, 118), a consonance which may or may not be enough to resolve the conflict summed up by the last appearances of the crux from the subject head (mm. 112 and 113). The harsh augmented second and strident diminished third between the first violin and the cello in extreme registers intensify the crux by their dissonances, which the tail attempts to ameliorate. The role of the tail in this attempted reconciliation is understood more readily because of its systematic opposition to the head since the beginning of the movement.

Any further markedness of the head itself might seem unlikely, since its configuration is from the beginning so quintessentially tragic. It is all the more remarkable, then, that the fugue presents just such a transformation, right after the exposition, which intensifies the tragic reversal of the original head. Although the exposition is completed thematically after the final entry in the cello (m. 16), closure is delayed by spinning out fragments of the tail for another few measures until the half cadence on the third beat of m. 20. At that point, an entry of the head in the first violin is significantly varied (fourth beat of m. 20 to the second beat of m. 22); instead of a *sf* emphasis on $\hat{6}$, there is a *subito piano* negation of the yearning aspiration ($\#\hat{7}$ to $\hat{8}$), supported by a tonal negation of the raised leading tone ($\natural\hat{7}$ to $\hat{6}$).

This reversal is supported by a similarly negative rhythmic gesture, anticipated in the cello release of m. 21, which seems to shrug in despair or exhaustion at the effort of continuation. Alternatively, the filling in of the tragic drop by a passing tone might be understood as mollifying the severity of the original reversal. The reversal of m. 22 is further highlighted by the abrupt release that leaves the subject head isolated, as though one had rejected the normalizing continuation (and its implication of "acceptance") provided by the tail at the beginning.

When further fragmentation reduces the head to three notes (m. 26), an expression of affirmation by the head becomes possible, since the first three notes by themselves exclude the tragic reversal of the fourth one. In a dramatic reversal at m. 27, the tragic drop is excised and the only undercutting that the aspiring B$\#$–C$\#$ receives is its harmonization with a simultaneous fragment of the head, G$\#$ to A in the cello. Together the two voices create, appropriately enough, the deceptive cadence earlier implied by the complete head in its opening form. But the upward move in the bass (from $\hat{5}$ to $\hat{6}$) substitutes a stylistic deceptive move for the strategic drop to $\hat{6}$ in the original subject. The new version is more positive because the move is up by step (in both voices) and not down by leap. The omission of the tragic drop in the continuation, together with the major mode setting in the sequential treatment of the tail, offers strong evidence for a more positive construal of this moment.

The subject head can also be "defused" to some degree by transformations substituting stylistically unmarked elements. This technique is illustrated by instances where the drop to lowered $\hat{6}$ is made less intense by the substitution of either raised $\hat{6}$ or the dominant scale degree. The first alternative occurs in m. 100, where the first violin entry of the subject substitutes D♯ for D (♯$\hat{6}$ for ♭$\hat{6}$), presumably to form a consonant interval with the B♯ from the augmented entry in the cello. The implied diminished third, avoided here, is realized in m. 113, where the climactic entry in the first violin pits a D♮ against the B♯ in the cello. Thus the earlier, less striking choice of D♯ may have had something to do with saving an especially marked interval (the diminished third) for an expressive climax (the crux in m. 113).

The second alternative for varying the head occurs in the second violin at the pickup to m. 110. It could be argued that this is a false entry, but its falseness is calculated in such a way as to save the marked harmonic intervals for the next few measures. The expected A♮ in the second violin at m. 111 occurs a half measure late, thereby avoiding a diminished fourth with the stretto entry in the cello (E♯). Instead, the second violin moves in parallel tenths with the cello, and the marked harmonic dissonances are saved for their crucial role in mm. 112 (augmented second) and 113 (diminished third).

This saving of expressive dissonance for the climax is hardly exceptional, and a theory of markedness simply confirms the obvious in such cases. What may be overlooked in traditional analyses, however, is the significance of moments that feature previously unrecognized stylistic types. One such example, involving the yielding/resignation progression, is found in mm. 106–107. In the fugal design, the cello is completing a climactic augmented entry. The expressive effect is triggered by a change in the last note of that augmented entry. The expected note in the cello at m. 107 is G♯; instead, a *rinforzando* G♮ intrudes, forming a crucial augmented fourth with the first violin. The resulting V$_2^4$ of the Neapolitan resolves to the Neapolitan in first inversion, and a descending sequence leads to a C♯ major chord (fourth beat of m. 110) that, as V/iv, sets up the last two entries in the subdominant (cello, then the first violin on the fourth beat of m. 111).

Besides leading to emphases on the Neapolitan and ultimately the subdominant (respectively summing up the tonal strategies of the movement and providing a cue for closure), the cello G♮ has an expressive role of its own. First it negates G♯, and then as the bass of a dominant four-two chord, it yields to the Neapolitan. The reversal suggests a possible turning point akin to the positive resignation, or abnegation, of the *Hammerklavier* slow movement. But because of the marginal tonal status of the Neapolitan (left behind in the inexorable descent and ultimately undercut as a scale degree by the dissonances of mm. 112 and 113), the reversal in m. 107 fails to sustain its claim to abnegation as a positive outcome to the spiritual dilemma of this movement. The "might have been" of the allusion to abnegation, however, may create a deeper sense of poignance by its very failure to hold.[15]

The significance of the progression to the Neapolitan is anticipated by the various yieldings that have undermined previous climaxes. Although one can analyze these passages purely "syntactically" as means of evading formal articulations such as cadences, or of promoting the continuity appropriate to a fugue, their "semantic," or expressive, role is too important to neglect. The yieldings serve to inflect the interpretation of those climaxes. It is this understanding, at a higher level than the mere tracking of consonance vs. dissonance or tension vs. relaxation, that enables the listener to participate in a richly worked-out dramatic scenario—not merely a topically flavored formal construct.

Since they often underlie and support more complex levels of marked opposition, such simple oppositions as consonance vs. dissonance, up vs. down, or major vs. minor can guide the interpretion of new oppositions that are not yet capable of determining their own correlations. For example, the climax at m. 54 is prepared by a direct, stepwise sequence involving the three-note fragment of the head in the cello (mm. 50–53). The climax occurs when the fourth note finally emerges on the downbeat of m. 54. Although earlier the first three notes alone (without the tragic reversal) were interpreted in terms of positive yearning (cf. m. 27), further support for that interpretation in mm. 50–54 is provided by the (positive) upward motion of the sequence, and the sequential mutations from minor to (nontragic) major accomplished by the viola.

The positive interpretation of the climax in m. 54 is supported by several other events. The first violin's imitation (in diminution, m. 54) of the complete head as stated by the cello prolongs the yearning effect. The major mode reduces the tragic effect of the drop to $\hat{6}$. The further diminution and sequence of the two-note yearning gesture in the inner voices enhances the rising gesture. And the second violin's minor-major mutation echoes the earlier mutations in the viola, prolonging the effect of clearing from tragedy to positive affirmation.

The latter mutation also serves a syntactic function, transforming the submediant of B major (G♯ minor) into the dominant of C♯ minor (G♯

major) and implying a return to the minor mode. The turn toward minor might appear to contradict the positive effects argued for above. But the identification of another yielding progression helps clarify the situation. The climax extends through the first three beats of m. 54, even as it is dynamically fading to *piano*. On the fourth beat a V_2^4 of C♯ minor, created by the beginning of the tail in the bass, provides a sense of yielding that complements the dynamic falling away from the climax. As the cello continues, sequencing a tail fragment, the upper voices join with tail fragments in diminution and sequence. The last, positively hopeful mutation (B–B♯) has been undermined by the V_2^4 continuation, and it appears that C♯ minor has returned. But a remarkable "after-glow" signals that the positive interpretation, while not a sustainable vision at this point in the drama, was correctly perceived as such. On the third beat of m. 55 C♯ minor is in turn undermined by a B♮, which gives rise to a B-major sonority in second inversion. The sweetness of the major, its appropriateness as echo to the climax on vi of B major, and its significance as a potential "salvation six-four" are blended here in a moment that, although neither climactic nor focal in terms of dynamics and structural placement, affirms that a positive moment has crested. Indeed, a similar stepwise sequence builds to the next climax (mm. 61–62), made positive by its move to A major. A transcendent affirmation immediately follows, cued by high register, major mode, and the resultant marking of the tail fragment as transcendent and serene.

There are similarities between the earlier climax at m. 54 and the one almost exactly twice as far into the movement, at m. 107. Both are preceded by stepwise ascending sequences that heighten the tension, as well as by registral leaps that thicken the texture. Both are "positive" reversals of the tragic. In the first case, the climactic crux is extended and then undermined by the V_2^4 of C♯ minor; in the second case, the V_2^4 of the Neapolitan is the marked crux, yielding to the Neapolitan in a manner reminiscent of the abnegation progression. Each climax, after being undermined, is ultimately surpassed by another climax reached soon after (mm. 61–62 and mm. 112–13.). In mm. 61–62 the climax is the first inversion resolution of a $vii°_3^4/ii$ (substituting for V_2^4/ii), with a sense of "willed" affirmation; in m. 113 the ultimate climax involves an inverted augmented sixth (diminished third) pulled to a V/iv, as though the "resolution" were simply a stable mean between two harrowing extremes. Both of these climaxes are repeated, the former echoed down an octave, the latter heard twice in the same extreme registers and then echoed in the inner voices by the less tense, diminished-seventh substitute. In both cases there is a sense of struggle for affirmation: the former achieves a resolution to A major, whereas the latter is tonally ambiguous.

If the movement ends problematically, it is not without some sense of the spiritually transcendent—a side that has been fully explored, if not definitively achieved, by the end of the first movement. The potential interpretation of the final C♯ major triad as a positive Picardy-third close is undercut by the context of its appearance—as resolution of an inverted augmented-sixth sonority, instead of closing a dominant chord in root position. Perhaps its marked context helps us hear the Picardy third as appropriately enigmatic. At any rate, something of the issue is left to be treated by the last movement of the quartet, where permutation of the head returns in C♯ minor, and a clear Picardy third ultimately closes the cycle.[16]

This expressivity of this movement is as much or more in the thematic surface as in the larger tonal and fugal architecture. The following outline lists some of the other means (both stylistically available and strategically invented) by which the surface is marked with such expressivity.

I. Marked sonorities
   A. The augmented triad of m. 27, which helps underline the aspiration of the B♯, while lending it greater anxiety, (see m. 14, where the augmented triad is produced by a retardation that overlaps the crux of the cello's entry with a hint of the yearning part of the head).
   B. The Mmm⁹ on the second beat of m. 36, which arrives just as a 4–3 suspension resolves and lends its traditional poignancy.
   C. Surprise major six-four "arrivals," such as that on the third best of m. 55, which suggest moments of affirmation or hope even when the resolutional closure they hint is neglected by ensuing events.
   D. The Neapolitan.
II. Marked tonal relationships
   A. Cross-relationships, such as that of m. 11, suggesting negations or cross-currents of the will.
   B. Mutations, such as the pair in the viola in mm. 50–51, where they undermine by their negation the positive hopefulness and excitement of the stepwise sequential acceleration.
   C. Diminished and augmented intervals indigenous to the minor mode (i.e., other than the augmented fourth or diminished fifth between $\hat{4}$ and $\hat{7}$), including the Neapolitan inflec-

tion. These are used both melodically and harmonically for their expressive intensity (anguish, etc.):

1. augmented second: melodically in mm. 12–13; harmonically in m. 6.
2. diminished third: (b$\hat{2}$–$\sharp\hat{7}$): melodically in m. 7; harmonically in m. 113.
3. diminished fourth: melodically in m. 6.
4. augmented fifth: harmonically in m. 27.
5. augmented sixth: harmonically in m. 27.
6. minor ninth: harmonically in m. 36.

D. Denials of implication (as noted above): mm. 107, 112.
E. Consonant interval to dissonant interval interpreted as nonchord tone to chord tone (reversal of consonance-dissonance relationship due to the emergence of a chordal level that goes beyond interpretation by interval alone): m. 24 (perfect fifth to augmented fourth, D–A to D–G$\sharp$, in the outer voices; the augmented fourth is part of a g$^{\sharp o \hat{6}}_4$).
F. Suspensions and appoggiaturas, especially chromatic ones.

III. Unusual textural features
A. Unusual doubling and crossed voices: third beat of m. 13, raised third in the second violin and the viola.
B. Parallel octaves: mm. 22–23, between the second violin and the viola.
C. Octave-displaced leaps: mm. 50–53, in the first violin.
D. Extreme registers: mm. 63–64, first violin.

These several expressive features require a semiotic assessment in terms of both their stylistic markedness (and correlations) and their strategic markedness (and contextual interpretation) that is not possible in such a preliminary study. The list is a reminder of the irreducible significance of the surface in conveying and inflecting musical meaning, giving it a specificity that often eludes paraphrase in language.

CHAPTER

VII

Beyond the Hierarchies of Correlation

Troping, Irony, Levels of Discourse, and Intertextuality

The development of correlations provides a stable framework for interpretive growth as further articulation of the hierarchy of oppositions. Thus far, that articulation has been modeled systematically, with new interpretations appearing as subsets of more general correlations. In the analysis of Op. 131, the tail of the subject, originally correlated with "nontragic," was further specified as "transcendently serene" on appearing in a higher register, major-mode setting. In such cases, the semantic field is enriched, but not substantially reshaped, by means of an orderly, hierarchical derivation process.

But another kind of interpretive growth may alter the constitution of semantic fields in more radical ways, suggesting the need for a more flexible model to complement the hierarchical one implied thus far. One possibility is that of the network. The semiotic theorist Umberto Eco (1984: 83–84) considers the universe of semiosis (human culture) in terms of a "network of interpretants" that is "virtually infinite" and akin to a "semantic encyclopedia." If previously unrelated correlations can interact without regard to their hierarchical derivation, then the meanings that emerge may in turn help reconstitute the semantic field in unexpected ways. The listener may be led to integrative insights or syntheses by such novel conjunctions of correlations from different parts of the semantic field.

The process is not unlike that of metaphor. As Eco (1979: 69) describes metaphor in language:

> The problem of the creativity of language emerges, not only in the privileged domain of poetic discourse, but each time that language—in order to designate something that culture has not yet assimilated . . . —must *invent* combinatory possibilities or semantic couplings not anticipated by the code.

While Eco may be going too far in considering all creativity in language as metaphorical, his emphasis on the pervasiveness of metaphor is apt. In what follows I will attempt to clarify the distinction between *correlation* and *metaphor* in music as analogous to the difference between literal and figurative in language. I will also consider whether the musical metaphor, or *trope*, can be understood in terms of markedness. Troping yields a synthetic specificity of meaning that is at the same time more complex and more peculiarly distinctive—a radical reinterpretation of the "narrower" range of meaning that markedness entails.

The remainder of this chapter examines two closely intertwined phenomena in music, ironic reversal and levels of discourse, closing with a brief consideration of *intertextuality* and *reflexivity of discourse* in music.

The Role of Metaphor

The prominent place given to metaphor and metaphorical thinking in recent theories of language and literature has led to a fresh perspective on the nature of meaning. For theories of language this has meant a reversal of the logical model of objectivist semantics that posits an objective content for each concept. Instead, for cognitive theorists like George Lakoff, concepts are better characterized in terms of prototypes or exemplars, not in terms of sets defined by presumably essential properties (Lakoff, 1987).

Ludwig Wittgenstein made much the same point years earlier with his notion of "family resemblances" as a way of characterizing a concept such as that covered by the common noun "game." He observed that "there is no single feature in common to all [games], though there are many common features overlapping. These cases of expectation form a family; they have family likenesses which are not clearly defined" ([1933–34] 1958: 20). At a larger level, the organization of an individual's "semantic space" is viewed by Eco as being more like an encyclopedia than a dictionary—with rich entries and cross-references rather than narrow definitions for each concept—and thus, as mentioned above, more like a network than a strictly logical hierarchy (Eco, 1976: 125–29).

Increasingly, figuration, including not only metaphor but also other tropes or figures, is viewed by linguists and literary theorists as being fundamental to the understanding of language and literature (Michael and Marianne Shapiro, 1976 and 1988; Lakoff and Johnson, 1980; Johnson [ed.], 1981; Lakoff and Turner, 1989).[1]

Such theorists have opened up promising new avenues of research into problems of linguistic and literary meaning. In turn, these new approaches might be seen as removing one of the typical charges brought against attempts to account for musical meaning—namely, that "extramusical" meanings such as expressive states are not precisely linked in unambiguous fashion with particular musical structures—in other words, that music is not referential in the earlier, objectivist sense. Certainly, attempts to approach musical meaning in terms of a lexicon of sound terms (Deryck Cooke, 1959) have not been entirely satisfactory. But reference is only one way meaning emerges; given that objectivist referentiality is under attack even for language, it follows that theories of music need not be held accountable for failing an already discredited standard of referentiality (see Chapter 9).

On the other hand, the temptation to consider all musical expressive meaning as metaphorical is also problematic. When Nelson Goodman[2] in his influential *Languages of Art* ([1968] 1976) proposes equating expression in music with metaphorical exemplification, he does so to capture those meanings (labels) such as "sad," which might properly be applied to musical passages but are not literally exemplified by the notes, as presumably would be the case for labels such as "loud." Unfortunately, Goodman offers no theory to regulate the proper application of his metaphorical labels. Their application appears circular: if the investigator believes a label applies to a musical passage, and that passage does not have an obvious similarity to the concept the label defines, then the presumed exemplification is "metaphorical"—whether or not one can demonstrate how the meaning is consistently cued by particular structural features or contexts in the music.

Despite his insistence that such labels apply truly or falsely, Goodman cannot provide music theoretical instructions as to how such determination should be made and must assume cases where it already has. Thus, his "metaphorical" exemplification has no explanatory content if the presumed connection between sound and meaning is not already obvious; and if there are other motivations for less obvious linkages, then we might dispense with such imaginary exemplification altogether.

A first-stage semiotic model posits obvious linkages between sound and meaning to be the result of similarity, as in Peter Kivy's (1980: 71–83) "contour" theory. Mark Johnson, in *The Body in the Mind* (1987) argues similarly for *iconic* and *indexical* motivations for basic metaphors in language, showing how many of our terms from various conceptual fields are mapped according to our bodily conceptions of space.

A second-stage semiotic approach to the problem of motivating the linkage between sound and meaning would supplement iconic with symbolic connections, as in Peter Kivy's (1980: 71–83) "convention" theory. By symbolic, I mean those connections that do not depend on likeness, but are the result of a habit that can be reconstructed as a stylistic convention.

Kivy correctly points out the cognitive status of much expressive meaning, regardless of whether its motivation is iconic or symbolic. We need not experience a given emotion as evoked by the music; instead, we often recognize emotional states without being moved, or choosing to be moved, by them. Kivy cites the Baroque theorist Johann Mattheson as the first to make this claim (Kivy, 1980: 39–42).

Chapter 9 offers a further refinement to Kivy's implicitly semiotic approach, based on a development of ideas from the American philosopher Charles Sanders Peirce (1931) that incorporates what might be described as a "symbolic iconism," or an isomorphism based on structural oppositions instead of properties. At this point, however, let us consider the difference between musical metaphors, on the one hand, and a more common kind of musical expressive correlation which is not essentially, or at least no longer, metaphorical at all.

For Goodman, any meaning resulting from the conjunction of two different domains is by definition metaphorical. The idea is not problematic for different domains within language (as, for example, in the metaphor "John is a tiger"), but Goodman wishes to apply the criterion to explain musical expressive meaning by considering music and emotions as the two domains. The difference in domain, however, is not analogous to the difference between two terms like "John" and "tiger," since musical events and labels for emotions are two different modes of expression, and to relate them involves a kind of translation, as well.

If conjoining music and another realm created metaphor in and of itself (even given Goodman's other criteria of reassignment and change in schematic organization due to the influence of one domain on the other), then metaphorically exemplified expressive meaning in music still might lack an essential characteristic of metaphor as it functions in literature and language—namely, its interactive force, or creativity, through which process fresh meanings emerge.[3]

If literality is simply the stage at which a metaphor, through usage, loses its original force (as in the life cycle of tropes documented by Michael and Marianne Shapiro, 1976), then one might hypothesize that music also has such "frozen" metaphors, or *correlations* (the term I have used for comparably "literal" meaning in music). The neutral term *correlation* is drawn from Eco's (1976) semiotics (influenced by the linguist Louis Hjelmslev): "A sign-function is realized when two *functives* (expression and content) enter into a mutual correlation; the same functive can also enter into another correlation, thus becoming a different functive and therefore giving rise to a new sign-function" (Eco 1976: 49). *Correlation* substitutes for more problematic terms, such as "reference" or "denotation," in dealing with this kind of musical meaning. Correlations in music are characterized by their immediacy—involving merely an act of recognition, as opposed to the cognitive reorganization and sense of novelty that would be involved in the interpretation of truly metaphorical musical meanings.

If correlations are encoded in a given musical style and transparently recognized by a listener, as could be argued for most assignments of the verbal label "sad," then metaphors require a more creative or integrative act on the part of the listener, one that leads to an *emergent* meaning—and probably a more complex meaning, as well (as, for example, the tragic grief ennobled by resigned acceptance that I have interpreted as "abnegation" in late Beethoven).

Although correlations provide for relative stability among expressive meanings, there is nevertheless a crucial difference in the way such stability is encoded, when compared with language. Correlated musical structures, unlike linguistic structures, may not have consistent forms; but they can exist as relatively stable *types* in the style, with a wide range of *tokens* of each type possible in various works in the style, as explained in Chapter 2. Competency in a style requires an ability to interpret the type from the token rather fluently—again, as transparently as an act of recognition. The meaning associated with the type is stylistically encoded as its correlation. That correlation, often rather general and perhaps not very interesting in itself, then guides the further *interpretation* required in accounting for variable features in tokens—or the influence of different contexts.

However, along with this level of relatively stable correlations and their contextual interpretations in given works, one needs to provide a level for more unstable meanings created by the figural play among musical types and their correlations. Something akin to creative metaphor in language may be achieved in a musical work when two different correlations are brought together to produce a third meaning. I will refer to such figuration of musical meaning more generally as *troping*, to emphasize the dynamic process involved, as well as to avoid confusion with other applications of metaphor to music.[4]

With respect to the latter concern, one should not confuse metaphors created by musical processes with Goodman's metaphors as labels for expressive meanings that are not literally exemplified in the music. The conventional status of some emotional correlations—i.e., the fact that they no longer appear to involve any literally exemplified features— should not lead to their construal as metaphorical merely because their original motivation has been lost or obscured.

It is also important not to consider expressive meanings as "extra"- musical simply because external verbal labels must be used to paraphrase their meaning. Language can be used as a metalanguage for musical meaning without necessarily being metaphorical (see Chapter 9).

Since metaphor is such an important part of artistic creativity, it would be worth salvaging the concept for those processes in music that most resemble it, rather than relegating it solely to the gap between language and music, or to the problems associated with using language as a metalanguage.[5]

To return to the problem Goodman failed to resolve: how can we explain the way expressive meanings are tied to structures such that his metaphorical exemplification can be musically motivated, and that it will support consistent interpretations by listeners? Goodman speaks of reference to a symbol system, and in a later article (1975) that symbol system is equated with an artistic style. But how does style, as a symbol system, work to keep expressive meanings coherent? The answer, I believe, is correlation. Oppositions in sound structure correlate with (cultural) oppositions in expressive structures by means of the more sophisticated iconism hinted at earlier. The American philosopher Charles Sanders Peirce characterizes such *structural* iconism as *diagrammatic* (1931: 4.347–573), although he does not put forward, as I do, the oppositional basis of each structure that coordinates the mapping of one to the other.

Another term for structural iconism is *isomorphism*. The important distinction to be made, regardless of terminology, is that correlation is not based on the structure of properties but on the structure of oppositions. Nevertheless, isomorphism may well be constrained by the *affordant limits* of such properties. For example, when Ernst Gombrich (1960: 370), taking his cue from Roman Jakobson and Charles Osgood, offers us a choice between only two words, "ping" and "pong," as names for an elephant and a cat, we are most likely to choose the name "ping" for the cat and "pong" for the elephant. I would consider this choice, which is indeed based on relating two scales of opposition, as also being constrained by the culturally ingrained tendency to equate high (as in high vowel) with small, and low with large. Thus, the chosen correlation is *motivated*, even though that motivation may not be conscious. In a purely systematic sense, the opposite correlation would have served as well, if the symbol system were a purely *arbitrary* code. It should be clear that my concept of *motivation* differs from Ferdinand de Saussure's ([1915] 1959: 67–69) notion of arbitrariness as a characteristic of the linguistic sign. Conventions may lose their original motivations over time, but they cannot move too far from the constraints of a deeply embedded cultural iconism.

Although one may observe a strictly hierarchical and logical derivation process, yielding increasingly more specialized subsets or subtypes of structures and meanings, one may also discover a more network-like, less predictable juxtaposition of disparate types. This network-like flexibility provides an extralogical, or perhaps supralogical, means of creating new musical meanings—not unlike the process of metaphor in language. When there are contradictions between juxtaposed correlations or their divergent realms of meaning, then conditions are ripe for a truly metaphorical interpretation.

Consider the distinguishing features of the metaphorical process in language. At its most powerful, a metaphor offers a novel insight by creating an interaction between two already established meanings that involves disparate, perhaps contradictory, domains of meaning, and that is brought together by a linguistic act of predication.

Is there a way that figurative interaction between meanings can occur in music? How can music, lacking verbal predication, bring disparate meanings together in a coherent way? Two examples by semiotic theorists will provide an orientation to the problems involved.

Vladimir Karbusicky (1986: 435–36) gives a humorous example of "purely musical metaphor": the concatenation of melodic fragments from Schumann's *Träumerei* and Dvořák's *Humoresque* by a salon pianist. The resulting monstrosity respects at least the harmonic aspects of music-syntactic construction and makes a point of the opposition between the expressive worlds of each piece by constant alternation between fragments. Despite his sensitive analysis of the "semantic charge" of each piece and the interaction of nostalgia (*Träumerei*) and cheerfulness (*Humoresque*)[6] that results from the intercutting of fragments, Karbusicky finds the example exceptional: "But these very correspondences with the linguistic metaphor as they appear in [this] caricature, indicate how much of an *exception* a 'metaphor' is in a purely musical code. [The restriction to] 'formulas' instead of . . . 'concepts' makes of it an intellectual game" (437).

Márta Grabócz, in her study of the piano music of Liszt (1986: 122–23), presents the idea of "bi-isotopies" (the superposition of two organizing categories that are concerned with musical meaning).[7] Her "semantic isotopies" are drawn from cultural units (semes) that cluster into larger realms of significance (classemes) such as the heroic, the religious, and the pastoral. These serve as higher-order types that can govern a complete musical utterance (not unlike what I have termed *expressive genres*). One such combination, of the religious and the pastoral, is termed the pantheistic and is considered by Grabócz as an *isotopy* in its own right (122). An example of a bi-isotopy would be the injection of the heroic at a climax in a work that appears primarily involved with the religious isotopy. I assume the interpretation of this fusion would be "triumphant religious affirmation," or something of that order.

In both Karbusicky's and Grabócz's examples, intriguingly, it is music that generates metaphor by its own internal processes. What I intend to contribute to the discussion is an analysis of the special requirements for musical metaphor at a semantic level (along the lines of Grabócz's bi-isotopies), and the importance of such metaphorical thinking in music (beyond the realm of artifice or caricature, as in Karbusicky's example).

In order for tropological interpretation to be warranted, there must be a musical event that contradicts stylistic expectation. Starting a movement with a closural theme might contradict a given stylistic expectation. But there must also be a functional location or process within which that contradiction can occur. In the Karbusicky example, the process of alternation serves this purpose. The beginning of a piece is also a functional location to the extent that for the Classical style one expects either an introduction or an opening theme. If a closural theme occurs, it exerts a figural twist between location function and theme function, as Judy Lochhead has argued (1979), and it is this interaction that demands interpretation. If successfully reconciled (whether by integration or higher synthesis), a new meaning has been troped from the contradiction of two older ones. That meaning might involve either a simple synthesis of two separate meanings ("my end is my beginning" or "in my beginning is my end") or a third meaning that emerges from their interaction ("nothing is ever finished," or the play of incongruity that yields humor).

In the former case, what I call the attribution model is involved. The troping is weak, in that either of the contradictory elements is understood as merely attributing a character to the other (a closural beginning, a beginning closure). In the latter case, there is a move by way of their interaction to a higher interpretation. I call this stronger kind of troping the speculative model.

Without a functional location or process to enclose the two terms or to set up a certain stylistic expectation, one could not claim the existence of contradiction. Instead, the "difference" would simply register as contrast, a common enough occurrence in music. Given the dialectical character of Classical music, as argued by Judith Eckelmeyer (1986) and Susan McClary (1986), the listener need not absorb a strong contrast merely as a syntactic feature of the style—as, for example, helping to clarify functions among themes, or setting up a balanced opposition between parts of a given theme (the beginning of Mozart's *Jupiter* Symphony). The opposition may also initiate an ongoing dramatic conflict of characters or agents, perhaps suggesting a dramatic program. In addition, the contrast may lead to a tropological interpretation that goes beyond the opposed correlations. Indeed, the piece that contains such oppositions might itself be interpreted as a high-level trope in that it accommodates, or even reconciles, the opposition.

Although the expanded concept of troping implied by that last conjecture is intriguing, let us return to the two conditions established earlier, adding a third that will account for higher-level organization:

1. The trope must emerge from a clear juxtaposition of contradictory, or previously unrelated, types.
2. The trope must arise from a single functional location or process.
3. There must be evidence from a higher level (for example, Grabócz's isotopies) to support a tropological interpretation, as opposed to interpretations of contrast, or dramatic opposition of characters.[8]

An example that illustrates these conditions is the Allegro theme, mm. 1–8 of the Finale from Beethoven's Piano Sonata, Op. 101 (see Example 4.5, mm. 1–8), where three distinct topics are conjoined in eight bars. The topics in the first four bars are heroic (fanfare-like, diatonic, *forte*), and learned (imitation, implied 2–3 chain suspensions); the second four bars present the pastoral (soft, musette-like syncopated pedal point, flowing sixteenths in simple stepwise motion). Ratner (1980: 260) claims that the theme has a rhythmic gesture typical of the bourrée; if so, bourrée becomes musette after four bars.

The pastoral topic is the governing expressive genre (isotopy) of the sonata as a whole, and the heroic and learned topics have already appeared in the second movement. Thus, in terms of a higher-level (dramatic or expressive) scheme, there is support for a tropological interpretation. Since these disparate topics are juxtaposed in the eight-bar opening Allegro theme (a single functional slot), their interaction is clearly at issue.

In the previous chapter the term *thematic integration* was used to describe the bringing together of previously opposed thematic material in a single context (whether in simultaneous or closely juxtaposed fashion). While the concept of integration may help explain how a more meaningful thematic closure is achieved, and achieved in a way that complements but goes beyond the "syntactic" tonal closure revealed by Schenkerian analysis, it may leave out of the account the expressive purport of the themes themselves, working instead within a more formal account of their conflict and resolution (although this need not be the case; compare the discussion of an integrative troping of hymn and aria in the recapitulation of the *Hammerklavier* slow movement). The Finale theme from Op. 101 has a particular expressive significance that also emerges from troping, not merely integration, of correlations associated with heroic, learned, and pastoral topics.

The heroic element suggests an interpretation of victory; the learned element (with a correlation of "authoritative") acts as an inflection of the heroic, and enhances the sense of determination (*Entschlossenheit*) that Beethoven specifies. This first trope is rather straightforward, along the lines of the attribution model, in which one element (learned) serves to inflect the other (heroic).

The second trope, formed by the interaction of learned-heroic and pastoral, is far richer in its metaphorical force, since there is a greater contradiction between the two (active vs. passive), and a greater cognitive task in accommodating the two to a larger significance. The nature of the heroic victory is one that must be possible within the realm of the pastoral. If the pastoral is interpreted for this sonata in the context of the spiritual ("raising" of pastoral to the high style, as supported here by the learned style), then the victory will be understood as an inward, spiritual one—a somewhat different perspective from the outward, heroic triumph of the Fifth Symphony's Finale.

The subtlety of a trope may well demand its working-out musically in the remainder of the movement. A composer is not likely to present such a productive trope and then neglect that productivity in terms of the subsequent musical-philosophical discourse. Although musical discourse is not, like language, propositional, it can nevertheless suggest a sustained argument composed of correlations, their development, and their tropological interaction.

A cultural meaning one might call "philosophical disputation" could be suggested as an appropriate general correlation for the fugato development section. The seriousness of the learned style, however, is mollified by continued pastoral influences: the answer is in C major, there is a move to F major before the third entry in D minor; and C and F major recur as subdominantly oriented reductions of tension. But the fugato achieves an intensification by means of stretto followed by a climactic augmentation, wedged between low dominant pedals in the left hand— thereby preparing for the appropriately triumphant return of the main theme with the recapitulation. The coda (recall Chapter 4) features the pastoral with a brief deflection to F major, cross-hand cuckoo effects, buzzing pedal trill, and decrescendo decay. Only the final *fortissimo* repetitions of block chords recall the heroic determination of the opening, but they are sufficient to support the trope of an internalized victory of the spirit.

This, then, is one of the ways that music has of creating its own metaphors and sustaining them through a movement. To summarize the argument, the musical trope I would call metaphor is derived from already established correlations that are brought together in a single functional location or process, where their contradiction provokes an emergent interpretation. Functional locations exist as a result of stylistic formal schema, or as a result of a contextual expectation set up by the piece. Tropes can range from the attributive to the speculative, and the latter can serve as a tropological premise that is worked out by the movement. Indeed, the higher-level contexts of dramatic or narrative schemas help justify, and guide the interpretation of, thematic tropes.

The collisions of meaning that speculative tropes produce may be considered supralogical in that correlations are brought together from disparate realms. A logical growth process for meaning would involve a strictly hierarchical derivation process, creating subsets of already established correlations. The power of nonhierarchical metaphors, on the other hand, may result in interpretive insecurity; juxtapositions may fail to trope, and there is a greater chance of misinterpretation altogether. Nevertheless, tropes have emerged at various levels of structure in each of the extended analyses from previous chapters. Clearly, tropological investigation can be an indispensable complement to formal and hierarchical systems of analysis, whether formally or expressively conceived.

Toward a Concept of Irony

Irony is a higher-order trope inaugurated by the contradiction between what is claimed (or observed, or done), and a context that cannot support its reality (or appropriateness).[9] The trope is interpreted by recognizing that something else is meant; thus, there is a figural twist on what cannot be taken literally or as fact. In the case of metaphor, something else is meant, as well. The claim, for example, that John is actually a tiger makes no literal sense. But for irony, there has to be a potential for reversal in interpreting what is "really meant" by the word or deed—a reversal that rhetorically enhances the intended meaning by the exaggeration of its opposite. That reversal is different from the interpretation of metaphor as meaning something other than its literal meaning. For metaphor, the correlations of John and tiger are interpreted interactively such that a contextually appropriate application of the properties of tigerhood to John is intended (this metaphor has become more attributive than speculative, in the senses defined earlier). But with irony, there must be an intentional inappropriateness, whether of literal or metaphorical meaning, such that we can interpret the contradiction as meaningful (or expressive).

There is a difference of levels between metaphor and irony. Consider the use of an "ironic" tone of voice in stating, "John is a tiger." If John is not, for example, aggressive, then John (through the exaggeration of contradiction) is decidedly *not* a tiger. Note that the metaphor must first be unpacked before its negation can be meaningful, implying two distinct levels of interpretation. One might model the situation as − (A + B), in which "A + B" is metaphor (attributive or speculative) and "− ( )" is irony (intended reversal of the meaning of a discourse or action).[10]

Irony can have degrees of power just as metaphors can be more or less creative. The power of a sustained ironic discourse may undermine an entire ideological system or reveal a stance as untenable. In one of its earliest characterizations (by Quintilian), irony is defined as a figure of thought, the "elaboration of a figure of speech into an entire argument" (Muecke 1970: 16). On the other hand, an ironic remark need not be skillful in its choice of exaggerated opposite in order to achieve a short-term effect of humorous deflation or insulting mockery. Irony is an easy refuge for the disenchanted; thus, its artistic value must somehow be related to the quality of its means and the worthiness of its ends.

More-artistic forms of irony may in turn provoke higher-level metaphorical interpretations. Rodway (1962: 113, cited by Muecke, 1970: 45), offers a prescriptive account: "irony is not merely a matter of seeing a 'true' meaning beneath a 'false,' but of seeing a double exposure . . . on one plate." This characterization suggests the potential for metaphorical development of the "double exposure," creatively producing a third. The troping of paradox, "of the ambivalent and the ambiguous, of the impossible made actual, of a double contradictory reality" (Muecke, 45), might be considered an interpretive product of such forms of irony.

Muecke (1970: 8–13) lists fifteen types of irony, including two that have an important and recognized role in music: dramatic irony and Romantic irony. Dramatic (or Sophoclean) irony is aptly defined as "the irony of a character's utterance having unawares a double reference: to the situation as it appears to him and, no less aptly, to the situation as it really is, the very different situation already revealed to the audience" (Connop Thirlwall, 1833: 490–91, cited by Muecke, 1970: 29). Applications to opera as drama are obvious enough. The orchestra may reveal, in dramatic-ironic fashion, the actual expressive state or the implied intentions of a character who pretends (in the kind of music sung, or at least in words or actions) to something other.[11]

Dramatic irony can be used for either serious or comic effects. The devaluation from pathos to bathos in Donna Elvira's learned-style arias from *Don Giovanni* may be tied to the lack of contextual support for the elevated register of her outrage over being dishonored—she is more upset about being abandoned than being seduced.

Romantic irony is a particular kind of irony fundamental to Romantic aesthetics.[12] As developed by Friedrich Schlegel (1772–1829), it moves beyond the figurative trope, or even sustained dramatic irony, to the level of the author's (composer's) detachment and self-critical consciousness, not only from writing (composing) but from life as well. Thus, irony is inflated to a kind of cultural trope at the level of philosophical contemplation.

The high seriousness of irony as a critical perspective, from a higher plane, on the workings of life or art suggests corresponding levels of discourse in the work. Such shifts in levels of musical discourse can serve as strong evidence of Romantic irony in music, as will be demonstrated by the following examples.

Levels of Discourse and Ironic Troping

Levels of discourse are created in literature by shifting from direct to indirect discourse or narration. Music may signal analogous shifts, although not necessarily narrative ones, by means of certain extreme contrasts of style or stylistic register: successively (in which case the latter music seems to "comment" upon the former), or interruptively (in which case an entity appropriate to a context is displaced by an inappropriate one).[13]

An example of the latter, discussed previously in Chapter 3, is the Turkish March from the Finale of the Ninth Symphony. The topical interpretation discussed earlier is funded by Romantic irony, a higher-level critical perspective that creates the trope. A self-deflating, and thus humanizing, irony undercuts the previous elevation of tone or stylistic register and provokes an interpretive synthesis as "all-embracing," a central metaphor for the movement ("alle Menschen werden Brüder").

The modeling of this process is the reverse of the one where a metaphor is ironized. Here, an ironic reversal is troped as a metaphor. Let A = high style, followed by B = low style. The listener first interprets B as "–A," an *ironic reversal* of A. The paradox or double exposure of A and "–A" may then be synthesized as "all-embracing," a trope on the interaction of A and B.

The strategy of undercutting a high point (whether by stylistic "register" or by pitch register) is a familiar one. A composer may defer a climactic arrival or closure by undercutting or interrupting, in order to leave room for further development. But this partial explanation, often couched in formal terms, may be supplemented by ironic and tropological understandings in cases such as the Turkish March. In the examples that follow, I concentrate on the cueing of Romantic irony; the next section will address ironic reversal and its interpretive consequences.

The Finale of the Ninth Symphony provides evidence for the appropriateness of a Romantic ironic interpretation, as well as for Beethoven's awareness of levels of discourse in a somewhat literal sense. The quotation of previous movements and the subsequent rejection ("Nicht diese Töne") by the soloist suggest the injection of a persona who can change the prevailing musical discourse. The approaches represented by each of the quoted movements are surpassed as the last movement finds a new expressive level—not *topically* transcendent, as in the slow movement, but tropologically more inclusive or "all-embracing." The trope of inclusiveness is also supported by the choral hymn. With its easily sung stepwise line and simple elaboration, the hymn suggests the widest possible inclusion of society.

The bass soloist employs recitative, the closest that music approaches to prose or declamation. Topically, recitative structures may, even without words or a singer, cue shifts in narrative or dramatic discourse.[14] Thus, in the String Quartet, Op. 131, one finds a recitative section not only providing a transition linking two movements (the second and fourth) but also injecting its reaction, from another level of discourse, to what has just happened.

The typical recitative chord (used as a formula for beginnings and "paragraph" breaks in operatic recitative) is the first inversion of the major triad. The chord is interpreted as a new dominant cueing a sudden tonal shift, corresponding to a shift in thought or utterance. Treated topically, a salient first-inversion major triad may well trigger a shift in discourse level simply by suggesting such a recitative-like initiation, with its corresponding change in musical style.

In the third movement of Op. 130 a sudden tonal shift from A♭ to F major is cued in this fashion (Example 7.1, m. 17). The dramatic effect, a sudden departure from the hardly completed imperfect authentic cadence on A♭ (dominant of the movement's home key of D♭), is marked dynamically by the first-inversion dominant. Further evidence for recitative as a topic is provided by the descending fourths, characteristic of opening as well as closing recitative lines. The abrupt, operatic interruption in m. 17 suggests a persona[15] "taking stock" of her own discourse, perhaps seized by a sudden thought from another realm of consciousness. The potential insight is not sustained but dissolves into a static quibbling (m. 18). A "significant" ♭6̂ at the end of m. 19 suggests a fateful warning that is placated by the return of the theme. The interruption, not in itself productive, highlights the tender naiveté of the theme and renders it all the more touching for its fragile hold on the discourse.

Compare now the opening of the movement (Example 7.2), a retrospectively understood two-bar transition from the previous movement (modulating from B♭ minor to D♭ major), that reinterprets 7̂ of B♭ minor as a poignant ♭6̂ (B♭♭) of D♭ major in an *empfindsamer* declamatory texture. This moment of melancholy gives way to the naively optimistic theme, similarly highlighting the fragility of the theme. Of course, the setting of the theme—*piano*, *dolce*, with delicate staccato-sixteenth accompaniment—contributes its share of expressive correlations, but the troping of a shift in discourse level adds something qualitatively beyond the presentational expressiveness of the theme by itself.

The accompanimental texture in mm. 5–6 foreshadows its later development into a "clockwork" (Ratner 1980: 391) accompaniment. This accompaniment suggests a certain artificiality, which could be tropologically interpreted not as artifice but, again, as a fragile and intimate personal emotion that is not sustained in the face of tragic reality. The implication of a music box also contributes to a childlike sense of naiveté.

Further support for discourse shifting as a compositional ploy for the movement is found in mm. 81 and 83 (Example 7.3a), where Beethoven contrives an allusion to the main theme of the second movement (Example 7.3b) in a texture germane to the third movement. This troping suggests the role of intertextuality, a concept that is explored in the next section. As a reminiscence, it demonstrates shift of discourse level; as a trope, it perhaps imports something of the obsessiveness of the Presto theme into a context where it is absorbed (reluctantly) by the persona as part of an external world and its reality (note the C♭–B♭ sigh in the second violin at the end of m. 81, which "comments" on the theme).

176 | Interpretation and Theory

Example 7.1. Beethoven, String Quartet in B♭, Op. 130, third movement, mm. 16–20.

Example 7.2. Beethoven, Op. 130, third movement, mm. 1–7.

Example 7.3. Beethoven, Op. 130. a. third movement, mm. 79–84; b. second movement, mm. 1–4.

a.

Example 7.3. (Continued)

b.

One last enhancement of the theme by means of a play with discourse levels involves a familiar disruption, the fermata, and the cadenza, which historically developed from it. Cadenzas are not necessarily ironic, but they do serve as means of commenting upon, or reacting to, aspects of the previous discourse. They allow the soloist of a concerto an appropriately persona-like projection, whether as composer-persona or as performer-persona. The cadenza offers that persona a field of quasi-improvisatory play on the themes of the preceding discourse, with a freedom that is not constrained by the form of the movement proper. The freedom is akin to being "outside" (or parenthetical to) the time of the movement itself.

In the third movement of Op. 130, the brief fermata elaboration by the first violin (Example 7.4, m. 65) provides a soloistic persona in rather literal fashion. Furthermore, the sweeping ascent to the expressive crux from the middle of the theme (see Example 7.2, m. 7) is a remarkable moment, like a gasp of awe-filled insight, that elevates the restored theme to a transcendent level. The key of G♭ is suitably subdominant, and the yielding V$^4_2$–I^6 that delays resolution of the dominant from the fermata until the end of m. 67 also contributes to the gentle resignation of this transcendent level of discourse.

To return to recitative cues, the opening two chords of Op. 59, no. 2 (Example 7.5a) not only announce the tonality (as in the first movement of the *Eroica* Symphony) but also set up a larger discursive context for what follows. The opening measure presents a move to the characteristic first-inversion dominant as well as an upper-voice leap of a fifth, clearly

Example 7.4. Beethoven, String Quartet in B♭, Op. 130, third movement, mm. 65–69.

Example 7.5. Beethoven, String Quartet in E minor, Op. 59, no. 2, first movement. a. mm. 1–16; b. mm. 139–44.

a.

Example 7.5. (Continued)

b.

cueing the recitative topic as enunciatory. Interestingly, the chords are also treated as thematic (note the cello's inverted thematic fifth in m. 15), and their eventual integration into a single level of discourse is accomplished by means of the spillover of sixteenths from the development into the recapitulation (Example 7.5b, mm. 139–42), filling the rhetorical gap, as it were, between announcement and message.

Use of the recitative topic at the beginning is not new for Beethoven. It plays an obvious thematic role in the opening of the *Tempest* Piano Sonata, Op. 31, no. 2. The opening of the Ninth Symphony, however, features rather enigmatic fifths. Their relationship to recitative is established only with the addition of a first-inversion D major chord, which lends the recapitulation its unmistakable air of climactic pronouncement. The D^6 is deferred in its resolution to a G minor chord, but it nevertheless suggests V^6/iv as well as Picardy third, combining with its cueing of the recitative topic to create a "super-trope." The multiple associations triggered by this chord are reflected in the striking interpretations it has evoked.[16]

Brahms gives evidence of the power of this trope to suggest a kind of annunciatory force in his appropriation of this technique for the opening of the D minor Piano Concerto. The first-inversion B♭ major triad is understood as VI in D minor, but its rhetorical function is to provide a strong, annunciatory opening to the orchestral introduction and exposition.

How Much Is Ironic?

It is the ability of a musical style to cue shifts in levels of discourse that helps support ironic reversal. But the operative level of irony must be interpreted in terms of the governing expressive genre. Two examples may help clarify the issue. In the first, I draw back from Wilfrid Mellers's inflated interpretation of cosmic irony in Op. 101. In the second, I move further than Rey Longyear in assessing the ironic consequences of an abrupt shift at the end of Op. 95.

Mellers sums up his interpretation of Op. 101 as follows:

> Opus 101 begins as a lyrical song that proves to be a dream; continues with a corporeal march which, especially in its trio, glimpses the Word through the Flesh; aspires to an aria-hymn that dissolves in harmonic deliquescence; attempts a sonata conflict which, beginning optimistically, lapses into farce; calls unsuccessfully on fugal unity to restore order; and assays sonata again, which this time flickers out in pathos and bathos. [1983: 161]

Mellers attempts to move the interpretation to a still higher level, and it is not this effort that I would criticize, but rather the particular interpretations that seem at times to be unwarranted. Conflicting interpretations are to be expected at the level of troping, and any critique must be grounded in correlations that in turn may appear rather speculative to the reader.

The notion of mixed genre (Chapter 3) may be inferred, with some stretching, from Mellers's account, which tropologically fuses the con-

Example 7.6. Beethoven, Piano Sonata in A, Op. 101, fourth movement, mm. 55–60.

horn fifths

cepts of high seriousness and play (1983: 162): "What Beethoven has done in the sonata is to accept this most basic of human 'failures' and, totally without evasion, to compose out of failure a work which is also an act of play." Mellers rejects a straightforwardly positive outcome (as he claims Donald Tovey and Martin Cooper espouse) because of his inability to "accept the coda's playfulness at face value" (161). His interpretation invokes a second level of discourse in its implication of near cosmic irony in the final movement, and it is this level that a critique must first address. If the coda of the Finale is somehow inappropriate to the context of the movement or cycle as a whole, then an ironic interpretation would be one way to reconcile that inappropriateness as a compositional effect rather than as a flaw.

Mellers's claim that the Finale of Op. 101 "lapses into farce" is based on his analysis of the "debunking" effect of the second theme and codetta of the exposition. Their inappropriately childish character deflates "both song and drama" (158). The ingredients of irony in the low *buffa* folk song and "irony that is witty rather than grotesque" at the cadence to the exposition suggest that Mellers is reacting to the shifts in levels of discourse. In Example 7.6 a *pianissimo* horn-fifth figure is immediately followed by a *forte* cadence. The effect of the contrast is heightened by the dancelike tune that follows. But something of the message is lost if one does not realize that the horn-fifth figure is treated as a quotation, interpretable as a typical pastoral figure that is mockingly rejected by the *forte* and tossed-off leaps of the cadence that follows. What is being debunked is not the optimistically triumphant and transcendent Finale theme, but the trite reference to a pastoral figure that has lost its potency. This irony functions more at the level of stylistic self-consciousness on the part of Beethoven than as part of the dramatic scenario for the movement. A miscalculation of the operative ironic level leads inevitably to Mellers's interpretation of the whole Finale as somehow ironically undermined in its high spirits. Instead, as was argued earlier, the use of low style and a *buffa* element can inflect the high heroic and transcendent elements in a way that is tropological, but not ironically reversed, in its emergent meaning: a unique spiritual victory is achieved, one that is grounded in the reality of everyday life and the vitality of a life tied to the natural order.

In this sense, Beethoven's loose description of the four movements—"Dreamy feelings," "Summons to the deed," "Return to dreamy feelings," and "The deed"—must in turn be interpreted.[17] The deed, or act, is to be understood as a positive outcome achieved through a "determination" (*Entschlossenheit*), that is enhanced by the Romantic-ironic projection of the persona above his own discourse. The recognition of a powerful will behind the music is one result of such an interpretation.

The last movement of the *Serious* String Quartet, Op. 95, has a remarkable addendum to the coda (Example 7.7). Rey Longyear, in his article on Romantic irony in Beethoven (1970), comments on what I would call a striking shift in stylistic register:

> Mozart, in the finale of his G major Quartet, K. 387, used the buffa melodies of his closing themes (measures 92–124) as an effective foil for a "learned" fugue, but Beethoven, in ending Opus 95, destroys the illusion of seriousness which has hitherto prevailed with an opera buffa–like conclusion. This ending exemplifies many of the other characteristics of romantic irony which Schlegel described: paradox, self-annihilation, parody, eternal agility, and the appearance of the fortuitous and unusual. [147]

Kerman (1966) suggests a distant motivic connection, or "reflection," of the opening movement's basic step progression from F to G♭ to G♮.[18] But he wonders how one could explain the "fantastic evocation of an opera buffa finale in which all the agitation and pathos and tautness and violence of the quartet seem to fly up and be lost like dust in the sunlight" (182). Kerman compares this "joke" to the more clearly earned "*volte face*" at the end of the Finale to Op. 132, suggesting that Beethoven somehow "solved" the problem with the latter work.

None of Kerman's stylistic and motivic rationales are convincing to me as explanations for the late shift in expressive direction in Op. 95. I agree with Kerman that one expects a change of emotional state in Beethoven's music to be earned through a progressive thematic dis-

Example 7.7. Beethoven, String Quartet in F minor, Op. 95, fourth movement, mm. 129–36.

course that ultimately rationalizes an earlier, sudden contrast. This is the case for the abrupt Neapolitan passage in the slow movement of the *Hammerklavier*. It is also the case for the slow movement of Op. 95, where the return section integrates aspects of the fugato's tragic searching, and only then works toward a serenely transcendent close. A similar rationale is not possible this late in the finale of Op. 95.

But I would argue that the *addendum* (not coda) to Op. 95 is neither a miscalculation nor a poorly solved problem. Note that the movement proper closes with a tragic fading to a unison (m. 131). The major tonic triad in m. 132 is not an unearned Picardy third but an anticipation (hence the *ppp*) of the addendum. The sudden change of tempo and character in m. 133 must be explained in terms of a shift in level of discourse, due to the utterly annihilating effect of the surprise ending for an otherwise tragic work.

Nietzsche's evidence for the Übermensch, (more akin to a fully evolved human consciousness than the Nazi perversion as racially "pure" superman) was his ability to laugh and thus shift to a higher, self-critical level of consciousness—literally, to project above even the most serious of tragic events and in some sense escape their limits altogether. There is indeed that kind of power here, since only a strong consciousness can be both fully aware of its own suffering and still capable of projecting above it. A Romantic ironic, Nietzschean interpretation moves one beyond the confines of a tragic-to-triumphant expressive genre. And since the ironic reversal does not lead to a worked-out, strategic troping on the earlier discourse, a mixed genre such as the tragicomic is ruled out. Instead, we find a radically different, "split" genre—in which the discourse is shifted to another plane entirely for the conclusion, and any ultimate integration in the mind of a listener is conceived as outside the work itself.

The Markedness of Tropes

A musical trope, considered as a potential type, is marked with respect to its origin; novelty, foregrounding, and salience are clearly characteristic of strategic markedness. It is difficult, however, to conceive of the narrower range of meaning of a trope when it does not organize itself as a subset or subdivision of a preestablished semantic hierarchy, but roams freely in its associative interpretive play. If that is the case, then the trope (although arising from the interpretation of a contradiction) cannot be defined oppositionally as a type. Thus, an original trope will not have a single, fixed correlation but will instead provoke multiple acts of interpretation.[19]

Although the trope may be unstable in its original appearance, it may be susceptible to growth. The process of identification of an entity, after all, is the first step in its generalization as a type (even if the type has only one token at first). Through frequent use, a trope may lose its interpretative freedom (or force) and acquire a more limited correlation. This process is comparable to the "life cycle" of a trope in language, as Michael and Marianne Shapiro (1976) have brilliantly analyzed. The cycle accounts for a gradual decrease in indeterminacy and a corresponding increase in definition as a result of frequent use. A "dead" or "frozen" metaphor is one that has become a relatively fixed correlation. Frozen metaphors can later be revived by redirecting attention to the figural motivation underlying a conventionalized meaning.

To return to the musical trope, when a given set of interpretations has become relatively fixed for a trope, then it will have an oppositional location in a new, or modified, semantic hierarchy. Until then, it may not be useful to specify the markedness opposition defining a trope, since in its most potent stage a trope eludes the simple oppositional definition for which markedness valuation would be appropriate. That is not to say that the interpretation of a trope does not take advantage of the marked relationships of its various components, since one cannot assume that the trope ever completely escapes the semantic universe in which it is created. Rather, the trope moves freely to combine or detach previously separate or attached meanings, working over the two-dimensional hierarchy of the semantic field and giving it the multidimensional flexibility of a semantic network.

Consider the following example, which illustrates style growth but not metaphorical troping. In the third movement of Op. 59, no. 1, a neighboring elaboration of the dominant involves a move to a German augmented sixth followed by V^4_3/V (Example 7.8a, mm. 19–20). The usual sequence for a syntagm involving these two chromatic chords is just the opposite, as one can observe in a typical passage from the same movement (Example 7.8b, mm. 36–37). Here, the vii°⁷/V is succeeded by the German augmented sixth; the sequence becomes more intense as it becomes more chromatic, with the A♮ in the soprano inflecting to A♭ in the bass (by means of a voice exchange).[20] This "normal order" is reversed in mm. 19–20, but the stylistic intensity values are clearly respected by the dynamic indications (*sf* for the A♭, decrescendo for the A♮ move in the bass). Thus, the hierarchy, or ranking, of the chords in terms of intensity is not reversed, but there is a reversal of their ordering, creating a new syntagm that is "tense to less-tense." This reversal is indeed marked, and clearly not fortuitous, as the dynamic indications reveal. But it is not a metaphor, since it has a straightforward correlation based on the understanding and application of stylistic correlations (of intensity) that have been respected in their ranking. The syntagm is new, and thus a new meaning has emerged, but the new meaning is built up from an elementary manipulation of the old, and the semantic hierarchy is instantiated rather than reformed. At best, it could be considered a *metonymic* trope, since there is a figurative play with syntagmatic order.

Example 7.8. Beethoven, String Quartet in F, Op. 59, no. 1, third movement.
a. mm. 16–21; b. mm. 35–37; c. mm. 124–26.

Interestingly, Beethoven exploits this new syntagm in a strategically marked fashion. The same progression appears, transposed to F minor, in mm. 124–25 (Example 7.8c). This time it serves as a hinge to the cadenza, which links with the Finale (the cadenza enacts a shift of discourse level, as well). Since the Finale is to be in F major, the Db in the

Example 7.8. (Continued)

c.

cello is diverted from its intense voice leading ($\flat\hat{6}$–$\hat{5}$; compare m. 37, A♭–G, in Example 7.11b), and raised to a D♮, which is not only less tense but also an appropriate preparation for F major. The potential lessening of tension from this reversal (D♭ to D♮, and the harmonic progression Fr^{+6}–V$^4_3$/V) is not realized because this time the *sf* emphasis occurs on the less-tense V$^4_3$/V (compare Example 7.8a, mm. 19–20). The effect is that of thrusting into a more positive realm. The subsequent cadenza offers a sudden insight (a new level of discourse) that escapes the tragic portentousness of the third movement and anticipates the joyous, pastoral exhilaration of the last movement, with its Russian folk tune.

To be a trope in the figurative sense defined above, the musical event must somehow produce an emergent meaning that crosses domains of the established correlational field. For example, the Mm^7 sonority built on $\hat{5}$ is the only Mm^7 in the major diatonic set. Its significance syntactically is well established as V^7 resolving to (and thus implying) the tonic. A deceptive cadence does not reverse this functional implication, but merely plays on the effect of its denial. But the use of a Mm^7 sonority in other than dominant-seventh circumstances could constitute a trope. Indeed, one such instance in the slow movement of Op. 95 (Example 2.3, mm. 149–50) was discussed as an uncharacteristically static sonority exploited more for its sonority than for its function. And in the first movement of Op. 101 the use of V_3^4 and V_5^6 for stasis was shown to undercut their still-present functional significance (Example 4.1, mm. 12–13 and 52). Several features may support the interpretation of a Mm^7 sonority as static, reversing its typically dynamic function. These include repetition, longer duration, resonant spacing, and a sense of expanding an area not focal to the prevailing key (i.e., creating a brief plateau at a new tonal level). Some combination of these may suggest a tropological interpretation.

Troping of harmony, voice leading, and thematized texture run consistently through the four movements of Op. 59, no. 2. The V^{m9} implied by arpeggiation in m. 4 of the first movement, and hinted by the $\hat{6}$–$\hat{5}$ voice leading in the bass in m. 12 (creating vii^{o4}_2 to V^7; Example 7.6a), becomes the crux of an intensification in the coda (Example 7.9a), where an extended arpeggiation of the dominant ninth begins as vii^{o4}_2 and ends up as a densely packed V^{m9}, *fortissimo*. Despite its tension, the harmony hardly seems resolved by what follows, but rather seems "stuck" in a kind of dense "black hole." Thus, the sonority and texture yield a new significance not predictable from earlier correlations.

The second movement, in E major, exploits the lowered sixth by modal mixture, and a prolongation of the V^{m9} is interrupted by the move from $\hat{5}$ to lowered $\hat{6}$ in the bass (Example 7.9b, mm. 74–76). This time the lowered $\hat{6}$ is harmonized with a stern iv^6, *forte*, resolving to V in a stylistic quote of the Baroque "Phrygian" cadence. Its use here, with the open fifth of the upper voices doubled to reinforce its "starkness," serves a similar role in shifting the discourse. The *subito forte* for the iv^6 and the *subito piano* resolution/restoration of V, along with the shocking contrast in texture, support the idea of an interpolation from another level. The effect is similar to the arrival of the stone guest in *Don Giovanni*; here, the interpretation might be "fateful warning." The extrapersonal attribution of fate is supported by the "authoritative" correlation of an older style and the "monumental" interpretation of texture and duration for the iv^6.

The shift to block chordal texture is thematized in the coda (Example 7.9c, mm. 138–43), as the main theme returns, *fortissimo*, with *sf* accents on dissonant, offbeat chords, for a dramatic summation of the tragic awareness only hinted by the earlier iv^6. Interestingly, in this passage the C♮ in the bass in m. 138 is reinterpreted as B♯, and the B♯ in m. 142 resolves as a C♮, troping by means of enharmonic interpretation the thematically sensitized, lowered $\hat{6}$ voice leading associated with V^{m9}.

Example 7.9. Beethoven, String Quartet in E minor, Op. 59, no. 2: a. first movement, mm. 230–40; b. second movement, mm. 74–79; c. second movement, mm. 138–43; d. third movement, mm. 21–25; e. fourth movement, mm. 354–60.

In the third movement the V^{m9} (Example 7.9d, m. 24) appears in a dense spacing reminiscent of the coda of the first movement, as the grinding crux after a "stuck" reiteration of the Neapolitan in the previous bars (heard as VI of A minor until that point). Again, C♮ to B is troped. The C♮ is harmonized this time by an F major chord, adding another colorful reinterpretation to its repertoire.

Finally, the last movement fulfills the logic of a trope that has become

Example 7.9. (Continued)

b.

Example 7.9. (Continued)

d.

e.

akin to a poetic conceit for the cycle, beginning in an apparent C major that is really an expansion of VI in E minor. Neapolitan expansions again play a role, linked to C as V/N. In one last reference to the block-chordal texture, a large-scale arpeggiation of the dominant (filled with chromatic passing tones in contrary outer voices) leads to a *sf* V_5^6 with the familiar $\hat{6}$–$\hat{5}$ motion in the viola hinting at previous V^{m9} usages (Example 7.9e).

Thus, troping may involve the concatenation of various musical elements, or the interaction of different realms of musical structuring, in a way that lends new significance to old structures.

An impressive trope at the level of formal structure and material function occurs in a movement analyzed in Chapter 6. The development of the first movement of Op. 130 combines the stasis of an ostinato (derived from the cadence gesture of a dynamic theme) with the instability of reversed metric placement and a mosaic of thematic fragments worked through various keys (characteristic of the typical *Durchführung*). It seems plausible that a kind of stratification occurs between background ostinato and forgrounded thematic fragments. But what emerges is far from either the typical development section's argumentation, or its *Sturm und Drang* or *Empfindsamkeit* topics (with their implied constrasts in expression). Instead, a kind of transcendence of discourse is suggested, perhaps modeled as stream-of-consciousness or pure contemplation.

In Chapter 5 the strategic matrix of material and location categorized this development section as closural material in a developmental location. At that stage of the investigation, only the simplest correlational mixing was suggested. The richer interpretation just given for the development section of Op. 130, however, demands more than a systematic logic of new meaning derived from the predictable mixing of stylistic categories. Instead, increasingly speculative interpretations emerge through a troping process that expands the semantic field in unpredictable ways.

Intertextuality

Musical discourse, as has been shown, may shift among different levels in a manner analogous to shifts in narrative discourse. Although contrasts may cue such shifts, Classical music is so full of contrasts that this consideration alone is not sufficient. In many of the examples we observed a higher-level contrast of styles or topics, including invocations of earlier styles (especially the Baroque), topics, and types (especially those associated with forms such as recitative or cadenza that typically cue such shifts).

Another important cueing of discourse level is achieved by quotation or modified reference to another work. This is to be distinguished from the general use of typical patterns or templates that are part of the

Example 7.10. Beethoven, String Quartet in A minor, Op. 132, third movement (subtitled *Heiliger Dankgesang eines Genesenen an die Gottheit, in der lydischen Tonart*): a. mm. 1–6; b. mm. 31–38.

a.   Molto adagio.

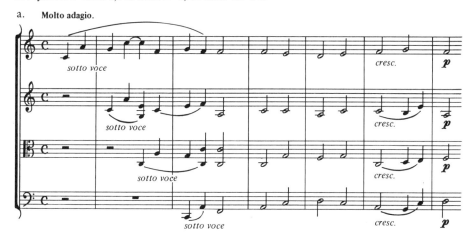

anonymous heritage of a stylistic language, unless (as was the case with the Phrygian cadence in the second movement of Op. 59, no. 2) the formula is derived from a different style than the one prevailing in the work.

The use of different styles or works to enrich the discourse of a given work may be termed *intertextuality.* Current intertextual theories in literature often go so far as to depreciate the individuality of the work in favor of its interpretation as the intersection of numerous interacting codes. This unraveling of the connotations and relationships among structural and signifying levels is pursued to a masterful end in Roland Barthes' analysis of a short story by Balzac.[21] Although there is future potential for interpretation in this approach to interacting codes, musical intertextuality might best be concerned at this stage with all the straightforward instances of appropriation from other works and styles, especially when those appropriations entail not merely syntactic borrowings but also borrowings of, or tropings upon, the correlations of appropriated material.[22]

A marvelous example of this kind of intertextuality is found in the third movement of Beethoven's String Quartet, Op. 132 (Example 7.10). Here, both Renaissance and Baroque styles are invoked for their strongly contrasted associations. The programmatic title provides a clue to intepretation: "Heiliger Dankgesang eines Genesenen an die Gottheit, in der lydischen Tonart" (Holy song of thanksgiving to the

Example 7.10. (Continued)

b.

divinity from a convalescent; in the Lydian mode). The opening section is clearly prayerlike, and although Beethoven's Lydian mode can
be rationalized in terms of F and C major, the unusual metric placement, voice leading, and harmonic succession of chords is marked
with respect to Classical norms. The slow tempo, *sotto voce* dynamic
level, self-conscious points of imitation, and subsequent hymn texture
all contribute to the evocation of a distant liturgical style, reminiscent
of Palestrina.[23] The evocation of such an early style (cf. Beethoven's
Missa Solemnis) carries a religious connotation from its liturgical asso-

ciation, and a near-mythic or mystic interpretation from its seemingly primitive, and thus "primal," pitch structure.

The contrasting section at m. 31 is entitled "Neue Kraft fühlend." Beethoven expresses new strength and vitality within the context of grateful prayer by the use of a stylized Baroque dance with its relatively faster tempo and activity levels. A comparable opposition within Renaissance styles may have been beyond his musicological awareness; thus, Beethoven chooses the more familiar but still historically removed Baroque style for a suitably energetic dance topic. This dance is the perfect blend of energy (trills and melodic figures in a vibrant triple meter) and dignity (stately tempo, with pomp in the alternating *forte* measures, and a "ceremonial" stepwise descent in the bass).

With the contrast of styles comes a contrast of discourse level, clearly interpretable from the programmatic labels. A similar example is found in the contrast between the *Allegro* first movement and the *Andante espressivo* second movement of the *Lebewohl* Piano Sonata, Op. 81a. The first movement is written in a relatively modern style, while the second exploits aspects of an older dramatic recitative couched within a pre-Classical *empfindsamer Stil* more characteristic of C. P. E. Bach. Again, the programmatic concept of absence suggests a change of rhetorical levels—expression of inner grief with an occasional outburst of anguish. Within the *Andante espressivo* a timeless waiting is suggested by the repetition of the initial motive and sequencing of the initial phrase. Temperamental outbursts (*sf*, mm. 19–20) occur above a Baroque-inspired walking bass, and the brief cadenza (mm. 13–14) shifts to a more interior response, or self-interrogation, as suggested by the softly arpeggiated diminished sevenths.

Rhetorical shifts based on self-quotation (of earlier movements) in the finales of the Ninth Symphony and the Piano Sonata Op. 101 have been mentioned. Another striking example, although less obvious as an exact quotation, occurs in the rhetorically shifting transition linking the third and final movements of the *Hammerklavier* (Example 7.11). This near-improvisatory passage has been discussed in illuminating detail by Charles Rosen (1972: 426–29), who emphasizes the "effect of the gradual creation of a new contrapuntal style," "taking shape, and growing organically out of unformed material" (428–29). The familiar ingredient of stylistic quotation is found in the interludes between chords descending by thirds. These interludes suggest (1) toccata, (2) "prelude-toccata," and (3) "invention-toccata," as numbered in Example 7.11.

Example 7.11. Beethoven, Piano Sonata in B♭, Op. 106 (*Hammerklavier*), transition to the fourth movement, mm. 1–5.

Example 7.12. Beethoven, Op. 106: a. transition to the fourth movement, mm. 9–10; b. first movement, mm. 81–84.

Unmentioned, however, is the "quotation" of a written-out fermata from the first movement (Example 7.12a, derived from 7.12b, mm. 81–84). The resemblance is striking when these excerpts are played one after the other. But the clinching evidence is the similar function of each of the two passages as a moment of insight, reflecting upon the previous discourse. The version in the first movement occurs after the second theme has collapsed in a chromatic sequence. It offers a moment of reflection before the closing themes of the exposition. The variant in the last movement serves not as a contrapuntal interlude but as a V_2^4 "cadenza" or elaborated fermata over a tonic pedal. Both versions have the familiar effect of ♯4 to ♮4 within their V^7s, hinting at yielding or relinquishing and a subdominant-side pull, each appropriate for such a reflective moment.[24]

Reflexivity in Musical Discourse

These various forms of intertextuality suggest a wealth of resources for signaling shifts in level of discourse, and they also point toward a broader concept of reflexivity in discourse.[25] Reflexivity extends the notion of Romantic irony as self-conscious awareness and commentary on the work as it emerges, either compositionally (as creative act) or temporally in performance (as ongoing discourse). Reflexivity includes those means whereby the composer "gets outside" the artificiality of the form to suggest either a greater reality of experience or an awareness that goes beyond the expressive discourse of the work.[26] His concern to exceed the expressive capacities of an already powerful style leads Beethoven to striking shifts in levels of discourse, including the use of self-quotation and stylistic allusions. The transition to the last movement of the *Hammerklavier* is reflexive in both ways. The shifts of an emerging consciousness are both represented (by the improvisatory shifts in style) and reflected upon (by means of self-quotation in the composed-out fermata).[27]

The literary theorist Mikhail Bakhtin ([1935] 1981) considers the play of styles and language types in literature as examples of "heteroglossia" (different voices), producing the dialogic play of discourse in the novel. One of the effects of such play is to parcel out meanings between different voices—not unlike the levels of discourse, or their implied personae, that I have investigated for Beethoven.[28] It is this dialogic play, more complex than mere "point of view," that enables the author to present a myriad of perspectives on the discourse of characters and the events of plot. More subtly than in the musical examples given here, the novel may alternate among several voices, and thus levels, within a single character. Nontexted music must instead signal its shifts by means such as those illustrated above: extreme contrasts in style or topic (especially where they suggest a reversal), cueing of recitative as a topic, direct quotation or intertextual importation, disruptions of the temporal norm, or even negation. But the capacity of music to cue these shifts, and the perspective on discursive depth that such shifts afford the competent listener, must be recognized even when their interpretation is more problematic, and their significance more elusive, than for literature.

CHAPTER

VIII

Analysis and Synthesis

The *Cavatina* from Op. 130

The previous chapters have outlined a multifaceted approach to musical meaning in Beethoven, ranging from basic stylistic types and thematic structures to topical fields, expressive genres, shifts in discourse level, and tropes. They have demonstrated the correlation of types and the interpretation of tokens, the establishment of stylistic markedness and the development of strategic markedness. These fundamental categories and concepts have served to organize the investigation of expressive meaning in the Classical style, its creative manifestation in Beethoven (especially in the later works), and its implications for style growth. These strands are now drawn together in a summary analysis of the *Cavatina* from Beethoven's String Quartet, Op. 130 (reproduced in its entirety as Example 8.1). The *Cavatina* had great expressive significance for Beethoven; he is reported to have said that the music always made him weep. Besides

Example 8.1. Beethoven, String Quartet in B♭, Op. 130, fifth movement complete (*Cavatina*).

its obvious expressive power, the *Cavatina* is an appropriate final example in that it synthesizes, in a remarkably integrated movement, many of the expressive strategies encountered in previous analyses. In addition, the search for expressive power sufficient to evoke tears in the composer will lead us far beyond the simple opposition between the tragic minor and nontragic major with which we began.

Example 8.1. (Continued)

Example 8.1. (Continued)

Overview of the *Cavatina*

The *Cavatina* is, not surprisingly, a slow movement. Slow movements often probe the greatest depths of expression because they can be highly configured with expressive turns and inflections. I am not alluding to ornamentation, but to the reversals and other marked musical events that are focal points for expression. A slower tempo allows for greater flexibility of expressive discourse, at least on the surface, since a listener has more real time in which to consider possibilities and absorb the effect of actual events.

As opposed to the more outgoing aspects of fast movements, slow movements are typically, and in terms of their genres, more intimate expressions. Varieties of quiet reflection—soul-searching, poignant remembrance, and the like—are culturally established in the literature as well as the music of the late eighteenth and early nineteenth centuries. Adagio movements are often synonymous with personal reflection, ranging among the following:

1. Tragedy (either directly expressed, through *Empfindsamkeit* and *Sturm und Drang* in the slow movement of Op. 10, no. 3; or as monumental and objectified in parts of the slow movements of Op. 101 and Op. 106)
2. Tragic awareness tending toward transcendence (Op. 106, III)
3. Assurance or reassurance (Op. 13, II)
4. Serene sanctity (Op. 132, III, A section)

The *Cavatina* is a unique blend of these types. The movement is in E♭ major, appropriately the subdominant of the home key of the quartet, B♭ major. A relatively diatonic tonality with only occasional chromatic inflections lends the *Cavatina* a more "primal" expressivity, akin to the slow movement of Op. 132 but without as direct a stylistic allusion to the past. Thus, the irruption of a recitative-like (*Beklemmt*, or "anguished") section is all the more effective as a contrast.[1] But how does the relatively unclouded, major-mode diatonicism of the movement proper achieve such poignance? I will return to this question below.

The emotional climate of the *Cavatina* would at first appear to be generically "serene." Chorale-like harmonic progressions and hymnic textures signal the high style, whereas the aria-like melody in the first violin introduces a more personal element (recall the "objective hymn vs. subjective aria" opposition in the slow movement of the *Hammer-*

klavier). Simplicity in harmonic progression provides an elevated pastoral contribution to the high style.

According to Koch's *Musikalisches Lexikon* (1802), a cavatina is "a short aria in which words are seldom repeated and melismatic extension of syllables seldom applied, and which in particular has no second section."[2] If we examine the form of Beethoven's instrumental "cavatina," we find that it clearly exceeds a single section, and yet its developing variation suggests a more organic expansion of a continuous discourse. Tonally, the *Cavatina* is unusual in that it remains largely in the key of Eb major. Except for the exceptional, rhetorically discrete *Beklemmt* section, there is only one passage that attempts a move away from Eb, and it returns before a significant new area can be established. Figure 8.1 illustrates aspects of part form and sonata in the design of this extended cavatina, which eludes both formal schemes.

The passage beginning with the B♮ in m. 12 would qualify as transitional in a sonata scheme, evolving as it does from a counterstatement of the main theme; but that hypothesis is undermined when the move to C minor is suspended on a cadential six-four (mm. 15–16) and diverted after the delayed half cadence (mm. 17–18). A circle-of-fifths sequence unexpectedly returns to Eb (mm. 18–23). Upon the return, the diverted transition to a new key area is retrospectively interpreted as a more parenthetical (if dramatically motivated) digression.

From a formal standpoint, the theme beginning in m. 23 could be heard as closural, but it has an expressive weight that is comparable to the main theme (the 2PK designation in Figure 8.1 indicates a closing theme in the original key). The first two measures are expressively and formally highlighted by their immediately varied repetition, expansion, and varied restatement.

Topically, the *Beklemmt* section is a dramatic recitative; it also functions as a brief *Durchführung*, shifting to Cb major and leading to Ab minor. This episode is not a straightforward B (or C) section, but more like a suspension of time (recall the trancelike development section in the first movement), cued by a recitative that itself appears to be in a different time from that of its background accompaniment. It ends appropriately enough with a Baroque-like Phrygian cadence, iv⁶–V, in Ab minor (recall the rhetorical use of this cadence in the slow movement of Op. 59, no. 2, analyzed in Example 7.9b). The cadential dominant is simply reinterpreted as the tonic for the return of the main theme.

A newly written closural section (mm. 58–end) follows the return of the theme, spinning out countermaterial from the theme and exploiting

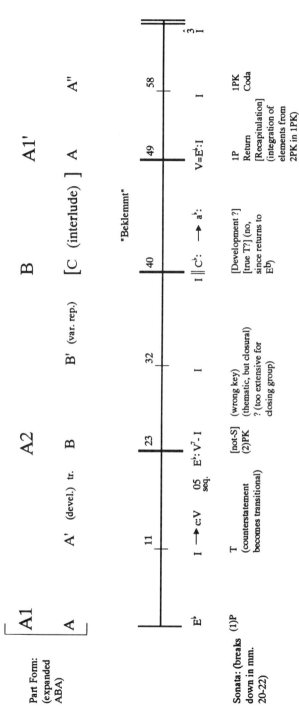

Figure 8.1. Diagram of the *Cavatina*, with unconvincing formal analyses revealing aspects of part-form and sonata schemes.

one of its characteristic points of expressive focus: the sudden melodic drop to a 6–5 elaboration of a deceptive move (m. 60, compare m. 6). The cadence (mm. 63–64) features melodic descent, triplet, and escape tone, familiar from the 2PK theme (mm. 23–24). Thematic integration has been shown to be a typical closural strategy in Beethoven's sonata forms, especially so in the first movement of Op. 130.

Although this movement is not formally a sonata in tonal terms, the rhetoric of thematic form draws notably from sonata schemes. The hybrid of aria, part form, and sonata[3] requires less support from oppositions of tonality because other expressive oppositions and an ongoing evolution of those oppositions are adequate in themselves. Since the "second" theme (2PK) was presented in the tonic, no tonal resolution is required to satisfy that principle of sonata form, and thus the 2PK theme receives merely an allusion, not a full return, in the closing section.[4] Its expressive derivation from the first theme, to be explored below, further rationalizes its role in the drama.

A Closer Interpretation of the Cavatina

In Nineteenth-Century Music ([1980] 1989), Carl Dahlhaus claims that motivic connections between themes in this movement serve to synthesize an instrumental idiom and a vocal model.[5] For Dahlhaus, the "poetic idea"

> remains strangely suspended between three poles: a stark realism, as is illustrated in the Recitative by the expression mark *beklemmt* ("agonized") at measure 42; a masklike aura pervading the vocal styles in their instrumental guises; and a spirit of reflection into whose coils Beethoven draws his quoted types of vocal expression by enveloping them in a web of specifically instrumental motivic relations. [85]

Applying Ratner's (1980) topics, we can go further than the previously noted high style (slow, *sotto voce*, hymnlike texture in the opening), and discover *empfindsamer* declamation in the melodic line (the rhythmically abrupt sigh and release in the melodic line in m. 3, and its subsequent drop to a sigh figure in m. 6).

If the sincerity of the high style is established by use of straightforward harmonic progressions at the beginning, it is weighted with intense feeling by the more individualistic melodic line. By comparison with the successive first themes of the slow movement of the *Hammer-klavier* (Chapter 1), the contrast in the *Cavatina* is simultaneous rather than successive. There is a background-foreground relationship between the unmarked hymn accompaniment (objective) and marked melodic theme (subjective). The resulting trope is similar to that achieved by the integrative recapitulation in the *Hammerklavier* movement.

The E♮ in the first measure comes too soon to be taken seriously as a functionally significant alteration; instead, it serves as a local intensifier, creating the sense of an introductory kernel phrase of one measure, complete with a miniature climax followed by a cadence. The first violin enters from within the texture of m. 1, launching from the premature cadential move in the lower voices (mm. 1–2). That solid harmonic progression reinforces the affirmational value of the first violin's opening melodic gesture.[6] Although it is secondary to the melody in the first violin, the melodic curve in the first measure also plays a thematic role; it provides the link between gaps in the main melodic phrases, as well as source material for thematic extension, transition, and the final closing section of the piece. In that it is stylistically unmarked melodic material, lending itself to both linking and closural roles, it plays something of the role taken by the tail of the fugue subject in Op. 131 (Chapter 6). This type of material, as noted earlier, is amenable to various kinds of strategic markings that allow it to fulfill other, more-specialized functions: in the *Cavatina*, the modulatory sequence in mm. 17–21 of the transition is built from this material.

The opening gesture in the first violin is characterized by an expansive major-sixth anacrusis to $\hat{3}$, leading in parallel tenths with the bass to a preliminary apex on $\hat{5}$, and falling off by step to $\hat{2}$. The somewhat abrupt breaking off in m. 3 hints at the kind of wrenching release observed in m. 21 of the Op. 131 fugue (Chapter 6). Here, however, the effect is considerably milder; nevertheless, the gasping effect created by the rest in m. 3 suggests the world of *Empfindsamkeit* by shifting from continuous aria melody to broken, declamatory utterance. Because the "open" ending on $\hat{2}$ is harmonized as part of a larger progression, rather than as a half cadence on V, the 7–6 suspension over ii⁶ creates a sense of expansiveness. Gentle poignance is added when the sigh, G–F, is echoed directly by the viola's G–F and then later in the measure by the second violin's D–C and A♭–G.

In Beethoven's compositional process, the climax of the phrase as a whole (mm. 2–9) resulted from three successively higher climaxes in the sketches (Example 8.2; Mies, 1929: 25). Mies demonstrates how the

Example 8.2. Two sketches and the final version of the *Cavatina* theme from Op. 130, mm. 4–6 (Mies, 1929: 25).

apex is made "more obvious by the drop that follows" (25), thus interpreting Beethoven's intention in the successive revisions as the intensification of a certain melodic design.[7] There is more involved, however, than just melodic interval succession or apex design in the expressive richness of this phrase.

The bass line in the first three measures offers a series of variations on a three-note stepwise ascent, but in the fourth and fifth measures the motive is inverted, first in the second violin, and then in the cello. The inversion in m. 5 is a reversal of the bass progression in m. 2 (note the stylistically unmarked progression involving a passing V_3^4). The resulting contrary motion intensifies the soprano ascent with a familiar expansion. When the melodic apex is gained in m. 6, the bass expands beyond the three-note model to reach its lowest point yet. But as soon as the outer-voice climax is exposed, and thus emphasized, it is undercut and dramatically reversed by the inward collapse of bass and soprano to a diminished seventh chord (vii°[7]/vi) and by the deceptive move implied by its continuation to vi. The effect recalls the moment in the opening of the *Hammerklavier* slow movement (m. 5), where a climax is left hanging by a sudden seizure of anxiety, or qualm of doubt. In the *Cavatina*, this qualm is mollified when the phrase continues smoothly with an expanded ii[6], a reassuring 7–6 suspension on the downbeat, and the integration of "accompanying" material into the main line (compare the melodic line in m. 7 with the second violin's connective tissue in mm. 1 and 3).

Such amelioration is appropriate to the generic character of the *Cavatina*. By virtue of its major key and its elevation of simple music to high seriousness, the movement appears to be in the nontragic realm of the transcendently serene. Like the first movement of Op. 101, however, elements of the tragic may be hinted, or allowed to irrupt, to provide a

Example 8.3. Anaylsis of the *Cavatina* opening theme, mm. 1–10, showing expressive focal points in the context of phrase-structural analysis and quasi-Schenkerian outer-voice reduction.

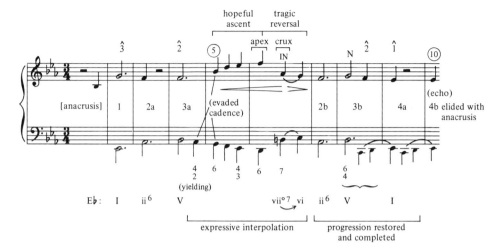

greater sense of the real world behind the elevated discourse of the *Cavatina*. And the immediate effect of the sudden collapse in m. 6 is unmistakably a (tragic) reversal, even in this serene environment.

Example 8.3 presents a reduction of the opening theme, indicating the importance of the events in mm. 5–6 in the context of typical voice-leading and phrase-structural norms.[8] The theme may be seen as an expansion of a $\hat{3}$–$\hat{2}$–$\hat{1}$ upper-line structural descent supported by I–ii⁶–V–I. Following the opening anacrusis (m. 1), an expected four-bar phrase is evaded in m. 5 by the familiar yielding progression in the bass (V–V$^4_2$–I⁶) and a melodic reversal in the melody that denies the expected closural $\hat{1}$. The extended four-bar phrase is harmonically restored in mm. 7–9, following an expressively motivated expansion in mm. 5–6.

A processive scan of the phrase structure based on a harmonic model (the numbers between the staves of Example 8.3) reveals the interpolation that creates a marked structural environment for the marked expressive crux.

A strong wedge motion in m. 5 expands registrally to the apex on the downbeat of m. 6, which is negated as a climax by the more intensely expressive crux created by the unexpected reversal (registral collapse) on the second beat. The "willed" (basically stepwise) ascent takes on a hopeful character supported by the stepwise bass. (Note that the wedge-like expansion "opens up" emotional as well as registral space, and overrides the potential "lament" connotation of a stepwise descent in the bass.) The reversal involves inward leaps of a sixth in the soprano and the bass that suddenly collapse the registral space and "constrict" the hopeful expansiveness.

Beethoven's dynamic markings clearly indicate that the apex is not the point of expressive focus. The harmonization of the last two beats of m. 6 not only reinforces the crux by chromatic intensification of a deceptive move but foreshadows the turn to C minor in the counterstatement/transition section that follows.

The stepwise motion in the bass from B♭ to E♭ (mm. 8–10) results in a less common I_4^6–vi^7–V^6–I cadence (mm. 8–9, reiterated in mm. 9–10), which undermines melodically the otherwise strong harmonic cadence.[9] In turn, the special mm^7 sonority of the (passing) vi^7 coincides with the temporary undermining of the cadential dominant degree in the bass. Later in the movement, that mm^7 sonority will prove to have been expressively prophetic, as a marked sonority taking on thematic significance and compelling an interpretation of its oppositional status.[10]

A varied repetition or counterstatement of the theme begins in m. 11, leading toward C minor by m. 12. As the vi region of E♭ major, C minor would appear to be an appropriate choice in light of the harmonic emphasis it has already received in m. 6. The region could also be motivated by the expressive value of the relative minor as an emotionally troubled opposition to the serenity of the major. But C minor, as we have seen, eludes cadential confirmation.

Another mm^7 sonority occurring on the downbeat of m. 13 is interpretable as iv^7 becoming $ii^{\varnothing6}_5$ (or simply $ii^{\varnothing6}_5$ with a 7–6 suspension). The sonority is familiar from mm. 8 and 9. The motivic sigh on the downbeat in the upper voice associates the sonority by its function with subdominants in mm. 3 and 7. But its continuation here is more emotionally charged. Instead of the reassurances following from m. 7, a partly chromatic 5–6–5 progression leads to an augmented-sixth highlighting of the cadential six-four in C minor.

The expected cadence is delayed by still another mm^7, interpolated in a way reminiscent of mm. 8 and 9, but functioning here as iv^7 instead of vi^7. Although simply a neighbor chord syntactically, the sonority has much deeper expressive significance. Features supporting the sonority as expressively marked may be summarized as follows:

1. dynamic, agogic, durational, and reiterational emphases, marking it as a salient event on the surface;

2. neighboring and interpolational status as a delay of expected cadence, supporting a construal as "parenthetical" or outside of the normal course of time, thus akin to "insight" in that it comes without logical necessity or a sequential train of thought;
3. previous thematization of the sonority, providing further strategic markedness and suggesting interpretation based on the relationship between current and previous uses;
4. subdominant flavor, suggestive of reflective rather than future-oriented temporal activity;
5. less actively dissonant sonority (mm⁷), yet distinctively oppositional to the brighter Mm⁷ or MM⁷ sonorities, thereby supporting an interpretation on the tragic side (broadly speaking).

Interactively interpreting these inflections of meaning, one might understand the resulting trope as "tragically weighted insight or reflection, expanding an instant that seems frozen within the flow of time." The duration and reiteration ensure time for its full import to be absorbed.[11]

After this expressively more focal digression, the cadential six-four moves to its expected V. But continuation to a minor tonic is denied. Instead, the C major chord hints at Picardy-third transcendence only to reveal its function as V⁷/iv, instituting the circle-of-fifths "retransition" to E♭. This transition undercuts the presumed cadence of m. 18 by sequencing the pattern beginning with m. 17. The twice-deferred cadence is formally troped by transformation from closural to transitional material. Finally, the melodic gesture of m. 18 acts as a denial of the hopeful melodic line from m. 17 (compare the head from the Op. 131 fugue), reversing direction and thus undermining C as melodic goal at the same time that C minor is undermined as tonic. These twists and turns configure the surface with irreducible significance, even as we hear the underlying structure from which they depart (Example 8.4).

As mentioned earlier, the linking eighth notes from the framing and introductory m. 1 are treated imitatively to create the background for this retransition. The first violin line in mm. 17–21, on the other hand, appears to be developing the expressive contour from mm. 5–6 of the theme. But there are significant differences between the expressive crux as transformed in m. 21 and the model in m. 6: a more declamatory rhythmic physiognomy and a pronounced avoidance of the previous deceptive move (vii°⁷/vi to vi) upon descending to A♭. At this point, the melodic drop is absorbed harmonically into the dominant-seventh pro-

Example 8.4. Reductive analysis of the *Cavatina* transition, mm. 17–22, showing development of the crucial ascent-reversal idea from mm. 5–6.

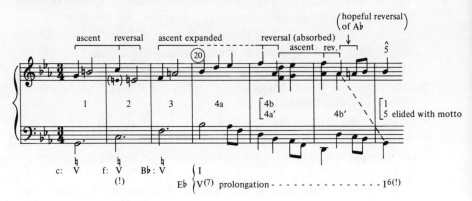

longation from m. 20 to m. 22 and echoed in parallel sixths by the second violin and viola. The subdued intensity and focus of the crux reduces its tragic effect in this location.[12]

With the entry of the second, or closural, theme in m. 23 comes one of the most heart-wrenching moments in all of Beethoven's music. But how can one claim such powerful expressivity when there seem to be so few clues in terms of marked or unusual progressions? The basically simple diatonic progression seems to offer little that would account for the overwhelming impression of poignance.

An analogous problem is presented by the much-debated aria "Che farò senza Eurydice" from Gluck's opera *Orfeo ed Eurydice*.[13] The problem there is resolved if the interpreter treats the disparity as a trope leading to an emergent interpretation: "grief that transcends the possible (conventional) modes of expression." The aria presents a protagonist devastated and reduced to a state of childlike innocence, and such utterance is wrenching in its dramatic ironic effect (see also the explanation offered in Chapter 2).[14] But the Beethoven example does not have as clear a dramatic scenario to motivate its quite different quality of expression—consoling at an immediate level, but wrenching in its poignancy at a higher level.

Owen Jander (1983) has written about the expressive genre Romance, defined in expressive terms by Rousseau, which achieves its effect through a simple melody that is repeated without ornamentation. For Jander, this poetic genre helps explain the intent of the slow move-

Example 8.5. Analysis of the *Cavatina* second theme motto, mm. 23–24.

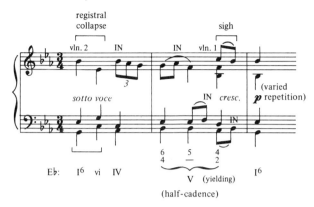

ment of Beethoven's Violin Concerto (along with another, more programmatic idea related to the Orpheus myth). If one were to mark such an effect in the *Cavatina* (which I do not claim to be a Romance, but rather to use the genre in a topical way), it would be in the treatment of the theme beginning in m. 23. A simple varied repetition (aab, twice) results in four statements of the eloquent two-bar motto. Although lightly ornamented, the two-measure utterance has a profoundly simple, sincere character, supporting the hypothesis that, as in the Romance, its continued reiteration might lead one to tears.

The consoling aspect is cued both stylistically and strategically. Stylistically, the *sotto voce* dynamic indication, chorale-like texture, simple diatonic progression, and the effect of varied repetition suggest an interpretation of reassurance. Strategically, the particular details of this passage (such as the initial absence of the soloist, the first violin), and its gestural relationship to an earlier expressive crux, make the consolation more specific and give it a clear dramatic motivation.

Gesturally, the first measure of the theme (m. 23) may be compared to the expressive crux in m. 6 in that the outer voices collapse inward (see Example 8.5). Whereas the effect of the collapse to a diminished-seventh "qualm" and subsequent deceptive move is unsettling in m. 6, the effect in m. 23 of the stable $\hat{5}$–$\hat{1}$ melodic drop, although harmonized with I^6 moving to vi, is much more reassuring since the vi is not so much deceptive[15] as it is a means of marking scale degree $\hat{1}$ with something of the earlier tragic awareness. Thus, the consolation in m. 23 is both realistic and relevant to the earlier disturbance in m. 6. Indeed, the

Example 8.6. Reductive analysis of the *Cavatina* second theme, mm. 23–31. Note sudden hopeful expansion in m. 27 and filled-in reversal in m. 29.

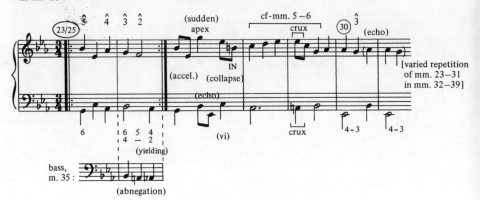

oppositional reversal is possible because such resemblances between the two locations allow one to infer a similar involvement with the tragic. In m. 23, however, the response differs in a way that can be interpreted as consolational.[16]

The continuation of this second, or closing, theme reveals further relationships or derivations from the opening theme that justify its presentation in the home key of E♭ major and the sense it gives of integrating or resolving tensions that were interior to the opening theme. On the third beat of m. 23, the 9–8 appoggiatura over IV recalls earlier subdominant uses, but this time the subdominant is subsumed on the weak third beat rather than placed focally on the downbeat. A comparison with the third beat of m. 2 reveals the triplet "softening" of a previous melodic rhythm. The next measure (m. 24) also features the thematized escape tone (IN) echoed imitatively in the lower voices. These are telling associations that one would expect in an integrational thematic passage.

The cadential ⁶⁵–⁴³ in m. 24 is evaded by a dynamically marked V⁴₂ (crescendo followed by a *subito piano* resolution to I⁶), a familiar progression whose interpretation also involves a sense of yielding. Indeed, the by-now-familiar V⁶₅/V to V⁴₂ variant occurs climactically in m. 35 (see Example 8.6) as the last form of the reiterated two-measure unit, cueing resignation-as-abnegation before the closural resolution of V⁶₅/V to cadential six-four and a perfect authentic cadence (mm. 38–39).

The closing theme group as a whole (Example 8.6) displays several important expressive features that derive from the repetition/variation process. The nearly exact repetition in mm. 25–26 is both compressed and truncated, leading to a completely realized four-bar phrase in mm. 27–30. In m. 27 the melodic fifth is compressed into one beat, and an expansive leap of a tenth to the apex is supported by a sudden crescendo to *forte*. The continuation of tonic harmony (delaying the less positive vi as an answer to an echo in the cello) underlines this "breaking of bonds" as a positive moment of heroic affirmation (within the contextual realm of the movement).[17]

Subsequent upward sighs in the melody supply the climactic realization of a similar urging in mm. 13–14, while miming the contour of mm. 5–6. When the apex of E♭ is reached in m. 29, its potential as a climactically resolutional goal is undermined by the A♮ in the bass and its subsequent falling off (E♭–C–G, first beat of m. 29); but the reversing drop is partially filled in by the soprano and further unsupported as tragic by the bass. The positive resolution of A♮ to B♭ in the cello confirms this transformation of tragic reversal to a more accepting resignation, reinforced by the abnegational treatment of A♮ in m. 35.

Finally, the richer harmonization of m. 28 in m. 37 entails an applied dominant of vi and the thematic drop of a fifth in the bass, enhancing the thematic recurrence of the submediant harmony. Once more, the vi chord provides its expressive inflection by undercutting the aspirations of the melodic sighs.

The *Beklemmt* Interlude

The agitated vocal recitative of this section shifts to a more-exposed level of discourse, almost a baring of the soul. The extraordinary rhythmic independence of the first violin, with its gasping bits of melodic utterance, comes close to modern conceptions of extreme, and perhaps psychologically dissociated, utterance. Conventionally, the section is a species of dramatic recitative; the other instruments are not merely accompanimental, but serve to create a background of equally divided beats against which the vocal utterance is rhythmically and metrically foregrounded. This stratification of temporality characterizes a section that is itself a temporal interruption of the prevailing texture and discourse. The recitative functions as a frozen moment in terms of the time of the piece; it is expanded musically to suggest virtual, or psychological, time.[18]

The pathos of the section is so well secured through rhythmic and textural design that the move to C♭ *major* can be accommodated. (Minor mode might have been expected, and indeed, the section ends in A♭ minor.) Since C♭ is the ♭VI of E♭, there is a thematic relationship with previous expansions of vi; the significant difference here is the shift of a half step, which also supports the interpretation of this section as coming from a different realm of discourse. The dramatization of mm. 5–6 appears here as a tentative, hesitant, almost questioning ascent in the first violin, which suffers a shuddering chromatic collapse in m. 44, then moves to a more sobering insight in the relative minor (A♭, the minor subdominant of E♭). The fateful monumentality of the Phrygian half cadence authoritatively seals this awareness.

Reinterpretation of the Return: Dramatic Closure

As mentioned earlier, the dominant of A♭ minor is simply reinterpreted as the tonic of E♭ major for the return of the main theme. After the first theme is recapitulated almost literally, a closing section begins in m. 58. Although the motive in the first violin reflects its contour in m. 42 (a point noted by Lockwood, 1992: 214), the focal points of this integrative coda recall earlier expressive gestures (see Example 8.7). Measure 59 presents an unclouded apex, appearing as a positive resolution; the echo in the first violin, however, is not only interrupted but further recalls the expressive crux from m. 6. The deceptive move from V⁷ and the thematic associations of the vi sonority (especially with added dissonance) support a tragic interpretation of the crux. But this time the harmonization is less intense, and dynamics are undercut as if to suggest a reminiscence of the crux.

The parallel moment in the varied repetition of this phrase (m. 63) drops to B♭ instead of A♭ to initiate a two-bar closural gesture. Now the expressive focus is shifted to the chromatic bass line (D–D♭–C–C♭–B♭), with its conventional closural emphasis on the subdominant and the thematic hint of abnegation (D–D♭–C in the subdominant). Note also the brief hint of vi⁷ with the premature move of the bass to C. The chromatic descent in the bass (a milder echo of the *Beklemmt* collapse in m. 44) is compensated by the strong scale-degree interpretation of the soprano in mm. 63–64 as a stable descent from $\hat{5}$ to $\hat{1}$. In other words, even though the $\hat{5}$ (B♭) in the first violin is quickly turned into an unstable seventh harmonically (either vi⁷ or 7–6 suspension over IV⁶),

Example 8.7. Reductive analysis of the *Cavatina* closing section, mm. 58–end. Note heightened summary of the crux in m. 60, coordination of crux and abnegation progression in m. 63, and poetic reminiscence in mm. 65–66.

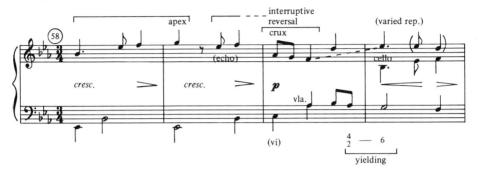

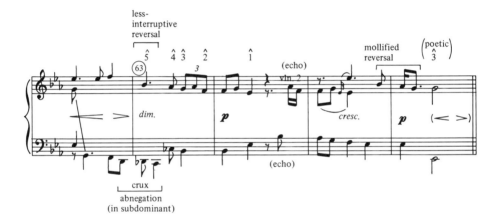

its clear structural role in the descent accommodates an expressively colored harmonization. That harmonization is in turn expressively motivated by the chromaticism in the bass (recalling, while helping to unwind the tensions of the movement) and the resulting mm⁷ sonority with its thematic associations.

The first violin line in m. 63 also brings back the triplet, practically the only distinct reminder of the first section's closing theme (mm. 23ff.), itself derived from the first theme. The escape tone elaboration of the cadence in m. 64 can be related to both themes, and thus it lends its hint of thematic integration to the closural process.

The move in the final bar to G in the upper line is thematically high-lighted by the pitch-class relationship A♭–G (here, as a 4–3 passing tone over the tonic, but obviously an expressive echo of m. 60). Just as the omission of the fifth and the doubling of the third of the final tonic were marked for "serene" closure in the second and third movements of Op. 131 and Op. 135 respectively (see Chapter 2), the close of the *Cavatina* is given a poetic reassurance by means of the reinforced doubling of the G in the final tonic. The melodic close on $\hat{3}$, although syntactically merely a tag to the structural close on $\hat{1}$ in m. 64, functions expressively as a benediction to the movement—the sweetness of serenity restored in the face of tragic awareness.[19]

Conclusion

From the standpoint of categories of genre, the *Cavatina* occupies a place roughly between the two movements analyzed in Chapters 1 and 4. Like the first movement of Op. 101, the *Cavatina* is a movement in a major key with a serene surface marked by numerous undercuttings of climaxes and cadences. The admixture of tragic elements in each of these movements (the two outbursts in Op. 101, the move to C minor and the *Beklemmt* episode in the *Cavatina*) does not divert the ultimately positive outcome of each movement. Rather, the irruption of the tragic gives greater depth to each movement's perspective. The result of mixing pastoral and tragic, or meditatively serene and tragic, is the elevation of the discourse to the high style in terms of serious spiritual intent.

Like the slow movement of Op. 106, on the other hand, the *Cavatina* is already a serious slow movement with intensely expressive intent (implicit in the tempo indications affixed to each movement: *molto expressivo* for the *Cavatina*, and *Appassionato e con molto sentimento* for the *Hammerklavier* movement). While the *Hammerklavier* movement struggles more strenuously in its move from darkness to redemption, the *Cavatina* reflects a subtle awareness of tragic insight within the realm of faith, an awareness that becomes even more intimate and vulnerable following the disclosure of the *Beklemmt* episode. Both movements trace the endurance of a fully tested faith as they arrive finally at glowing, major-tonic sonorities. Neither proposes nor achieves an easy or definitive resolution to the tragic, which is more subtly, and perhaps more affectingly, expressed in the *Cavatina*.

The profound inwardness that merges lyric contemplation and dramatic struggle may well account for the *Cavatina*'s special poignance, as evidenced by Beethoven's own emotional response. Even more so than the first movement of Op. 131, the progressive treatment of a marked expressive event in the *Cavatina* forges a dramatic and expressive coherence that does not depend on the dialectical tonal drama of sonata form, but draws upon the resources of a stylistic language that can thematize generative oppositions at any level. This thematically conceived expressive language had profound consequences for style change in the nineteenth century, as uniquely realized in the styles of Wagner, Brahms, and ultimately Schoenberg.

Historical and Theoretical Perspectives

The final two chapters of this study range widely from the historical to the speculative. Chapter 9 presents a broad defense for a semiotic approach to musical expressive meaning as drawn or diverging, from significant antecedents in the nineteenth and twentieth centuries. Chapter 10 offers a more speculative series of theoretical observations. It begins by exploring two perplexing intersections between music and language—the depreciation of meaning in music when compared with meaning in language, and the problems associated with using language to label or communicate expressive meanings. Next, it expands on considerations of stylistic growth first touched upon in Chapter 2; specifically, it demonstrates how Charles Sanders Peirce's categories of Firstness, Secondness, and Thirdness can help explain several varieties of creative type-generation in music. Finally, it develops a general theory of motivations for semiosis, with implications for music cognition as well as music theory. These topics complete the general overview of markedness theory as part of a larger semiotic model encompassing style growth and change, as well as expressive meaning in a given style.

From the Aesthetic to the Semiotic

The theory of musical expressive meaning outlined in the preceding chapters is grounded in correlations mediated by the markedness of oppositions in the style and manifested in acts of interpretation involving such larger contexts as expressive genres, thematic (or strategic) markedness found in the work, tropes (metaphor, irony), shifts in discourse level (Romantic irony), and intertextuality. While not every musical style may encompass all of these possibilities, I have shown for Beethoven (and by implication, for tonal composers immediately before and after) how these theoretical components may contribute to a competent interpretation of expressive meaning.

To the extent that a stylistic competency moves beyond a "lexicon" of types, or a "grammar" of their sense, to a "poetics" of their significance, competency becomes harder and harder to capture systematically. Thus, an attempt to reconstruct a style competency must admit a sizeable speculative component. This component I call the *hermeneutic*, and it is characterized by a creatively inferential process that provides hypotheses about potential correlations or interpretations. Hermeneutic hypotheses may be drawn from any part of the contemporaneous cultural universe, including connections or evidence from other arts, other realms of discourse, biographical information—in short, any relevant area that may have contributed to the expressive field of a musical style or work. The structuralist concern, then, is with the appropriate mapping, or correlation, of expressive meanings onto a systematic base of oppositions in the style. The reconstructed system of correlations in turn informs further hermeneutic investigation by ensuring that interpretations are coherently developed and tropes are properly grounded.

What should be clear from the conduct of the analyses in earlier chapters is that a hermeneutic investigation often precedes the systematic formulation of markedness, providing intuitively reasonable categories and differences in structure. Markedness theory is then employed to map the coherent organization of those categories in terms of their complementary oppositions. Ideally, these two components of a semiotic approach are intertwined, leading to a mutually supportive fabric of inferences.

I do not claim to provide discovery procedures for those inferences. A rule book cannot guarantee sensitive or profound interpretations. Nor has it been my task to follow interpretations all the way to a completely specified or subjective end. Yet it seems clear that an intensely personal experiencing of the music was part of a musical aesthetic held by Beethoven and many of his contemporaries.

Unfortunately, that aesthetic was not sustained through the nineteenth century, when philosophers found loose claims of expression in music to be unsupported. Without the insights of semiotic theory, it is not surprising that alternative approaches to the theoretical formulation of expressive meaning could not go very far. In the face of a more rigorous philosophical discourse, aesthetic theories of expressive meaning began to fall outside the pale of respectable discourse among music scholars, as well. Indeed, music scholarship is just beginning to recover from the repression of expressive discourse fostered by a formalist aesthetics. The errors of formalism have been compounded by a kind of scientism within the discipline, involving a preference for "safer" facts (and the theories that can be "proven" by those facts) in order to secure a respectable place among the scholarly disciplines.

In deploring a similar bias of music analysis toward structure, Joseph Kerman (1985a: 73) is outspoken:[1]

> Music's autonomous structure is only one of many elements that contribute to its import. Along with preoccupation with structure goes the neglect of other vital matters—not only the whole historical complex [lesser music, performance conditions, economic, social, intellectual, and psychological forces] . . . , but also everything else that makes music affective, moving, emotional, expressive.

Carl Dahlhaus ([1980] 1989: 9) goes even further with respect to the urgency of expressive interpretation for Beethoven's music:

> Beethoven . . . claimed for music the strong concept of art, without which music would be unable to stand on a par with literature and the visual arts. . . . Beethoven's symphonies represent inviolable musical "texts" whose meaning is to be deciphered with "exegetical" [read: hermeneutic] interpetations.

Criticism of Beethoven's day could move smoothly between structural and expressive interpretations, as E. T. A. Hoffmann demonstrated.[2] The problem was that critics did not have a theory adequate to the consistent relation of expression to structure, and philosophers offered little beyond the theory of musical mimesis, or imitation of the passions (Neubauer, 1986: 159).[3] Thus, when the first great formalist aesthetician, Eduard Hanslick, examined the presuppositions underlying current expressive discourse, he found them illogical and thus to some degree illusory.

These concerns of nineteenth-century aesthetics will be addressed in the next two sections.

Early Nineteenth-Century Approaches to Musical Meaning

Although my approach to musical meaning may appear somewhat new, the underlying commitment to expressive motivations for formal structures is consistent with Beethoven's comments reported in earlier chapters and with contemporaneous criticism of Beethoven's works. In an illuminating study, Robin Wallace (1986: 149) concludes:

> The first critics of Beethoven tried to link what would now be called symbolist and descriptive [read: formalist] approaches to his music, both in the interpretive and in the analytical sections of their reviews. Thus [A. B.] Marx, despite the sectionalized, somewhat static view of musical form which he set forth in his theoretical writings, is able in the biography to link form effortlessly with the dynamic, psychological processes which he finds in the Fifth Symphony. Likewise, [E. T. A.] Hoffmann links his metaphysical fantasies to explicit details of the musical structure.

Scott Burnham (1990: 191) goes further, indicating how A. B. Marx understood expression in Beethoven to be dramatically motivated (as opposed to a more "lyrical" motivation in Mozart):

> With Beethoven's music, Marx feels something more momentous than a pleasing array of feelings; he feels the succession of states of the soul. By using the expression "soul state" (*Seelenzustand*), Marx implies something deeper than a *Gefühl* or an *Empfindung*, words he uses when describing the content of Mozart's music. The states of soul allegedly expressed in Beethoven's music represent more than merely personal feelings. Marx often identifies them with supraindividual, heroic values.

The kinship between this account of successive states and my theory of expressive genres in Beethoven should be obvious.

My approach to musical meaning is also consistent with another great exponent of Beethoven's music, a composer with the rare ability to examine and explain his own musical practice. Robert Schumann revered Beethoven and pursued similar expressive strategies in his own symphonies (for the C major Symphony, see Newcomb, 1984a). Schumann's aesthetic is revealed by his perspective on the thorny issue of musical programs, as clarified by Leon Plantinga in his study of Schumann as critic (1967: 123): "If the music itself were not communicative, Schumann insists, attaching a program or evocative title to it would be as futile as writing a poetic critique of it." A program is, in this sense, another construct that can evoke emotions or suggest states of being analogous to those signified by the music itself. Thus, a deeper meaning is understood to underlie both program and music:[4]

> A program or suggestive title, according to Schumann's notion, acts very

much like the poetic descriptions of creative criticism. The Jean Paulian "poetic counterpart" could serve equally well as a descriptive assessment of a composition or as a program for it; in Schumann's work as a composer and critic, it did both. Thus the music does not denote or portray the program; something like the reverse is true: the program suggests and clarifies certain qualities of the music. [Plantinga, 1967: 120]

It is clear that Schumann, as distinct from the formalist Eduard Hanslick, thought that music could elicit emotion; but something more was involved, corresponding to my model of a musical style in which oppositions articulate ever-more refined states of being. Support for this claim comes from Schumann's article "The Comic in Music" (1834: 10, translated and cited by Plantinga, 1967: 121):

Less well informed people usually tend to hear in music without text only sorrow or only joy, or that which lies halfway between, melancholy. They are not able to perceive the finer shades of passion, as in one composition, anger and penitence, in another, feelings of satisfaction, comfort, and the like. Because of this it is very hard for them to understand masters like Beethoven and Schubert, who could translate every circumstance of life into the language of tone.

Note that Schumann says "perceive," not "feel," suggesting a degree of aesthetic distance akin to a cognitive understanding, and not necessarily an empathetic re-experiencing, of those "finer shades of passion."

The difference between Schumann's kind of poetic criticism and my own interpretation of Beethoven is that I have tried, where possible, to correlate each cultural unit with an opposition in the style or the work, thereby tying an otherwise subjective discourse to a theoretical framework. This framework enables one to talk about the structure of meaning for a given style or work, provides consistency in interpretations, and promotes a more rigorous debate of the semiosis leading from sound to content (of whatever sort).

Hanslick's Problematic Legacy

Eduard Hanslick (1825–1904) was the first great formalist aesthetician of the latter part of the nineteenth century. His *Vom Musikalisch-Schönen* of 1854 is worth considering here because of its profound effect on theoretical and philosophical thinking about music and musical meaning, even today.[5] In his essay Hanslick was interested in refuting the notion that music could represent or evoke emotions in more than trivial ways. He believed that unsubstantiated and inconsistent ideas about musical expressiveness had contributed to a decline in the artistic quality of music. Hanslick criticized Italian composers for concentrating entirely on the attempt to express emotions or achieve effects, often to the neglect of purely musical development of themes.

With the appearance of Liszt's tone poems and Wagner's music dramas in the second half of the nineteenth century (and already with *Lohengrin*, earlier), this argument began to take on the dimensions of a crusade against musical infidelity. Now German musicians were perverting the techniques of purely musical development in order to represent or express ideas having a verbal and/or dramatic specificity. Worst of all, they were succeeding with audiences, gaining a popular legitimacy for this "Music of the Future." The future of music was at stake for Hanslick as well, not just in terms of aesthetic theory, but in terms of compositional practice. With the New German School, Hanslick faced a far greater challenge than the one posed by Italian operatic license; the future of the German instrumental tradition was in danger. Because of the position he took in *Vom Musikalisch-Schönen*, Hanslick was well positioned to become the chief polemicist for the conservation of purely musical values, which he interpreted as the beauty of sounding forms removed from superficial ties to the real world.[6]

On the nature of the beautiful in music, Hanslick writes:

> *Its nature is specifically musical.* By this we mean that the beautiful is not contingent upon nor in need of any subject introduced from without, but that it consists wholly of sounds artistically combined. The ingenious coordination of intrinsically pleasing sounds, their consonance and contrast, their flight and reapproach, their increasing and diminishing strength—this it is which, in free and unimpeded forms, presents itself to our mental vision. [[1854] 1974: 47]

In this classic statement of an extreme formalist position, Hanslick claims that music is autonomous as an artistic arrangement of sounds. But Hanslick was not that strict in his position. He was willing to admit the possibility of music's representing those aspects of external reality that were like music—that is, based upon what today would be called synaesthesia, or intermodality. In the case of emotions, it was possible for music to represent "the motion accompanying a feeling" but not "what is felt" (37). In other words, music could represent the "dynamic element of an emotion" (37). Nevertheless, one could not claim that a definite (specific) emotion was the object of a musical passage.

Hanslick bases much of his argument on the fact that the same music can mean different things. For example, Handel's reuse of music from several secular duets in *Messiah* is considered by Hanslick as evidence of music's lack of specificity with regard to meaning; music does not have a subject and is unable to represent a definite emotion. Since to represent something indefinite is for Hanslick a "contradiction in terms" (37), the beautiful in music must not be deduced from a supposed emotional element that cannot be represented specifically.

Hanslick pursues his argument about beauty in music by introducing analogies with an arabesque and a kaleidoscope. In enjoying the patterns, one appreciates the forms or colors in their changing arrangements without regard for direct symbolism of emotional or external meanings. The autonomous colors and forms constitute for the viewer "a complete and self-sufficient whole, free from any alien admixture" (48). A similar autonomy for the musical patterning of sounds and forms is argued to be richly "intellectual." Indeed, Hanslick claims his contemporaries have underrated the capacity of the human imagination, "which is so constituted as to be affected by auditory impressions . . . , delights in the sounding forms and musical structures and, conscious of their sensuous nature, lives in the immediate and free contemplation of the beautiful" (49).

Though music is untranslatable, and all our "descriptions, characterizations, and periphrases [*sic*] are either metaphorical or false" (50), music nevertheless has a logic and a meaning. Like language, we can "speak" music and understand it, according to its own laws of organization. The explanation of music, however, must be in terms of musical organization and not in terms of the organization of language or the mathematical relationships of the pitches and durations. Nor can it be in terms of the composer's biography or the presumed feelings (intentions) of the composer.

Hanslick argues that the "proximate cause [of the] thrilling effect of a theme is owing, not to the supposed extreme grief of the composer, but to the extreme intervals; not to the beating of his heart, but to the beating of the drums; not to the craving of his soul, but to the chromatic progression of the music" (54). This claim would appear to admit the possibility of emotional meaning as long as it is explained in terms of musical elements and forms, rather than the emotional intent of the composer. But when Hanslick clarifies the distinction between music and language, he denies this possibility: "While sound in speech is but a sign, that is, a means for the purpose of expressing something which is quite distinct from its medium, sound in music is the end, that is, the ultimate and absolute object in view" (67). The misguided limitation of semiosis to language is a result of Hanslick's assumption that all signification is modeled after referentiality in language. Naturally, music fails to conform to that model. "All laws of speech will turn upon the correct use of sound as a medium of expressing ideas," he writes, but "all specific laws of music will center in its independent forms of beauty" (68).

Hanslick uses the opposition of language and music to emphasize the unique character of music. Although as stated the opposition is too extreme, Hanslick's differentiation between everyday language, which allegedly deals closely with the world, and music, which is somehow removed from such common concerns, is sharply ingrained in subsequent philosophies of music.[7]

Hanslick also argues against emotion as a proper aesthetic value for music, even though the physical effects of sound on the body may well be linked to the experience of emotions. Instead, he proposes a theory of musical expectation anticipating Leonard B. Meyer's (1956); but unlike Meyer, Hanslick makes no reference to the direct triggering of emotion: "We here refer to the intellectual satisfaction which the listener derives from continually following and anticipating the composer's intentions—now to see his expectations fulfilled, and now to find himself agreeably mistaken" (98).

Hanslick's continuation reveals the shallowness of his understanding of such expectations, which are to be kept strictly on a "higher" mental plane, operating at a faster, purely mental pace: "It is a matter of course that this intellectual flux and reflux, this perpetual giving and receiving, takes place unconsciously and with the rapidity of lightning flashes" (98). One cannot help but sense the incongruity between this description and the "pure contemplation" Hanslick would have us hold as the highest aesthetic value. Something is missing; namely, how it is that these lightning flashes (of "unconscious" cognition) offer something higher (or are translated into something more significant) that is deserving of our "conscious" contemplation.

Hanslick returns to the comparison of language and music in a later chapter on music and nature, but with a different aim from his earlier separation of the two. Since they are both man-made, and thus artificial, language and music are now viewed as analogous with respect to their evolution (108). Thus, changing musical values are accommodated in terms of different stages (styles?) in a musical language. Hanslick evades in this way any universal or time-bound concepts of musical Beauty.

In practice, however, Hanslick's blindness to Wagner's musical values contradicts his own allowance for divergent values. The very possibility that Wagner might have accomplished such a change in musical values (misleadingly construed as moving from absolute to programmatic), and that quite a few people might have gone along with the change, seriously undermines Hanslick's theories from the start by exposing their prescriptive roots.

From a semiotic perspective, music is what a given culture, or some part of that culture, understands as such, not what it should be according to some grand scheme. And if musical systems, or musical values, can change over time, then more than one set of values may coexist at a given time.

Furthermore, if a group of listeners clearly value expressive content in a work of music, such content is not external to the musical experience. Instead, the expressive content must be accorded status as a (semiotic) fact about the group's understanding of the work.[8] One cannot presume to judge in advance the character of such facts with respect to various musics or peoples or cultures. As the anthropologist and ethnomusicologist remind us, ethnocentricity tends to hamper our ability to unlock a musical style, especially if we cannot accept (or comprehend) its aesthetic presuppositions. The latter may be the case even when the style in question is not that of a different culture but exists during the lifetime of the critic, as with Hanslick.

Although one need not presume that music is identical to language in its use of signs, one should be wary of denying music the symbolic capacity for a comparably wide range of expressive (not referential) possibilities. Nor should one assume that those ranges for music and language must be the same, or that they should involve any particular or prescribed overlap (see Chapter 10).[9]

"Beauty" is the term with which Hanslick captures the ultimate value of music, stemming from its "true" nature. As an aesthetic category, "beauty" became a catch-all term with prescriptive value for any aspect of music's significance: meanings, significant form, values, properties, qualities. Thus expanded, the concept of beauty has become as vacuous as the concept of emotional expression had become for Hanslick.

Despite the corrective merit of Hanslick's arguments against poorly formulated notions of expression, then, I would set aside his overcorrective bias against other kinds of musical values; clearly, those values could not be accommodated by the philosophical aesthetics he espoused. Attempts to restore the balance have been made by Suzanne Langer's iconic theory of musical expression, the more cognitive approach to emotion in music by Leonard B. Meyer, Nelson Goodman's theory of expression in music as metaphorical exemplification, and the arguments of Peter Kivy for expression and representation in music. Each of these approaches offers a piece of the puzzle of musical expressive meaning, as semiotically understood.

Early Symbolic Approaches: Langer, Meyer, and Goodman

Suzanne Langer (1953) argues that "significant form" (the term is from Clive Bell, 1914) is significant in terms of emotional experience, and not merely in terms of the play of forms. Her claim is that music can be a tonal analogue of the forms of emotions, rather than evoking them directly in a stimulus/response model, and thus that there is a symbolic component to musical understanding.

Langer's use of the term "symbol" must be understood as iconically motivated, rather than arbitrary or conventional (see discussion of Saussure and Peirce, below), since the motivation for the relation of her symbol and object is "formal analogy, or congruence of logical structures" (1953: 27)—what one might call isomorphism today. Because anything having the same formal structure can be symbolized by a musical structure under this theory, she considers music to have a nondiscursive (i.e., nonpropositional) logical expression based on its articulate form (31). Thus, by contrast with language, music has no words that can be defined as "independent associative symbols with a reference fixed by convention" (31).

This restriction of symbolism is unfortunate, as should be apparent from my theoretical argument for correlations. It stems from a confusion (similar to Hanslick's) that concepts in language have "unequivocal reference" (31), and it fails to recognize the possibility of less-specific, nonreferential, but oppositionally supported correlations. As I have argued, if one reserves specificity for the token, the type need not be other than general in its correlation.

While Langer's tonal analogue conveys significance, it is not to be construed as "meaning" (in the referential, truth-conditional sense) but rather as "import," and import is defined as "the pattern of sentience" (31):

The tonal structures we call "music" bear a close logical similarity to the forms of human feeling—forms of growth and of attenuation, flowing and stowing, conflict and resolution, speed, arrest, terrific excitement, calm, or subtle activation and dreamy lapses—not joy and sorrow perhaps, but the poignancy of either and both—the greatness and brevity and eternal passing of everything vitally felt. [27]

This is indeed an important aspect of musical meaning, and one that under this description would seem to be amenable to psychological study. But Langer's theory is clearly semiotic, not psychological, since it goes further than perception in assuming a critical cognition of articulated forms. Her warning is telling, even today:

The psychological approach, dictated by the general empiricist trend in philosophy, has not brought us within range of any genuine problems of art. So, instead of studying the "slight changes of stimuli" which cause "unpredictable and miraculous changes" in our nervous responses, we might do better to look upon the art object as something in its own right, with properties independent of our prepared reactions—properties which command our reactions, and make art the autonomous and essential factor that it is in every human culture. [39]

By "autonomous" Langer means simply that artistic experience is distinct from basic forms of experience to which earlier psychologists and sociologists had attempted to reduce it—for example, the direct satisfaction of pleasure, or the fulfillment of biological needs. With her definition of art as "the creation of forms symbolic of human feeling," Langer moves away from Hanslick's more restrictive view of music's autonomy. Nevertheless, Langer's symbolic theory accounts only for the iconically motivated forms of semiosis, neglecting motivations that stem from other aspects of structure and that may correlate with contents other than the emotive.

Leonard B. Meyer's theory of expectation in *Emotion and Meaning in Music* (1956) is far richer in this respect, although Meyer is primarily concerned with showing how Gestalt perceptual strategies play an important role in our expectations of musical outcomes. Chapter 10, below, considers such Gestalt strategies as *affordant* to higher levels of (*emergent*) cognition. For now, the argument concerns emotion in music, and for Meyer this results from the denial or deferral of expected outcomes. His approach thus draws on a theory of emotion stemming from the frustration of expectations. This perspective leads him briefly to an account of meaning influenced by information theory (Meyer, 1967), in which the predictive processes in the brain might be calculable on the basis of the information available to a listener at each point in the unfolding musical work.

Meyer also distinguishes designative from embodied meaning. Briefly, designative meaning occurs when the stimulus "indicate[s] events or consequences which are different from itself in kind, as when a word designates or points to an object or action which is not itself a word" (1956: 35). Embodied meaning, on the other hand, is "of the same kind as the stimulus itself" (35). Extramusical meaning would be an example of the former; other musical events which are about to happen an example of the latter. Indeed, for an absolutist, Meyer claims that the "musical event . . . has meaning because it points to and makes us expect another musical event" (35). It is this kind of meaning that Meyer spends the most time examining, but one should not assume that his position is that of an absolutist. Nor, on the other hand, is his position on expression limited to the evocation of affect (as stimulus and response). His discussion of objectified meaning adds a cognitive component to expressive meaning: "meanings become objectified only under conditions of self-consciousness and when reflection takes place" (39).

In a final, brief chapter entitled "Note on Image Processes, Connotations, and Moods," Meyer addresses an array of musical meanings other than those statable in terms of purely musical events. Connotations fall under the designative category, and Meyer sounds quite semiotic in his discussion of associations created by contiguity and similarity (two semiotic motivations discussed in the last part of Chapter 10, below). Indeed, although he does not pursue the analysis, Meyer touches on what I have referred to as salience—his expression is "divergence of the elements of sound from a neutral state" (263)—as basic to the specification of a connotation (what I call the articulation of meaning or the further interpretation of a correlation): "In general, the more markedly the elements of a sound pattern diverge from neutrality the more likely they are to evoke connotations and the more specific those connotations are liable to be" (264). Although the statement sounds prescient with regard to markedness theory, the "markedness" here is really salience; as in information theory, divergence is simply one more kind of perceptual "information" that can be measured in terms of its relative predictability.[10]

That Meyer's salience is at the level of gross perceptual differentiation is clear from the following claim: "For the connotations aroused by a piece of music which, on the whole, employs normal ranges, moderate tempi, and so forth will be determined more by the disposition and susceptibility of the particular listener than by the nature of the musical organization itself" (264). The analysis in the previous chapter would suggest that this is not necessarily the case, since subtler kinds of markedness were shown to be powerful in creating the remarkable expressive poignance of the "second" theme in the *Cavatina* of Op. 130 (Chapter 8).

But Meyer's valuable study points the way to a more intensive investigation of the oppositions in a style and their salience in the context of a musical work. His broader perspective on the varieties of musical meaning appears all the more remarkable when we consider the book's early date of publication—only three years after Suzanne Langer's *Feeling and Form*.

In Nelson Goodman's *Languages of Art* (1968), a little over a decade later, Meyer's clear distinction between designative and embodied meanings is not strictly maintained. Goodman's pair, denotation and exemplification, are conceived in such a way that each could involve what Meyer calls designative meaning. Exemplification occurs as a result of possession, not merely as a result of the object's being of the same media (Meyer's embodied meaning). Thus, music may exemplify either because the music literally possesses a feature (e.g., fast or slow) or because the music metaphorically possesses a quality (e.g., happy or sad). Unlike Langer or Meyer, Goodman does not attempt to justify, or motivate, this "possession"; it is enough that there is intersubjective agreement as to the appropriateness of the metaphor (in the case of expressive qualities). Thus, Goodman's theory would be fundamentally helpless in investigating meanings for which there might not be such agreement in advance (for example, the concept of *abnegation* in my semiotic interpretations). But Goodman qualifies his claims for possession, since reference is also involved: "just which properties of a symbol are exemplified depends upon what particular system of symbolization is in effect" (1968: 53).

In a later article, "The Status of Style" (1975), Goodman develops this important constraint on exemplification. He proposes that formal features of works are among those literally exemplified. Once again, it is by determining the style that we are led to understand what relevant qualities or features a musical event possesses, and thus what it can exemplify. But the mere identification of stylistic features offers no explanation of their expressive significance, even after they are plugged into the exemplificational model.

Since expression is equated with metaphorical exemplification, it is disappointing to discover that such an important aspect of music is simply "assumed"—and that important questions are begged.

First, Goodman claims that it must be appropriate to apply a predicate to the work of art (the predicate must properly denote the work of art). But according to whom? What if the appropriate, competent listeners are no longer around for us to ask? Next, Goodman claims that the predicate can be appropriate if the work possesses that property metaphorically. But how? And through what linkages with structures in the music? Goodman concludes that if metaphorical possession of a predicate is appropriately claimed for a work, then the work can in turn refer to the predicate by means of a species of reference termed exemplification.[11]

The answers to questions about appropriateness, in my view, emerge from a reconstruction of style and a hermeneutic investigation of works, with attention to *motivations* for expressive associations. The answers to questions about linkages belong to a structuralist theory of correlations as coordinated by *markedness* relationships. Such answers are difficult, but possible to advance, as I have shown in earlier chapters. While Goodman may not be able to delimit the "appropriate" application of nonliteral labels, he rightly points to a system of symbolization, or *style*, that must underlie such linkages.

Kivy on Expression and Representation

Peter Kivy has pursued the problem of expression in *The Corded Shell* (1980), outlining expressive theories from the early Baroque through Hanslick. His own summation of two basic kinds of theory has a familiar, if unacknowledged, semiotic echo:

> the "contour" theory (or model) of musical expressiveness . . explains the expressiveness of music by the congruence of musical "contour" with the structure of expressive features and behavior . . . . [T]he "convention" theory (or model) of musical expressiveness . . . explains the expressiveness of music as a function, simply, of the customary association of certain musical features with certain emotive ones, quite apart from any structural analogy. [77]

A semiotic theory would consider "contour" as *iconic* and "convention" as *symbolic* (the symbol entails a conventional relation between signifier and signified). Thus, Kivy's summary is neither new nor unusual from a semiotic standpoint.

Kivy's contribution lies in his historical research into the appearance of a *cognitive*, as opposed to a simplistically emotive theory. Kivy first finds this perspective in the work of Johann Mattheson (*Der vollkommene Capellmeister*, 1739). Kivy summarizes the cognitive theory of expression as follows:

> (i) Music is not primarily a stimulus; and its emotive expressiveness is not manifested in an emotional response. (ii) Music, in its structure, bears a resemblance to the "emotive life"; and the primary aesthetic response is a cognitive response: a *recognition* of the emotive content present in it. [39, italics added]

These points had been anticipated in earlier theories, but Kivy clarifies the historical significance of Mattheson's synthesis.

In a discussion of Langer and Goodman (60–63), Kivy inveighs against Langer's assumption that isomorphism is symbolic and Goodman's that exemplification is symbolic. His critique of Langer has the merit of pointing out the overgenerality of her "symbolism" as embracing the emotive life in general.[12] But his complaint against Goodman is unfounded, since Goodman clearly states that exemplification requires a system of symbolization (even if Goodman is unable to work that system out for music). Furthermore, the only exemplification that Kivy concerns himself with is that of the sample (Goodman's example is a tailor's swatch), hardly a fair construal of Goodman's exemplification in art works. Kivy does point out the need for "some psychological link between the music and what it expresses" (62), which I would interpret as some kind of motivation for the interpretation of an expressive state.

Kivy is more charitable toward isomorphism in his next book, on representation in music (1984). But he is clear about the need for some description (comparable to a key or a legend for a schematic design) to translate the isomorphism involved in representation when it is abstract, or lacking in obvious "pictorial" realism. Whether abstract or "realistic," his concept of representation emphasizes the kind of isomorphism that goes beyond mere imitation: "What is needed . . . for representation in any kind of detail, of a structure or system of elements, is *another* structure or system of elements that can more or less be isomorphic with it" (73). This kind of isomorphism is clearly what Peirce had in mind when considering the *diagrammatic* as an extension of the iconic (see

Chapter 7, above). Kivy also touches what Peirce would call the *indexical*, namely, representations by conventional association, such as patriotic tunes or chorale melodies (with their texts). The motivation here is contiguity, as Meyer (1956: 259) has already observed.

The interpenetration of expression and representation is one reason why I have avoided discussing varieties of musical meaning; instead, I have labeled musical meanings more neutrally in terms of correlations with cultural units. Kivy (1984: 124–42) also treats the problem of interpenetration in his later study on representation, concluding that expressiveness may contribute to the success of musical representation, but that not all representations are expressive (although expressive representations appear to be preferred by composers).

Goodman (1968: 46) considers the possibility that representation involves concrete objects or events and expression involves abstract states, feelings, or properties; but he argues that the distinction cannot be maintained in terms of what is symbolized. Rather, it is the direction of the symbolism that is important. For representation, the direction is from the signifier (music) to the signified, whereas "exemplification implies reference between the two in both directions" (59). And if the object being represented does not exist, then representation reduces to exemplification (66).

In terms of my theory, the conventions of expression (expressiveness) and representation, however different they may be, are coordinated by the same principles of markedness. I have not attempted to delineate these two kinds of meaning, but have concentrated on the pragmatic correlations and interpretations involving expressive meaning. In turn, the concept of *motivation* to be developed below addresses the kinds of evidence supporting such linkages without foundering on the philosophical problem of distinguishing them. This is an important advantage, since the focus is on establishing linkages for a given style, rather than distinguishing them as representations, denotations, exemplifications, or expressions.

Correlating Sound and Content: A Semiotic Theory

The philosopher Charles Sanders Peirce (1839–1914) has been recognized as one of the founders of semiotic theory. Active during the same time as Ferdinand de Saussure (1857–1913), the Swiss linguist whose similar concept of semiology first attracted scholarly attention, Peirce

Saussure (dyadic)	Peirce (triadic)	Applied to Music
1. signifier ⟶	1. sign vehicle	= musical entity
2. signified ⟶	2. designatum	= correlation (cultural unit)
	3. interpretant	= interpretation
	ground	= interpretive competencies of both <u>style</u> and <u>strategy</u>

Figure 9.1. Categories of semiosis.

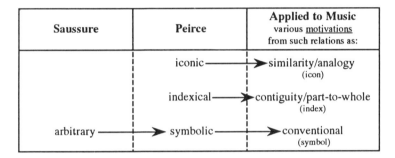

Figure 9.2. Potential relations motivating semiosis.

developed a more-sophisticated theory of signs, which has only recently been applied to the analysis of human semiotic systems. Whereas Saussure emphasized the dyadic nature of signification, divided into signifier and signified, Peirce had the crucial insight that semiosis is triadic (Figure 9.1). For Peirce (1931: 2.227 ff.), a sign (vehicle) is related to an object (designatum) in such a way that it brings forth an *interpretant* for a knowledgeable user (interpreter) of that sign; in turn, the interpretant is brought forth according to the ground of the relationship, its "rule of interpretation." For music this can be translated as follows: A musical *entity* (patterned sound serving as a sign vehicle) *correlates* with a cultural unit) that suggests further *interpretations* as mediated by the "ground" of *style*, and the further "ground" of the emerging *strategy* of a particular work. Figure 9.1 illustrates the linkages between Peirce and Saussure, and my translation for music theory. Figure 9.2 indicates the nature of the relationship(s) between signifier and signified, or sign and designatum, for each theory respectively. I use the term *motivation* in place of such inappropriate scientific terms as "cause." That which is *motivated* is merely that which has certain reason(s) for being, as indicated partly by its origins, but more importantly by its functions. Any truly complete explanation would involve an exhaustive account of all the motivations justifying the vehicle's relationship to its interpretants. Usually, however, one is quite content to achieve a semiotic understanding of an entity's functioning in the "code" (style) and in a particular "utterance" (strategy of a work). The distinction between various kinds of "causal" explanations (necessary, sufficient) is here superceded by a practical distinction. The effort to uncover determining "causes" (as in a scientific model) is futile; it is more fruitful to attempt to reconstruct functional explanations (as in a semiotic model) in terms of styles and strategies (Hatten 1982: 177).

There are three immediate advantages of Peirce's construal of semiosis as opposed to Saussure's:

1. The triadic conception avoids a behavioristic (stimulus and response) reduction of the relation between vehicle and meaning; indeed, the tendency toward psychological reduction in general is averted altogether.
2. The notion of interpretant promotes greater attention toward the way a sign is "meant to be taken" or toward meaning as "meaning-for" someone. Peirce called this the pragmatic dimension of meaning, and it influences one's reconstruction of the syntactic and semantic dimensions.
3. Since one interpretant can give rise to another, creating a chain of semiosis, Peirce's theory avoids the simplistic or mechanical one-to-one mapping of a rudimentary code (as, for example, in Deryck Cooke's *The Language of Music*, 1959) and provides for more richly significant languages or styles.[13]

Umberto Eco (1976) has drawn heavily from Peirce, particularly in terms of the *interpretant* and the "unlimited semiosis" it entails. He views an interpretant as that which "*inferentially* develop[s] all the logical possibilities suggested by the sign" (70)—not merely the connotation of a denotation, but that which can "explain, develop, [and] interpret a given sign," "beyond the rules provided by codes" (71). In conjunction with the notion of a cultural unit, the interpretant characterizes semiosis:

[A] cultural unit never obliges one to replace it by means of something which is not a semiotic entity, and never asks to be explained by some

Platonic, psychic or objectal entity. *Semiosis explains itself by itself*, this continual circularity is the normal condition of signification. . . . [71]

I have not fully explored the richness of this concept in my model, other than by making use of a somewhat comparable term, *interpretation*, to label the further articulation or development of a correlational meaning. And yet my interpretive analyses have demonstrated an ongoing semiosis, by interpreting correlations in terms of other correlations, overarching expressive genres, thematic markedness, or troping. This inferential development is also entailed by the working out of musical "ideas" in a work. Finally, I have purposefully avoided the further reaches of individual, subjective interpretations, instead reconstructing the intersubjective (shared, or shareable) interpretations of competent listeners in a style. For more on Eco, as well as Peirce, see Chapter 10.

The third major source underlying my semiotic orientation comes from the work of Michael Shapiro (1976, 1983) and his student Edwin Battistella (1990) on markedness in language and literature (developing the original concept as found in Trubetzkoy and expanded by Roman Jakobson). I will not rehearse the theory here, since it has been a central focus throughout the course of this book. Instead, I offer a few closing observations: Just as Peirce goes beyond Saussure with his triadic conception of the sign, Shapiro goes further than Saussure by suggesting the asymmetry of oppositions that systematically motivate Saussure's "arbitrary" sign and by specifying the relative range of meanings between oppositionally related signs. Furthermore, in helping to explain how new structures and meanings emerge from asymmetrical oppositions (see Chapter 10), markedness provides a systematic motivation for change (what I have termed *growth*) within a *synchronic* state such as a grammar or a musical style. In other words, markedness can capture the changes that develop a system, not just those that lead to the creation of a new one, as in a *diachronic* investigation. For Shapiro, such development is inherent in the teleology of the sign and in its purposive growth of interpretants.

Further Perspectives on Musical Meaning and Cognition

This final, more speculative, chapter contains three related sections. The first examines the issue of musical meaning as related to meaning in natural language, and the added problem of languaging about meaning in music. The second section develops a model for the emergence of varieties of musical meaning in a style, applying the ontological categories of Charles S. Peirce and the asymmetrical oppositions of markedness theory. The third section broadens the model by considering the kinds of motivations underlying artistic interpretation as a special case of interpretation in general. The ideas presented here are contributions toward a semiotic of artistic cognition, with implications for theories of cognition in general.

Music and Language

Both ordinary language and music are pliable in that they can be stretched to almost any semiotic end. I do not attempt to delegate possible, or even appropriate, realms of meaning for either of these forms of human semiosis. Rather, I shall examine several problematic issues about the use of language to talk about musical meaning, and the resulting confusion between linguistic and musical meaning. I further challenge the argument, stemming from Hanslick, that because music lacks referentiality as in language, it lacks expressive meanings of the kind I have interpreted in Beethoven.

It does not follow that simply because we cannot securely state in language the expressive meaning of a musical passage, we do not know it or cannot have access to it as it relates to a cultural universe. The confusions arise from several related issues:

1. the near-exclusive use of language as a metalanguage for music;
2. the widely divergent ways in which expressive terms may be construed—either as translations, paraphrases, metaphors, literal terms, labels, or tentative markers for musical meanings;
3. the different ways a semantic space may be organized by a musical style as opposed to a language in the same culture;
4. the misunderstanding of referentiality in language;
5. the problem of varying expectations for specificity, concreteness, and precision in characterizing musical expressive meaning.

1. Charles Seeger ([1935–75] 1977) was not the first to be concerned about the theoretical bias produced by our use of language to describe music. Theorists from Rameau to Heinrich Schenker and Hans Keller have sought ways to employ music or its notation as a metalanguage for music, either through musical analytical symbols[1] or through the ostension of recorded excerpts and their juxtaposition for aural comparison and inference (as in Keller's "wordless functional analysis"). Although Schenker ([1933] 1969) and Keller (1957) believed that a music theory could be developed in which words would be superfluous, in practice most theorists have been unwilling to give up the descriptive and argumentative resources of language. Indeed, one might argue that some kinds of musical meaning simply cannot be captured by notationally derived music-analytical symbols that are restricted to the indication of syntactic relationships among notes. For example, the concept of "undercutting," discussed in relation to the first movement of Op. 101,

can be expressed through a wide variety of tonal and other events. Thus, a single notational form would fail to capture the generality of the concept.

How might one explain a semantic dimension, such as the pastoral, without recourse to words? If one showed pictures or ran a film of idyllic scenes while the music was playing, would the association be enough to indicate the connection? Not unless one could convey an intent to symbolize (recall Peter Kivy's observation with respect to isomorphism, in Chapter 9). And how could one indicate which features of the music cued the pastoral?

Alternatively, one could play the excerpt in question and follow it with excerpts from increasingly better-known works which could serve as a kind of dictionary of rough synonyms for the concept, subject to listeners' abilities to infer the relevant invariance. But the listeners would still have to have the relevant concept in their understanding for at least one of the excerpts used, or the series might simply imply similarity between examples without ever conveying the particular significance under consideration. Even if the listeners were sensitized to common traits (pedal points, for example), the connection to a larger cultural concept of the pastoral, as developed in literature, could not be made. Nor could the further interpretive development of the pastoral as a *topic* be conveyed.

Indicating by pointing to something (deixis) or using something as an example of itself (ostension) is too primitive a means of signification for discourse about music. Besides being cumbersome and time consuming, neither deixis nor ostension can explain relationships between adjacent musical excerpts. One needs such basic logical relations as "is like/ unlike with respect to [play extract of relevant entity]" or "can follow . . . " or "implies . . . " or "interrupts. . . . " Even with this primitive operative language, the appropriate relationship still might not be inferred without further verbal explanation.

How, then, does a musical style become understandable for a listener? Much of the general expressive significance of tonal music did not have to be directly taught; it was enculturated through progressive inferences about its use and contexts. But for probing those aspects that are not immediately, or iconically, available to us—and for communicating our findings—language is crucial.

A difficult problem for cognitive theory is how we ever learn a concept without already understanding the concept.[2] A semiotic theory skirts the issue of conceptual genesis by assuming that a listener uses acquired codes to learn other codes, and that cultural codes such as those of literature and art can and do play an important role in providing the cultural concepts that correlate with musical structures. By beginning "in the middle" of a rich array of established styles and cultural understandings, the music semiotician need not be hampered by an inability to explain such a fundamental philosophical question as the genesis of understanding.

If language is understood as but one access to musical understanding, and we are willing to subject verbal discourse to a process of correction and revision as interpretive understanding grows, then the danger of a linguistic bias is not compelling enough for us to relinquish language's powers of explanation.

2. On the issue of language providing a kind of translation of musical content, should this translation be considered a paraphrase, or a metaphor, or merely a label or marker for music's own construal of content? There are several parts to this issue. First, each of these functions is a metalinguistic one, although their status and underlying claims may differ. If we say "this musical passage is sad," we may mean several things, ranging from attributing a property to the passage (either literally or metaphorically exemplified, for Nelson Goodman [1968] to claiming an effect that the passage has (either for me personally, or for any competent listener). Given this range of senses, it is not surprising that confusions arise. For purposes of comparison, let us restrict the sense of "this musical passage is sad" to that of a correlation between the musical passage and a cultural unit, "sad," that is relevant to the symbolic functioning of the musical passage as music. What might the advantages be in considering this term variously as a translation, a paraphrase, a metaphor, a label, or a marker?

As a translation of (one of) the meaning(s) of the musical passage, we assume we have found in "sad" an equivalent linguistic term for the concept that the passage brings to mind. As a paraphrase, we recognize the appropriateness of the term, but not a close equivalence to the concept with which the music correlates; we assume, however, that translation would be unproblematic were such a term available.

With a metaphor, we are led past prosaic paraphrase to an imaginative participation in the meaning of the passage, and by offering a nonequivalent linguistic formulation, we play upon the figurative resources of analogy and creativity to "recreate" the vital impression of the meaning by throwing light on it from a different perspective. But "sad" is a "literal" cultural unit, and "this musical passage is sad" could not be construed as metaphorical (recall the argument in Chapter 7).[3]

"This musical passage is filled with *les derniers soupirs* of Romeo and Juliet from the tomb" would, on the other hand, be quite metaphorical, and appropriately applied to the close of the second movement of Beethoven's String Quartet, Op. 18, no. 1. We know that Beethoven actually wrote the French phrase on an early sketch for the end of the movement, and he told Amenda "that he composed the piece with the vault scene of Romeo and Juliet in mind" (Kerman, 1966: 36).

We need not pin down a metaphor in full flight, shutting down its dynamic life in order to display a more static beauty. The end of the movement does not literally mean "les derniers soupirs"; rather, that poetic conceit is a key to understanding a related kind of experience (recall Schumann's observation about poetic criticism in Chapter 9). Public misunderstanding of the elusive richness of metaphor may lead composers to protect their intimate inspirations or personal interpretations by withdrawing programs attached to their work, as Berlioz did with his extensive program for the *Symphonie fantastique.*

A more neutral linguistic usage is that involving labels. A label is merely a tag for identification, recognition, and efficient communication about a musical entity. As such, it need not reflect any of the possible meanings of a musical entity. In the case of building blocks such as chords, whose meaning or significance depends so heavily on context (either higher systematic contexts or immediate strategic contexts), a descriptive label is desirable. Basic terms such as triad and seventh chord, or in the twentieth century, trichord and pitch-class collection, leave the door open for a wide range of interpretation. Expressive terms such as "sad" can also be used as labels, but since the structure of a sad passage is not as clear as the structure of a triad, and since there is clearly some attempt to capture an expressive content, a better term than "label" might be "marker"—in the sense of a place marker that designates a conceptual space, not in the sense of markedness. The use of "sad" as a marker for a musical passage would indicate that the theorist is uncertain about the appropriateness of the term as a translation or paraphrase of the meaning of the passage, but is willing to risk categorizing the passage, and similar ones, as "sad." Choice of markers should be motivated not only by their intuitive appropriateness at the given level of investigation, but in terms of the oppositional structures that help keep them coherent. In the case of "sad," some feature (such as minor mode) must be understood as oppositional to another, with which a semantic opposition (sad-happy, or tragic-nontragic in my formulation) can correlate.

3. This leads to the third point, the different ways in which music may articulate its semantic universe as opposed to language. There may not be a suitable musical opposition that can adequately distinguish, say, jealousy from envy; in such cases either term could be a suitable marker for that musical content. At first a musical style may need only four temperaments in order to categorize the range of emotional expression in pieces. Later, further subdivisions may be needed in order to reflect the more refined articulation of emotional states in a given style (recall Schumann's claim, cited in Chapter 9). In neither case should it be assumed that the musical articulation of a semantic universe is equivalent, or need be equivalent, to a linguistically articulated universe. The linguistic organization of cultural units, however, can provide some of the best clues for appropriate musical correlations.

4. Most comparisons between music and language emphasize that language is referential and music is not (except for trivial cases). But in language, excluding cases of ostension (where the referent is present to the speakers), even names lack the referential precision that has been claimed when making such unbalanced comparisons with music.

As the philosopher Saul Kripke has noted (1972: 269), proper names should be thought of as "rigid designators." They secure the identify of a particular person even when our discourse involves that person in hypothetical situations that have not, or will not, occur. Names serve to fix a reference (277) despite the transformations involved in a person's everyday life. Consequently, the most important properties distinguishing a person are not necessary ones but contingent ones (289). Kripke concludes that reference depends not just on what use we make of a name but on its cultural trappings—both the current sense of the name and the "history" of our acquisition of the name, whether through introduction to a person or through the written record of an individual (301).

With his admission that "more exact conditions [for delimiting the reference of a name] are very complicated to give" (301), Kripke in effect undermines the last bastion of scientific precision or security in semantics. Theories of musical expression, then, should not be faulted for failing to attain, or even attempt, a degree of precision or referentiality that can no longer be supported for language.[4]

Cognitive theorists are also struggling with the problem of reference from the standpoints of concept formation and the organization of conceptual understanding.[5] Their approaches include constructing a hierarchy of semantic features; positing a cluster of salient properties associated with the concept, or noting which exemplars of a class are prototypical[6] (for example, "robin" is a much more prototypical exemplar for "bird" than, say, "ostrich"); and constructing probabilities for inclusion or exclusion of certain entities as instances of a concept. What is emerging from such studies is further recognition of the degree to which the use of ordinary language involves metaphor, as well as referential imprecision and unscientific categorization, however much one might prefer airtight and scientific solutions to problems of definition and reference.

Words correlate most immediately with prototypical categories, not unlike what Eco (1976) calls cultural units. These categories of language inform our meanings even when we refer to actual objects in the world. Most people consider a tomato a vegetable, although it is actually a fruit. The former is its cultural classification, the latter its scientific one. The scientific falsity of the former category is irrelevant, for a language community, to the reality of its cultural or semiotic meaning. Thus, that a tomato is a vegetable is a semiotic truth insofar as it is an accurate account of common usage. In music, the principle is the same. The scientific fact that a perfect fourth is an acoustical consonance may conveniently be ignored when its semiotic (cognitive) construal is as a dissonance against the bass.

The lesson to be drawn from the cognitive theorists is that which was drawn from the linguistic philosophers. If we relinquish the notion of precise referentiality in language, then we are under no obligation to sustain such a standard of precision for those contents with which music correlates. The referential model of signification must not be allowed to cloud the issue of how or whether music can correlate with such content, especially when that model is shown to be inadequate through an overemphasis on precision in defining its object of reference.

Eco (1976: 58–68) argues that what he considers a "referential fallacy" can be corrected only by the notion of correlation with cultural units, because "every attempt to establish what the referent of a sign is forces us to define the referent in terms of an abstract entity which moreover is only a cultural convention" (66). If such is the case, then music may well be analogous with language in that regard—and music's nonreferentiality will not be seen as an obstacle to the teasing out of its meanings.

Music is not involved in naming or the referential manipulation of cultural units the way language is, to be sure, but the difference between music and language is in the use of the correlations possible between sound and content, not in the more basic semiotic mechanisms that organize those correlations. Music (at least in some styles) may be more concerned with presenting or dramatizing its correlations, but that is not to say that the competencies underlying our access to those correlations are not in some ways related to those underlying language or, more fundamentally, culture.

Indeed, many of the confusions about expression, representation, and the like are plagued with the same miscalculations I have documented with respect to reference. That is why, as mentioned earlier, I have chosen to focus on correlation.

The concept of cultural units for emotional states is a useful theoretical alternative to the evocation of actual emotions in music. Buck (1984: 11) considers emotions as cultural contents, expressed but not induced. He cites the case of Bertrand Russell, whose dentist gave him an injection of epinephrine. He subsequently experienced nervous excitation but was surprised to discover that "epinephrine was insufficient to cause a full-blown emotion because the cognitive element was lacking" (1984: 58). The excitation had no focus and thus could as easily have been interpreted in terms of sudden anger as of sudden elation.[7]

5. In considering the degree of specificity appropriate to the description of musical meaning, if referential precision is not possible, how can one delimit the indefinite or slippery correlations with emotional states that one finds in music? Two confusions can lead to near-paralysis in such attempts. The first concerns the degree of generality appropriate to an inquiry. As Aristotle so eloquently observed in the *Nicomachean Ethics*, "It is the mark of an educated man to look for precision in each class of things just so far as the nature of the subject admits; it is evidently equally foolish to accept probable reasoning from the mathematician and to demand from the rhetorician scientific proofs" (Book One, 1094b; cited by Hernadi, 1972: 154).

Stylistic types and strategic tokens require different degrees of generality in accounting for their expressive correlations. Since style structures are abstractions, and generalizations from, actual structures, we should not expect characterizations of their "potential for meaning" to be any less abstract or general. Strategic implementations of stylistic structures, on the other hand, demand further specification and interpretation. For an example of further specification, recall the doublings of closing triads

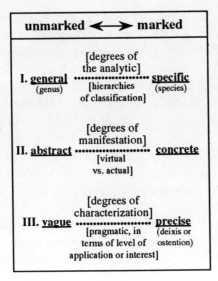

Figure 10.1. Three oppositional axes in the characterization of musical expressive meaning.

examined in Chapter 2; for examples of further interpretation, recall the speculations of Chapter 7, in which troping served to expand or enrich expressive meanings in less predictable ways.

In the case of further specification, a more specific term is obviously desirable; in the case of further interpretation, however, a more abstract term may be called for, or perhaps a metaphor that can help recreate in language the leap of meaning the music has achieved.

But consider the different senses attributable to abstract vs. concrete, as opposed to specific vs. general, or precise vs. vague (Figure 10.1). These oppositional axes can become confused when the theorist is enjoined on the one hand to be more precise (less "impressionistic"), and on the other, to avoid overspecificity (or "referentiality"). Small wonder that no one has met Hanslick's exacting standards for claims about musical expressivity.

To illustrate the ways in which these oppositions may interact, consider the abstract noun "turbulence." It can be used as a general term (the concept of turbulence), it can be made specific (the turbulence of water), or it can be made indexically precise (the turbulence of the water at Fingal's Cave during a particular storm). What should be noted is that the general appears vague only if we are expecting, or for some reason require, the specific or the deictically precise. A concrete noun, such as water, can be general, more specific (the waters of an ocean), or deictically precise (the waters in Fingal's Cave).

Now, if asked to characterize the correlation (to a cultural unit) of the opening passage of Mendelssohn's *Hebrides Overture*, some may feel more comfortable with an abstract/general answer (the concept of turbulence), others with a concrete/precise answer (the turbulence of the waters in Fingal's Cave). Others might argue that the essential meaning or interpretation has little to do with water or its turbulence, but that the title merely suggests an appropriate poetic conceit, one that is interpreted by still other cultural units such as "spiritual turbulence" or, more generally, "Romantic longing" (with regard to the restless aspect of such longing).

If we study the score (see Example 10.1), we would probably all agree with Peter Kivy (1984: 138–39) that there is a representation of waves rippling and heaving. Kivy considers the music illustrative because the expressive character of the music is "dark, brooding, melancholy, like the expressive quality of the Hebrides' seas themselves." In the third measure I might interpret a ray of "light" cued by the sequence to the relative major and the momentary displacement of the bass by the pedal A in the clarinet.[8]

With these observations, Kivy and I have pursued interpretations of the music in ways that encompass presumed representation or illustration, the expressive character of the music, and the expressive connotations (spiritual turbulence) suggested by the represented object. It would be impossible to choose in principle among these three ways of construing the meaning of the passage, since each answers a different query about the work. All are parts of the whole, and each can be supported by musical structures (in their stylistic and strategic oppositions). In accepting the possibility of one, we accept the possibility of the others; there is no greater claim for an interpretation simply because it falls within some privileged zone of specificity or generality. Which kind or degree of musical meaning will be the aesthetic focus of a historical period, or will come to be valued most highly, is the subject of historical inquiry, not a universal aesthetics of music.

If we collate the evidence of Mendelssohn's titles with an understanding of the cultural context of Romanticism; knowledge of specific works, such as his sketch of the site (Todd, 1979: 205) and "McPherson's pseudo-Celtic poem, *Fingal*" (Todd, 201), on which the early title, *Fingal's Cave*, is based; an understanding of the musical style and the correlations it has inherited from earlier styles; and a careful analysis of the sketches and final version, we can perhaps reconstruct the relevant levels of specificity for both illustrative and expressive meanings in this passage.

Example 10.1. Mendelssohn, Overture, Op. 26 (*The Hebrides* or *Fingal's Cave*), mm. 1–5 (from Kivy, 1984: 139).

The titles in this case are part of the guiding "poetic conceit" for a stylistic interpretation of the work. A part of the aesthetic experience of the work is stimulated by the title, as well as by the particular associations it may hold for the composer. Music does not have to supply its own conceits in order for the experience of such conceits to be valid. On the other hand, the interpretation of emotional turbulence is so ingrained in the style that it is not likely to be missed even if the connotations of a given locale (or its mythic resonance) are not available to a listener.

In summary, then, the use of language in discourse about music is indispensable, both metalinguistically and poetically. Language that characterizes correlations with cultural units may be more general than language that metaphorically interprets musical expressive meanings. The problems of specificity or generality are directly related not only to these varied uses of language, but to the operative level of analysis: whether stylistic or strategic, types or tokens. But in either case the construal of content in terms of cultural units, rather than of objects or emotions, avoids problems having to do with referentiality or psychological processes.

Freed from crippling demands inappropriate to the nonscientific status of semiotic inquiry, the theorist may probe a far richer field of cultural correlations and interpretations than Hanslick might have supposed. If the price is uncertainty, the reward is a correspondingly greater depth of musical understanding.

The Growth of Markedness and Musical Meaning

Markedness, with its fundamental asymmetry, has been shown to foster a specification of meaning as well as a progressive "articulation" of the expressive field, leading to *style growth*.[9] This is a crucial point. If meaning and its growth are kept coherent by the same fundamental semiotic mechanism (Shapiro, 1983), it is because that mechanism has a basic dynamic—stemming from the asymmetry of oppositions—that can both particularize meaning and provide an immediate niche for new entities in the semantic universe of a style.

Remarkably, it is this inherently dynamic form of opposition that characterizes a stable correlation in a style and enables the incorporation of unstable novelties. The same design may be seen to underwrite the systematic coherence of correlations while at the same time fostering interpretive and, ultimately, stylistic growth.

The process of growth may be understood from a complementary perspective, as well—that of Peirce's categories of being. It is possible to integrate markedness and Peirce's categories into a model of growth to explain how various kinds of musical (expressive) meanings can be interpreted in a work, and can become established as correlations in a style.

It should be clear that such a comprehensive model completes the larger theory of musical meaning projected in the present study. In addition, the model can help resolve some of the difficulties encountered in using language to describe meanings, by establishing a kind of "geometry of meaning" for new structures (to the extent that they can be derived oppositionally). Such a model can only suggest *how* meanings are systematically organized, not what they are, or whether they should be interpreted in one way or another. At best, the model offers a systematic motivation for the coherence of expressive correlations in a style, not for their particular content. But coherence (regardless of our labels or markers for particular meanings) is what ensures consistency in interpretation. It is also what enables a much richer expressive language to emerge than would be possible if interpretation relied merely on associations or habits. (I return to the issue of motivations in the next section).

To understand Peirce's conception of sign growth, it is necessary to introduce his ontological categories of Firstness, Secondness, and Thirdness (1931: 2.233 ff.). Peirce conceives of Firstness as pure quality or feeling—"essence" in that near-unimaginable state before opposition or difference begins to define it.

Secondness is the dynamic, oppositional relationship between two entities (events or objects, *designata* in general), for example, "action-reaction," "stimulus-response," or "X vs. not X." This category could also be characterized as dyadic, and thus not adequate to a theory of signification. Thirdness provides a triadic structure, and the interpretive mediation of duality or opposition. Thirdness is also the arena of rule or codified habit; it is here that one finds signs and semiosis in music and language.

Peirce derives his famous trichotomies recursively (2.243 ff.). Thirdness at the foundational level engenders further levels of First, Second, and Third (see Figure 10.2). Peirce's distinction between token and type is based on the difference between the manifested (sinsign) and the generalized (legisign). "Icon," "index," and "symbol" are each defined according to one of three motivations: likeness (qualities, properties, or structure), in the case of the icon; dynamical connection (the wind turns the weathervane that signifies wind direction), in the case of the index; or convention or habit (exclusive of iconic or indexical associations), in the case of the symbol. Signs may be multiply motivated, and the sign vehicle may in turn signify in more than one way. As an example, Peirce offers the footprint, which can be interpreted iconically (the image of a foot), indexically (made by the dynamic action of a foot), or symbolically (for Robinson Crusoe, signifying the presence of another human on the island).

To be properly interpreted, all signs rely on some degree of conven-

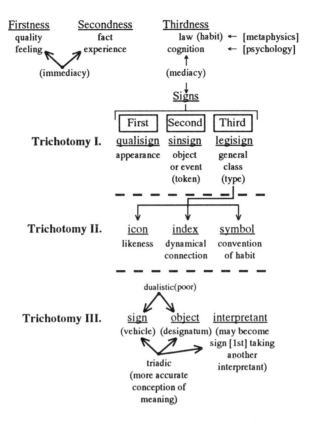

Figure 10.2. C. S. Peirce's categories and some trichotomies.

tion. There are conventions of interpretation even for iconic and indexical signs in a culture, conventions which help the interpreter select the relevant similarity or dynamical connection. In the strictest sense, stylistic meaning is by definition conventional, since it is based on a semiotic system of correlations. But conventions are not arbitrary, in that they have generally been motivated by iconic or indexical associations, whether or not those associations still play a role in interpretation. For example, I need not know that the word "bedlam" was originally motivated by indexical association with St. Mary of Bethlehem Hospital, where the insane were housed in London, in order to understand its conventionalized meaning: "any place or condition of noise and confusion."[10]

For the uninitiated, Peirce's categories may appear mystifying, and I

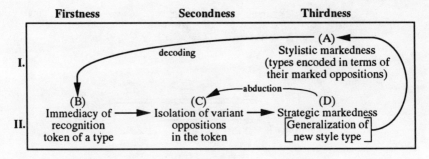

Figure 10.3. Model of growth in a musical style.

do not intend to pursue the trichotomies here. The following examples will apply the rather general model of Firstness through Thirdness to the development of a new musical structure or event—from its inception as seeming novelty to its encoding in a style as a systematic opposition. The road from Firstness to Thirdness moves from impression of qualities, through oppositional definition, to strategically marked meaning. If the strategically marked meaning fills a useful niche in the semantic universe, then it is likely to become part of the style, as well.

In the course of this exploration, I consider two kinds of growth processes, that of the unit, or entity, and that of the temporal process. These two levels of language are called *paradigmatic* and *syntagmatic* by Saussure. An entity is understood in terms of its oppositions with other entities, as well as in paradigms (model patterns), such as the classes of linguistic categorization—noun, adjective, verb—that determine its substitutability with other entities in a paradigmatic slot. A process (which can be understood as an entity at a higher level) is created by the association of two or more entities in a temporal sequence, or syntagm. For music, the implication or function of an entity would be its *syntagmatic* meaning.

Typically, a new entity is marked by its oppositional definition. Markedness, as a valuation of an opposition, should be considered a Third. It is, in effect, a systematic mediation of an opposition, providing the interpretation of the opposition. Figure 10.3 offers a general model for the development of a type from a token, as elaborated for the triad doublings in Chapter 2.[11] Note that the token is already mediated by its place in the style, a higher level of thirdness labeled (A) in Figure 10.3. As encountered by a listener for the first time in a work, the firstness of a musical event would involve its immediacy of identification as a token of a type in the style, e.g., tonic triad. Its secondness would involve the raising of dynamic opposition in one of its variable features, e.g., its distinctive doubling. If that doubling has interpretive significance, e.g., as serenity or starkness, then there is thirdness of strategic markedness and the potential that the previously variant opposition may be considered as invariant—e.g., as crucial to the definition of a new type. Finally, based on further use of that type, it may be said to have entered the style. Thus, creativity that has as its immediate goal a more highly expressive musical event may also have consequences for style growth.

Whereas Saussure posited the importance of opposition in his maxim that meaning is difference, Peirce had the insight that meaning emerges, or grows from, mediated oppositions (see Figures 9.1 and 10.2). But how might one recognize the significance, or pertinence, of previously variable features of a token—or imagine a meaningful role for potential opposition—without further inferences? Peirce considered this problem, concluding that the process of growth involves *abductive* inferences (hypothesis forming): "The second does not spring out of the first directly; but firstness looked at from a second point of view gives birth to a thirdness and the secondness comes out of the thirdness. This is the true logic of events" (MS 943).[12] Peirce appears to be addressing the cognitive sequence, not the deductive reconstruction, of the mind's acquisition of new knowledge. Thus, although one begins with knowledge of the style (Figure 10.3, A) and must first hear the unique token (B), the interpretation of significant differences among variable features of the token (C) requires some hypothesis as to what those differences might mean (D). Indeed, such hypotheses may be guided by (A); but only by abductive hypotheses from (D) can new meanings emerge.

The stylistic level should be assumed as a final-stage incorporation of various growth processes. In what follows I will concentrate on how marked entities emerge at strategic levels.

Considered from a paradigmatic standpoint, the growth or development of a new entity can be understood in two distinct ways: It emerges as a true novelty (with respect to the given style), or it emerges in relation to already existing entities, as modeled above. In the first category, we can place the products of invention, experimentation, and borrowing from other styles (ignoring, for the moment, other motivations, such as analogy, that may be at work as well). Such an entity, if it is to become a part of the style in a systematic way, must have some feature, Y, which can be marked with respect to its absence in another entity in the style. If we consider the growth process from the standpoint of Peirce's three categories, the process can be visually represented as in

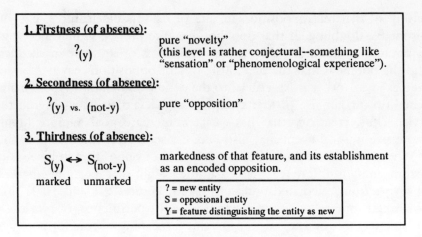

Figure 10.4. Development of a novel type in the style.

Figure 10.4. A novelty becomes an opposition which is then given a value (marked). Only at the third stage does the dyadic opposition become triadically mediated by a "rule of interpretation." The generalization of a type has been achieved; but whether the novelty in a work results ultimately in style growth depends on that type's becoming part of a stylistic competency, in turn guiding the interpretation of future works in the style.

True "novelties" are rare in music, since composers have not been as interested in this form of creativity, at least not until the twentieth century. Consider the use of white-key clusters in Berg's *Lulu*. As an initially novel sound (for European audiences unfamiliar with Cowell and Ives), the cluster quickly moves beyond a qualitative to an oppositional niche in its environment, and that opposition is marked as a consequence of several factors. As a primitive or "crude" noise, it is opposed to more-sophisticated atonal sonorities, which offer a greater potential for significance than the relatively undifferentiated cluster. When by *association* with a character on stage we grasp the leitmotivic connection with the Animal Trainer, it is easy enough to establish the proper *interpretant* for that connection—namely, a crude, unsophisticated, blunt, crass personality. Although the "novel" cluster sonority, as well as its particular timbre on the piano (suggesting the child who smashes a fistful of notes at random), achieves a strategic markedness in the context of the opera, the opposition is perhaps too asymmetrical to be productive beyond the scope of one work. Until composers such as

Penderecki explored the paradigmatic and syntagmatic possibilities of clusters, they lacked sufficient variety to be of much use compositionally. Compare, on the other hand, the more balanced asymmetry between tonal and atonal styles that is so effectively exploited in *Wozzeck*. Obviously, the internal articulation of each style supports a richer semantic field than mere opposition between the two, yet that opposition is productive of expressive meaning in its own right. In *Wozzeck*, tonal styles are used for source music or suggestions of an earlier, or literary, time; and an atonal style is used for present time in all its psychological intensity.

The second and more common growth process for a new entity is that of derivation from a preexisting entity. This process is the one modeled in Figure 10.3, involving the distinction between type and token. The generation of a new type from a subset of an older type, as shown in Figure 10.5, accounts for the doubling examples in Chapter 2. Note in this case that the new type, though derived as a subset of the original type, may escape from its original type categorization and become independent of any implied subordination to the original type. Variations on the process in Figure 10.5 are displayed in Figure 10.6.

The processes outlined in Figure 10.6c are akin to Umberto Eco's (1979: 23) concepts of "blowing up" and "narcotizing," with reference to a text's influence over the way readers actualize the potential semantic properties of its words or other entities. The unfeatured ("narcotized") properties are not eliminated by focus on the actualized ("blown up") ones; they remain available for future actualization by the text.

In John Crowe Ransom's example from Tennyson, "murmuring of innumerable bees," the sonic properties of the words are actualized because they are relevant to their semantic meaning (here, by a device known as onomatopoeia, or imitation of natural sounds).[13] By contrast, the "murdering of innumerable beeves" may contradict the claims of onomatopoetic meaning in language (Ransom's point), but for Eco, the sonic properties would merely be "narcotized," or ignored, because they do not support the semantic sense.[14] Although Eco's theory is conceived at the level of interpretation, his ideas apply equally at the level of type generation.

Turning to temporal or syntagmatic processes, we see that a new entity can arise by replacing the expected event in a temporal sequence. This substitution, often suprising, may then serve as an oppositional negation of the expected entity. For example: X implies Y (in the style);

1. Firstness of subset:

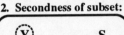

token (x) of a type (s).

Figure 10.5. Derivation of a type from further articulation of an existing type.

2. Secondness of subset:

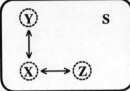

differentiation from other tokens (y, z) of the type.

3. Thirdness of subset:

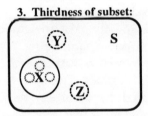

generalization of a new type, as subset of the original type, and having its own tokens.

X is followed instead by Q (in the work); Q is understood as an opposition or negation in kind of Y; therefore, Q is marked with respect to Y (see Figure 10.7). Even if Q already exists as a paradigmatic entity, it may take on a new syntagmatic function, and thus a new paradigmatic role, as a result of its substitutional usage.

The various possibilities underlying temporally based growth include the following:

1. Growth by negation (Q becomes a new entity defined as "not Y")
2. Growth by endowing a contextual location with markedness potential for any entity used as replacement for Y (for example, a cadential location)
3. Temporal expansion, understood as a strategy in which Y is under-

A. Growth by subtraction, division, or part-for-whole.

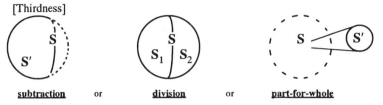

subtraction   or   division   or   part-for-whole

B. Growth by extension, addition, or ornamentation--with new features being "featured".

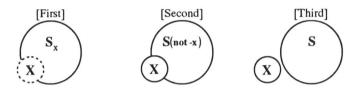

C. Growth by raising previously irrelevant features to a new relevance, or the opposite, lowering previously relevant features (type generalization).

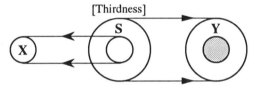

Figure 10.6. Other derivations of a type.

stood as displaced to a later point (not merely replaced)—for example, a delayed resolution or Schenkerian prolongation.

Perhaps the most common growth mechanism, since it can be invoked as soon as any of the other mechanisms have produced a new entity, is the fundamental operation of *analogy*. Its operation may occur either from a spatial (paradigmatic) or temporal (syntagmatic) perspective, as shown in Figure 10.8.

As an example of syntagmatic growth by analogy, consider the analogy between V to I and ii to V (both related by root motion at the interval of a descending perfect fifth). This shared relationship might have suggested the growth of a new kind of ii, one which strengthens the move from ii to V along the lines of V to I. The result is the familiar secondary or applied dominant built on scale degree $\hat{2}$.

But the substitution of terms based on analogy does not always guar-

1. Firstness of replacement:

temporal sequence: X———Q
      implications: "→Y"   "?!"   Q as surprise.

2. Secondness of replacement:

    sequence: X———Q
implications: "→Y" "∅Y" Q as "not Y".

3. Thirdness of replacement:

    sequence: X———Q   Q marked as a negation of Y
implications: "→Y" "not-Y" (e.g., a deceptive cadence); Q=not-Y.

Figure 10.7. Development of substitutional opposition.

A. Paradigmatic Substitutions

1. $X :: A$ X is like A,

2. $A \rightarrow B \rightarrow C$
     ↓   therefore, X can substitute for A;
   $\boxed{X} \rightarrow B \rightarrow C$

3. $X : Y :: A : B$ (or) X is to Y as A is to B,

4. $X : A$ $A \rightarrow B \rightarrow C$
          ↓   therefore, X may substitute for A.
       $\boxed{X} \rightarrow B \rightarrow C$

B. Syntagmatic Substitutions

1. $X \rightarrow Y :: A \rightarrow B$ X leads to Y as A leads to B,

2. $X \rightarrow B$ or $A_x \rightarrow B$ therefore, X may lead to B,
                   (or) A_x may lead to B.

Figure 10.8. Analogy as a means of growth.

antee success: "ii is to V as V is to I" does not yield the transitive result of ii leading to I. The reason is that analogy is neither a logical model nor a deductive syllogism, but a logic of possibilities. Theoretically understood, the analogy is not a rule or guarantee, but a mode of explanation which must be complemented by a statement of the relevant aspect(s) underlying the analogy (see discussion of motivations, below).

In this case, what underlies the analogy is the functional fifth-relationship between pairs of diatonic chords. That relationship may have led to the functionalization of ii–V; it certainly supports the extrapolation of a dominant relationship to that position, as V/V–V.

The new, by whatever means it comes about, will at least initially be marked with respect to the old. Besides the creation of new entities, however, there are other means of marking material: rhythmic placement; delay of resolution or arrival; contrasts created by dynamics, articulation, instrumentation, register, texture, or tempo; and thematization itself, as exemplified in earlier chapters. Some basic principles underlying marked materials in a style are set forth below. Even when their expressive force is no longer immediate (salient or new), the resulting markedness of oppositions may become systematic in the style. If this happens, the opposition and its correlative meanings will continue to function, but competition from other or newer events in a work may shift the expressive focus. Although immediate expressive effects can be achieved by "foregrounding" (making salient), a sufficient explanation of expressivity and other kinds of musical meaning must take account of the markedness values at all levels, whether salient or not.[15] Only by respecting the markedness of no longer salient events can one understand the stylistic surprise of, for example, a deceptive cadence long after it ceases to be an actual surprise.

The basic principles for markedness in other "parameters" may be laid out as follows:

1. Rhythmic placement: Y is marked with respect to its displacement to an (immediately) earlier location—syncopation, Classical rubato; or displacement to an (immediately) later location—hesitation, delay, syncopation.
2. Delayed resolution/arrival:
   a. Y is unmarked with respect to its (marked) absence when implied but interrupted by marked material.
   b. Y is unmarked with respect to the marked material between its implied location and its ultimate (nonimmediate) restoration.
3. Contrast: Y is marked when it is given emphasis by a sudden change from the prevailing:[16]
   a. dynamic level becoming (either louder or softer, although a greater contrast is required for softness to have the same marked effect)
   b. articulation

	Motivations	
same level	similarity	contiguity
hierarchical	analogy	synecdoche
different domains	metaphor	metonymy

Figure 10.9. Motivations for associations (leading to signification).

    c. instrumentation
    d. timbre
    e. register
    f. texture
    g. tempo
4. Thematic markedness, based on:
    a. location, as constrained by formal schema
    b. usage; significant strategic involvement in the working out of the "discourse" of the movement
    c. characteristic figures, topics, styles
    d. salience, as achieved by 1–3 above

A clearer definition of thematic markedness, or a discovery procedure for determining thematic markedness, is not possible since its assessment depends to some degree on the premises and strategies of a work. The thematic discourse of a work involves unique situations as well as contexts larger than those invoked for other forms of markedness (see Chapters 5 and 6).

Motivations

The larger contexts involved in interpretation are theoretically unlimited. They can be understood as drawing upon a few basic kinds of motivations, as illustrated in Figure 10.9. These kinds of motivations support the association of sound and content, in turn relating them to the larger tropes that they may fund (compare Jakobson and Halle, 1956). The different terms for similarity relations, for example, are based on a distinction between association of entities at the same level, as opposed to different levels.

A correlation is simply an association that has become symbolic (i.e., a conventional part of the style); for music, I use this term for systematic, or coded, associations between sound and content that are part of a stylistic competency (organized according to marked oppositions).

Before correlations can be established by a listener or theorist becoming acquainted with a new style, however, some kind of phenomenological interpretation must take place. This basal interpretation is an attribution of meaning by association of some sort; at this level there is an element of Firstness, and such conjectural graspings are often incoherent. Eco (1976) calls the process "undercoding":

> the operation by means of which in the absence of reliable preestablished rules, certain macroscopic portions of certain texts are provisionally assumed to be pertinent units of a code in formation, even though the combinational rules governing the more basic compositional items of the expressions, along with the corresponding content units, remain unknown. [134–36]

Once correlations have been provisionally established, the lowest level of interpretation is decoding—identifying and recognizing types among the tokens of a work. This level involves a somewhat less artistic reading based on systematically defined categories and relationships in the style. The categories are learned, and coherent (to the extent that the style is coherent), but not yet aesthetically interesting.

It is only at the level of (stylistically constrained) interpretation— attribution of meaning through a deeper associational process (involving tropes as well)—that interpretation of a work becomes artistically fruitful. Interpretation is a creative reading of a work based on the kinds of growth and creativity constrained by the style. Here it is crucial that style be understood as a competency, entailing *principles* of organization, not strict *rules* or purely systematic correlations. It is at this level that strategic interpretations and historically "appropriate" interpretations occur. Indeed, the interpretative labor ranges from type generalization of undercoded entities to interpretations of emotional, psychological, or spiritual states (as cultural units) and progressions among those states. Because this interpretation is an artistic process and

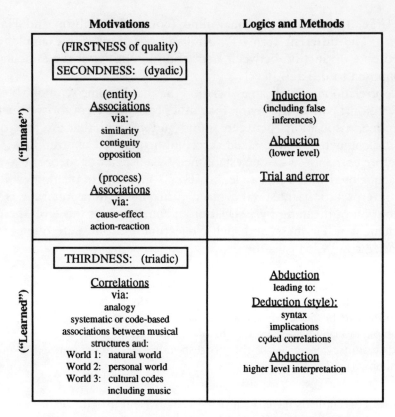

	Motivations	**Logics and Methods**
("Innate")	(FIRSTNESS of quality) SECONDNESS: (dyadic) (entity) Associations via: similarity contiguity opposition (process) Associations via: cause-effect action-reaction	Induction (including false inferences) Abduction (lower level) Trial and error
("Learned")	THIRDNESS: (triadic) Correlations via: analogy systematic or code-based associations between musical structures and: World 1: natural world World 2: personal world World 3: cultural codes including music	Abduction leading to: Deduction (style): syntax implications coded correlations Abduction higher level interpretation

Figure 10.10. Continua of innate and learned motivations and methods of interpretation.[17]

not merely an identificational decoding, it will be less secure or certain. There may be "leakage" in the form of other associations that may contradict correlations. Indeed, the work may "play" against the systematic correlations of the style and achieve coherence at a different level from the purely systematic.

Still further interpretation, moving beyond the original style altogether, is legitimate in two realms (neither of which has been the focus of this study):

1. Understanding the work in terms of a later style, for example, rehearing the Beethoven quartets from the perspective of the Bartók quartets, or (to borrow T. S. Eliot's perspective on literature) allowing each new work that enters the "canon" of great music to inflect our understanding of every previous work.

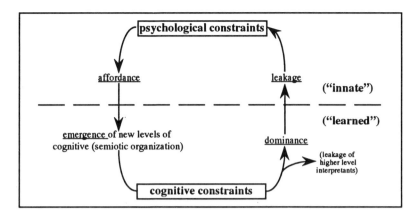

Figure 10.11. Cycle of affordance, emergence, dominance, and leakage.

2. Understanding the work in terms of private, subjective codes or needs, or overly precise programmatic interpretation.

Figure 10.10 deals with speculations as to the innateness of motivations and what could be called logics or methods of understanding. Obviously, no clear distinctions can be drawn between what is innate and what is learned, but the continuum may be useful in distinguishing between association and correlation, or between phenomenological interpretation and decoding-plus-stylistic interpretation.

Abduction, Peirce's term for the inference involved in hypothesis-forming (1931: 5.171), appears at several levels in the chart. As the inferential method underlying the process of interpretation, abduction is both a means of reconstructing the style and a means of going beyond it.

Figure 10.11 offers a revision of the distinction between innate and learned, in terms of a cyclic process of interpretation. The *affordance* of uncoded, prestylistic competencies (such as the ones Gestalt psychology reveals for fundamental perceptual acts) provides a starting point for a listener who must go further to abduce the *emergent* cognitive organization of a style. Cognitive (semiotic) competence, once learned, then dominates the subsequent processing (interpreting) of associations, overriding gross Gestalt perceptions when the two are in conflict. But an exception must be made for leakage, in which the basic affordant perceptual (or other) competencies reassert themselves. Leakage occurs when an overly artificial style can no longer support complex cognitive organization at the expense of more affordant perceptual competencies. For example, a succeeding generation of musical listeners not exhaustively trained in a complex style may "default" to more-basic Gestalt perceptual strategies, thereby missing crucial segmentations or entities. Leakage is characteristic of the average listener's approach to serial music. Leakage also helps explain the historical simplifications in styles immediately following highly complex ones (reduction in contrapuntal complexity may be found in both early Baroque and early Classical styles).

As the parenthetical note in Figure 10.11 indicates, leakage may involve associations that are simpler or more "natural" at higher levels of interpretation, as well. A musical work may not be able to support the ambitious program ascribed to it by its composer, as Schumann often complained in his reviews (Plantinga, 1967: 123).

Figure 10.12 generalizes the notions of affordance and emergence to help differentiate the kinds of meaning investigated by the sciences as opposed to the humanities. Peirce's semiotic was conceived as embracing not only logic but pragmatics (meaning as relevant to its use by an interpreter; i.e., meaning defined by use). The humanities are, or should be, more concerned with pragmatics than with logic. A structuralist account of music that is not fully informed by interpretive potential is a science of the coherence of phenomena in themselves, which may not be entirely relevant to their coherence as understood (interpreted, or used) by a listener.

Generative/reductive accounts informed by the intuitions of competent listeners (Lerdahl and Jackendoff, 1983) may be overly structuralist, as well. Even if the rules of a generative process are fine-tuned to lead to an intuitively satisfying "output" (as in Chomsky's generative syntax for linguistics, an inspiration for Lerdahl and Jackendoff), there is no way to claim the empirical reality of those rules for a listener, for two reasons already put forward in the case of generative syntax in linguistics. One, the chains of inference are too long to be directly tested (Janet Fodor, 1977: 105). Two, "generativism is unacceptable as a methodological postulate because it confounds logical necessity with empirical necessity" (Shaumyan, 1987: 29).[18]

But suppose there were a way to test such inferentially complex claims. There are three good reasons why an exclusively experimental approach to the cognition of Beethoven's style, for example, might still fail to capture the kinds of expressive meaning I have put forward in this more speculative study: the music is historical; it is artistic; and its style must be learned. History is contingent, not logical, in its growth and change. Artistic works are creative, and thus even more unpredictable.

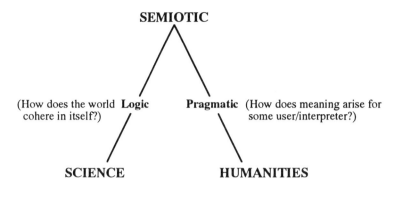

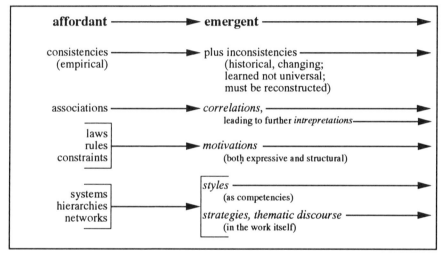

Figure 10.12. From science to the humanities: affordant and emergent aspects of two approaches. (For further discussion and definition of some of these terms, see Glossary.)

And a style must be learned in its full reconstruction. If my interpretations are any indication, we have yet to fully reconstruct the expressive competencies involved. One cannot assume that present-day listeners either have a fully internalized competency in a historical style or that they are not going to be influenced by later stylistic competencies in their interpretation. Thus, psychological testing would probably reveal more about the capacities of listeners than about potential stylistic interpretations of a work.

All of these considerations underline the undeniably speculative nature of theorizing about stylistic competencies and expressive meaning in music, and the importance of artistic interpretation at all levels of theory building. Accepting uncertainty as a fundamental condition of music theory has a positive side, however: one remains oriented toward the vastness of possibilities—the unlimited semiosis of interpretation— and less likely to neglect expressive meaning in music simply because theories of expression can never be airtight.

Conclusion

Meanings are not the equivalent of sounding forms. The linkage between sound and meaning, though mediated by forms, is also mediated by habits of association that, when stylistically encoded, produce *correlations*, and when strategically earned (inferred through a stylistically constrained interpretive process) produce *interpretations*. Although iconic motivations (similarity, analogy) may account for the origin of many musical signs, the ultimate status of the musical sign is symbolic.[1] Musical correlations are capable of transcending their original iconic linkage, but they are never completely arbitrary. Though original motivations may be lost, correlations retain the systematic motivation of their markedness. And markedness, central to this study, offers a semiotic explanation for the systematic organization of musical meanings, regardless of their original motivations.

Correlations may develop new interpretations by a growth process based on the inferred markedness of new or previously disregarded oppositions. Indeed, once one has a sufficiently coherent system of forms and meanings, then interpretations may be generalized as correlations, even without direct iconic motivation. The iconic persists, however, as a check upon the artificial growth of a style, as well as a motivation in its own right.

The possible meanings of any musical entity are drawn from syntagmatic relationships such as implication, larger schemes such as expressive genres, and ultimately tropes and shifts in discourse level. The description of musical meanings may range from abstract to concrete, general to specific, and precise to vague according to one's level of investigation. But musical meanings need not be referential, since correlations with cultural units are not the results of meaning. Whatever the motivations for correlation, musical meaning is inherently musical; thus, music is not an autonomous art form in Hanslick's sense.

We may now incorporate Saussure's famous insight, "meaning is difference," into the following extended statement of the model for musical meaning developed in this study, as applied to Beethoven's style:

1. Musical meaning is difference
2. structurally conceived and interpretable as asymmetrical opposition
3. marked within a cultural style system
4. correlated with marked oppositions in hierarchies of:
    a. formal (syntactical, functional)
    b. expressive (emotional/spiritual states that are cognitively recognized and culturally coded)
    c. dramatic, and
    d. narratalogical dimensions, and
5. further interpretable according to contexts (interactive environments) regulated by strategies of:
    a. thematization
    b. expressive genre (as negotiated with formal genre)
    c. tropological figuration (musical metaphor, irony, shift in level of discourse, reflexivity), and
    d. intertextuality
6. at any and all levels of complexity, from the most affordant perceptual levels to the more emergent cognitive levels of listener interpretation; and from the simplest oppositions of sound (duration, frequency, amplitude, timbre) to the most complex interactive network of a late Beethoven quartet.
7. Furthermore, the stylistically motivated and historically reconstructed meanings explored in this book do not exhaust the wealth of legitimate interpretations conceivable within the frameworks of later stylistic competencies and/or individual chains of increasingly subjective (personal) interpretants.

One might speculate why markedness is so valuable as an explanatory model for musical meaning. I have shown how markedness can help account for growth of meaning in a style by regulating the further articulation of oppositional types. I suspect that markedness can also help explain the way individuals learn to distinguish concepts, and thus the structural vehicles for those concepts, whether in language (the meanings of words), nature (the properties of objects), or music (the significance of sounds). It is tempting to imagine the operation of neurons in terms of marked/unmarked oppositions, but it is also clear that the brain has other, more networklike (or even holographic) means of organizing information.[2] Nevertheless, the decoding and interpretation of many of the oppositions analyzed in this book would seem to require a fine-grained perceptual and cognitive capacity for interpreting uniqueness against a backdrop of the familiar, and that is where markedness operates most obviously. Whether as a uniquely manifested token of a stylistic type, or as a typical (even prototypical) token transformed by its environment, or (far less often) as a brand new entity, musical events may be marked by any differences which are potentially significant.

I have concentrated on expressive meaning for the interpretations in this book because this kind of meaning has been unjustly neglected, particularly from a structuralist perspective. The exploration of expressive meaning from a hermeneutic perspective may have been suppressed by a climate of scientized formalism in past years, but hermeneutic methods were not necessarily in conflict with structural analysis—rather, hermeneutics was devalued because the apparent (and often quite real) subjectivity of its approach made its results suspect.

Markedness, as it arises from salience, has much to offer any theory for which the salient event is by definition "expressive." This concept is enunciated in Mathis Lussy's (1873) theory of expressive performance, in which the singer is instructed to project the salient or unusual events (articulatory, dynamic, agogic, harmonic) as indicated by markings in the score or as interpreted by a stylistically informed musician. Markedness helps explain expressiveness of this kind by suggesting the narrower range, and thus the greater specificity, of meaning in "foregrounded" events. Salience created by deliberate distortion or "making strange" became an aesthetic credo for Slavic poets in the early part of the twentieth century, as theorized by the Russian Formalists. Roman Jakobson developed his linguistic theory in that formative environment, and it is not surprising that he should have extended Trubetzkoy's concept of markedness in phonology to the domains of syntax and semantics. Michael Shapiro was a student of Roman Jakobson's, and Shapiro's extension of markedness to poetics marks a full circle from the inspiration of poetry in the development of the concept.

But markedness is more than salience, as pointed out in Chapter 2, and expression is more than that which is "pressed out" by surface emphases. By reconstructing marked oppositions at all levels of structure, one begins to understand how musical meaning at all levels is kept coherent. Older marked oppositions may lose their immediate expressiveness in terms of foregrounding as they are displaced by newer oppositions that further articulate the semantic space. But those older oppositions continue to differentiate meanings, even when those meanings are no longer expressively focal. If this were not possible, there would be no way of building a functional syntax or any of the hierarchies of a style. As expressive meaning shifts to more-focal oppositions (whether new stylistic oppositions, or old oppositions "renovated" by thematic markedness), the oppositions that are increasingly "backgrounded" may come to appear purely formal, as if they merely provided a structured background or grid against which foregrounded events might be featured as highly expressive. But that construal forces a misconception, since we do not listen to music merely to pluck the fruits of expressivity off the branches of structural trees.

Expression, in its deepest sense, involves the integration of all aspects of an art work, not the isolation of a single "level of attending" (although the latter might well represent a listener's initial appreciation of a work). A theme (such as the opening of the slow movement of Op. 7, analyzed in Chapter 2) does not reduce to its expressive crux any more than it reduces to a fundamental *Ursatz*, in our interpretation of its expressive meaning. Integratively, the expressive meaning of such a theme is irreducible, since every detail, whether nonstructural in a Schenkerian sense (yet "expressively salient") or backgrounded in an expressive sense (yet "structurally significant"), has artistic value. As Roman Jakobson phrased it, everything in art is pertinent.[3] In music, as in art, that which is structural *is* so because of its expressive significance, and that which is expressive in turn depends on a structuring which enables us to infer (differentiate, mark as oppositional, correlate, and interpret) its expressive meaning.

If the foregoing discussion has begun to blur the distinction between expressive and structural meanings, then perhaps what is needed is a new vocabulary that does not preserve the outmoded opposition between the two. I have been unable to dispense with these troublesome terms; historical contingency and the desire to communicate has led me to offer new meanings couched in a vocabulary that tends to work against me. My concern for less-loaded terminology has led me to implement the term "correlation" in place of terms such as "expression," "reference," "representation," and "exemplification"; and I have tried to handle differences among correlations by distinguishing among the various kinds of "motivations" involved. But even the term "correlation" implies a connection between separate things. And separation has led in the past to a misconstrual of meanings as somehow "extramusical." Yet if musical structures could not have originated without the meanings that help to define them, then no musical meaning is "extramusical," regardless of how far down a chain of interpretants one must go to retrieve it.

What semiotics can offer music theory is the realization that structures and meanings arrive in a single package, wrapped by a symbol system (style) and unwrapped by a series of interpretive acts (presumably guided by the style). Although it can happen that a particular period's aesthetic will weight, for example, mathematical values above expressive ones (Xenakis), those values are inevitably negotiated with expressive values the composer already holds (as witnessed by the subtle changes Xenakis makes in his notational realizations of computer-generated algorithms).[4] The problem is that without a shared stylistic competency, listeners may not be able to appreciate the expressive, or indeed the mathematical significance of novel styles. Thus, I have limited my investigation to the more common situation where there is a shared symbol system sufficient to ground the kinds of interpretive claims I have made for works of Beethoven.

A cautionary note is in order, however, with respect to hermeneutic license. It is possible for expressive approaches to engender their own dogmas—and not merely at the level of overly ideological "readings" of "texts."[5] Just as the structural organicism of orthodox Schenkerian theory has often directed listening and analysis toward the coherence of structural pitches and hierarchies of voice leading as the "true content" of music, the "hermeneutic windows" of Lawrence Kramer (1990) or my own tropological interpretations may lead to an equal if opposite extreme—privileging the idiosyncratic. We must not neglect the explanation of marked and unmarked oppositions that have lost their "stylistic salience" or that are part of the background in a work—and not solely because they provide for underlying coherence. Coherence must itself be understood integratively—neither as "structure" nor as "expression" alone, but as a product of the marked and correlational organization of musical meaning. Thus, I offer a theory that claims to be both structuralist and hermeneutic, but that expands the range of these complementary approaches. The theory is structuralist in its further pursuit of the structure of expression, and hermeneutic in its further pursuit of the expressiveness of formal structures.

It is this interpenetration of meanings, this thorough integration of means, that has been my guide. If the investigation has led at times to painfully detailed theoretical reconstructions, or overly intricate interpretations of works that convey their riches far more eloquently, then it may be helpful to remember that Beethoven's compositional process was no less exhaustive, and his eloquence was earned through a series of painstaking revisions. Directed by a deep spiritual commitment, this devotion to compositional craft enabled Beethoven to express the most profound passages of the spirit, while touching the simplest chords of our common humanity.

Reconstruction of musical meaning can never be completely exhausted by the disciplines of music history and theory. For reconstruction is also an invitation to reexperience—to reinvigorate our listening or performing at the springs of Beethoven's inspiration and through the roots of his musical style. If that reexperiencing is to be expressively fruitful for us, we must bring something more than structural recognition or "safe" formal analysis to the enterprise. No musical reading that insists on literalness or factitious security can ever fully ripen into a satisfying expressive interpretation, for either the performer or the listener. Instead, we must be willing to participate in an artistic transaction in which "validity" is no longer a barrier to the imagination. Such creative engagement can and should absorb the results of hermeneutic inquiry and structuralist formulation as pursued so exhaustively in this study, but it must also be open to other interpretants that arise from individual experience. Beethoven's music—indeed, all music we value highly—encourages self-inquiry and personal growth as we internalize what Beethoven called the poetic meaning of his music. For competent listeners, personal meaning will inevitably be shaped, and enhanced, by stylistic meaning. But the threshold of an individualized interpretive journey marks the semiotic limit for my investigation of stylistic interpretation. Beyond that threshold we are witness to the mystical fusion of sound and significance, as music embraces

> The art and the ear,
> of earth and the heart.[6]

And as theory gives way to poetry, the theorist must end in respectful silence.

Abnegation and the New Genre

What Beethoven Might Have Learned
from Reading Goethe's *Wilhelm
Meisters Lehrjahre*

As a cultural unit, abnegation is related to Christian notions of sacrifice and spiritual surrender, although it has its secular counterparts in the nineteenth century. An example of abnegation with respect to love is familiar from Wagner's *Die Meistersinger*, in which Hans Sachs forgoes (with some inner struggle) his opportunity to win the willing hand of Eva, in order to help Walther achieve what is clearly in Walther's and Eva's best interests. Thus, Sachs's frustration is transcended by his self-denying love, resulting in the happy ending of comedy (a wedding), as opposed to the tragic aspect hinted in the Prelude to Act 3 (portraying Sachs's emotional state during his inner struggle).

In terms of its underlying dramatic structure, an abnegational genre may be understood to comprise three parts: a reversal (from what is desired), a sense of either willing that reversal or accepting it as if from an external source, and a positive (higher) outcome of what otherwise would have been a tragic situation resulting from the reversal. The distinctiveness of this dramatic genre is threefold: the tragic is not dismissed (as in comedy), or allowed to overwhelm (as in tragedy), or added in judicious doses (as in tragicomedy), but rather transcended. In this sense, the abnegational genre is structured like religious drama.

As structurally defined, abnegation may be generalized to any number of situations—just as religious drama, with its sacrifice leading to transcendence, offers a structural model for secular plays or novels. Ultimately, the abnegational tragic-to-transcendent genre finds a musical realization in works such as the slow movement Beethoven's Piano Sonata, Op. 106.

It may be helpful to consider influential works that might have inspired Beethoven's unique realization of this genre. Goethe's famous novel *Wilhelm Meister* is one such work. Part I, the *Lehrjahre* (apprenticeship) was completed in 1796. Beethoven recommended it to Therese von Malfatti in a letter of 1807: "Have you read Goethe's *Wilhelm Meister*, [or] the Schlegel translation of Shakespeare; one has much leisure in the country, and it will perhaps be agreeable to you if I send you these works."[1]

Goethe's novel is a *Bildungsroman*, or novel of personal development, involving the education and maturing of the protagonist. The plot of the *Lehrjahre* hinges on fundamental reversals in the life of the protagonist. By the end of his apprenticeship, Wilhelm undergoes initiation into a quasi-Masonic brotherhood, the Society of the Tower, and recognizes his own inadequacy in the world of the theatre (as both actor and playwright). He voluntarily renounces his self-chosen profession, whereas a marriage to his ideal love, Natalie, is renounced for him, since Natalie recognizes that Wilhelm's spiritual maturation is not yet complete. He must first travel to Italy for his *Wanderjahre* (the term for the next stage in an apprentice's education before acceptance by a guild).

The *Wanderjahre*, or Part II, was completed some thirty years after Part I, so Beethoven could not have read it before completing his late works. Nevertheless, it is revealing in its subtitle, "The Renunciants," which confirms Wilhelm's acceptance of what might otherwise have been a tragic reversal of both his professional and his personal aspirations in Part I. That renunciation has a positive outcome, as Wilhelm gains insight into a range of topics of interest to Goethe during that time (notably, aesthetic education).

If Goethe had permitted Wilhelm to be happily married at the end of Part I, the genre would have been akin to comedy; if he had opted for Wilhelm's suicide in utter despair (as was the case in his *Sturm und Drang* novella, *The Sufferings of the Young Werther*, 1770), the reversals or deferrals might have been legitimized as tragedy. With either comic or tragic endings, however, the novel would have been closed in terms of its genre. Instead, a new conception, related to the genre of religious drama without being specifically Christian,[2] is brought to bear, creating the novelistic genre known as the *Bildungsroman*.

The *Bildungsroman*, as Goethe develops it in *Wilhelm Meister*, also includes a negative reversal early in the career of its protagonist. Wilhelm is shattered by the discovery that his beloved Mariana is still sexually involved with a wealthy lover. His severe disappointment leads him to renounce both Mariana and his early efforts at writing poetry, since his artistic life is intimately linked in his mind with love. This renunciation, followed by a return to the world of his family's business, is soon recognized as improperly motivated, and thus Wilhelm embarks on a sequence of experiences with the theatre in its many forms. Through these experiences he appears to be led through a progressive education in art and life.

But this education, or perhaps its deeper lessons, are lost on Wilhelm, for whom a prime motivation for becoming a man of the theatre is to see himself (on stage at least) as an aristocrat, rather than as the son of a middle-class merchant. Despite his many insights into life, Wilhelm remains a dilettante of the theatre. He is finally led to that recognition by the Tower Society, which has been watching over him throughout his "education." His initiation completes the "apprenticeship" with a positive renunciation of his quest to be a playwright.

Hans Vaget (1983) emphasizes the aspect of dilettantism which is revealed by Goethe as "fruitful error," since it eventually leads to maturation. Vaget suggests that "the traditional term *Bildungsroman* should not be applied to the *Lehrjahre*. . . . What we witness is a process of successful socialisation with the focus on the ambivalent role of dilettantism in that process" (14).

Jane Brown (1983) emphasizes the dramatic element in the novel, not simply in its subject matter, but in "a series of allegorical scenes with a didactic purpose" (the initiation) and "a dramatized ritual, rather along the lines of the earliest church drama" (Mignon's funeral). Her observations support my claim for a new underlying *dramatic genre* for the novel, but with different emphases:

> In the parts of the novel where Wilhelm mistakenly pursues his theatrical mission we find contemporary Aristotelian forms [of drama], where he pursues more important things the drama is non-Aristotelian. The theatrical mission of the *Lehrjahre* is to return the drama from Aristotelian neoclassical forms to the indigenous tradition of allegorical and festival drama which Mignon's funeral approaches, to drama which still has a religious and social function. [81]

Brown argues that Goethe moves away from Aristotelian tragedy because, as Goethe writes in his essay "Nachlese zu Aristoteles' Poetik" (1827), tragedy does not affect the spectator (in his time) deeply enough with respect to emotion or catharthic improvement. Only "the reader's intellectual response to the work" (84) can enable a more profound impact.

Wilhelm's experiences with love lead to the heights of true devotion to Natalie; but with a parallel recognition that Wilhelm is not ready to be the husband she deserves, he is led to defer their marriage. Benjamin Sax (1987) explains the role of Natalie as a model of the integration that Wilhelm must achieve: "Natalie instructs him through the model of her own life that identity is found in the recognition of one's Gestalt or 'inner form'" (69). For Sax, Natalie provides Wilhelm "a model of *Bildung* as an integration of inclination and object, of action and perception, yet how this model is to work in his own life is left open" (69).

Wilhelm has matured to some degree by the end of Part I, and the positive aspect of his renunciation is signaled by his reunion with the young Felix, the son he had only lately realized Mariana had borne him before her death. But further growth is still required. His *Wanderjahre* involves a tour of a model school for the aesthetic and moral, as well as practical, education of children. This and other utopian projects to which he is exposed place the second part of the novel in a more transcendent realm topically, and they serve as a positive affirmation of the higher purposes of renunciation.

Clark Muenzer (1984) has explored the issue of renunciation in Part II, the *Wanderjahre*, at the levels of deferred aspiration of the protagonist and an analogous deferral in the open-ended structure of the novel itself. The plurality of genres suggested by the episodes in the *Wanderjahre* produce "essential detours and serve as reminders of the need to renounce all ultimate meanings, even as they are pursued" (107). Thus, renunciation is a theme that is pursued "self-reflexively" by the novel itself (recall the discussion of self-reflexivity at the end of Chapter 7, above).

Goethe was himself influenced by the anti-Aristotelian perspective of Sanskrit drama. Ekbert Faas (1984: 156–59) has documented this connection in terms of both poetics (Bharata's first century treatise, *The Art of the Play*) and drama (Kālidāsa's fifth century drama, *Sacontalá*, available to Goethe in G. Forster's 1791 German translation of an English translation).[3] Faas, drawing on Erich Heller (1962), concludes that Goethe's *Faust* is not tragic, because there is "no catharsis, only metamorphosis," and Faust is not "purified in a tragic sense" but rather follows, in Heller's words, a "never-ending voyage of self-exploration" (1962: 479). This is similar to the concept of *Bildung* in *Wilhelm Meister*, if at a higher dramatic pitch.

There are other striking parallels to *Wilhelm Meister* in the *Faust*-Kālidāsa connection. As Faas elaborates: "Goethe's paradise, like Kālidāsa's, is not a transcendent stellar universe of disembodied perfection but a world in which we try to perfect and purify ourselves. Both plays suggest this by emphasizing the notion of teaching and learning" (174). To support this perspective, Faas quotes the following from *Faust*: "He who strives and ever strives,/ Him we can redeem./ And if love from on high/ Has also taken his part/ The blessed host will meet him/ with a warm welcome" (lines 11934–41).

The emphasis on striving, coupled with the grace of love, is a formula found in Beethoven, as well (though he could not have read the completed *Faust*). The heroic fugal finale to the *Hammerklavier* is the height of learned style, the emblem of a process of intellectual as well as spiritual striving. When the heroic first subject is ultimately integrated with the redemptive second subject (recalling, as was argued in Chapter 1, the resignational second theme of the slow movement), then we have a musical encapsulation of these two means of transcending the tragic.

Schiller's essay "On the Sublime" (1794) recalls Goethe's emphasis on education as leading to a personally achieved state of abnegation. In speaking of man's freedom over the powers of nature, gained through moral education, Schiller writes:

> But to attain to this state of mind, which morality designates as *resignation* to necessary things, and religion styles absolute *submission* to the counsels of Providence, to reach this by an effort of his free will and with reflection, a certain clearness is required in thought, and a certain energy in the will, superior to what man commonly possesses in active life. [137; italics added]

And that "moral aptitude" is supplemented by "an aesthetic tendency" which "can be cultivated to such a point as to become a powerful ideal development" (recalling the concept of *Bildung*).

Beethoven's renunciations in his personal life are well known. In the Heiligenstadt Testament of 1802 Beethoven gives up all hope of a normal social life because of his deafness, dedicating himself to composition. In 1812 he also chooses to relinquish his "immortal beloved," identified by Maynard Solomon (1977: 158–89) as Antonie Brentano, perhaps the first woman he loved who felt as deeply about him. Unfortunately, and for various possible reasons (Solomon [1977: 184–85] suggests Beethoven's reluctance to break up Antonie's marriage, his doubts stemming from previous rejections, and his fear of changing the circumstances of his life), renunciation is the thrust of his letter: "Look out into the beauties of nature and comfort your heart with that which must be."

At other times Beethoven wrote in terms of submission to Fate, on the one hand, or Providence, on the other. In the sketch books of 1816 (cited in Schauffler, 1929: 358) he writes: "Submission—submission! Thus may we win something even in the deepest misery, and make ourselves worthy to have God forgive our shortcomings. Fate, show your force! We are not lords over ourselves. What is determined must be, and so let it be!" And even earlier, in 1801, in a letter to Wegeler (cited in Newman, 1927: 63), he states, "I have often cursed my existence. *Plutarch taught me resignation.*"[4]

Thus, we have clear evidence of Beethoven's personal experience of resignation and his ability to generalize the concept in terms of both the secular (Fate) and the sacred (Providence). It is not unreasonable to assume, given the potential influences of Plutarch, Goethe, and Schiller, that Beethoven might have sought musical means to portray the experience of abnegation. Musical strategies might range from the more local (an immediate chord progression, found as early as the slow movement of the Piano Sonata, Op. 7, analyzed in Chapter 2), to the more global (the expressive genre of a movement, as in the case of the slow movement of Op. 106, analyzed in Chapter 1). In the latter case, the troping of the resignational second theme with the transcendent Neapolitan key area resulted in positive resignation, or abnegation, at a thematic level; the same progression found in Op. 7 then serves in Op. 106 as a hinge for the abnegational move to F♯ major in the recapitulation's thrust toward transcendence.

The new genre that appears to emerge, for Goethe as well as for Beethoven, is one in which tragic events are subsumed under a larger scheme that transforms them by abnegation, conceived as positively resigned acceptance that leads to a higher or better state. For Goethe that state resulted from striving toward improvement, understood in *Wilhelm Meister* an integration of the whole person. For Beethoven, it meant the serene transcendence of a spiritual victory, won not only through heroic striving (as in the *Hammerklavier* fugue) but through profound abnegation in the face of a tragic reality that cannot be cancelled.

GLOSSARY

The following terms are defined according to their semiotic use or sense in this study. Some of them have been appropriated from other fields, where their definitions may differ. Here, they form part of a coherent system, and thus their meanings interlock. The figure at the end of the glossary may be helpful in summarizing relationships among key terms.

ABDUCTION. Peirce's term for the kind of inference akin to hypothesis building, in which the theorist proposes a general principle to account for a series of observations. According to Peirce (1931: 5.171), abduction "is the only logical operation which introduces any new ideas; for induction does nothing but determine a value, and deduction merely evolves the necessary consequences of a true hypothesis."

ABNEGATION. Willed resignation as spiritual acceptance of a (tragic) situation that leads to a positive inner state, implying transcendence (see Appendix).

AFFORDANT. Adapted from Gibson (1966), used here to refer to those perceptual interpretive abilities that enhance and constrain our processing of sound through time. Affordances (such as those organizational feats Gestalt theory predicts) are the "default" level of physical processing, whose limits can be transcended by (emergent) cognitive acquisitions, such as the competency of a style. But extreme demands on cognitive (learned) organization may result in leakage, through which basic affordant modes of listening are reasserted by default.

ANALOGY. A logic of possibilities, based on the complete range of motivations (similarity, contiguity, etc.), and having the form A is to B as X is to Y. Analogy is in turn a higher form of motivation, but at best a provisional argument for reconstructing correlations or stylistic interpretations (i.e., more abductive than deductive).

ANOMALY. Aspect of a work which is antithetical to its presupposed style. Unusual events are often considered anomalous, especially when style is conceived as a set of prescriptive rules; such unusual events are often

287

merely atypical, since they conform to deeper principles, or they are stylistically accommodated by surrounding events (*see* COMPENSATION).

APEX. The highest pitch-registral point of a phrase or gesture. Not always the point of expressive focus (*see* CRUX).

ARBITRARY. According to Saussure, the state of most linguistic signs, as unmotivated other than by habit or usage. But since even habit and usage are motivations, arbitrariness is perhaps misleading (*see* CONVENTIONAL; SYMBOLIC). Furthermore, systematic motivations are usually active even if original motivations have been lost over time.

ARRIVAL SIX-FOUR. Expressively focal cadential six-four serving as resolution of thematic or tonal instabilities, often with a Picardy-third effect. Need not resolve to V; its rhetorical function may displace its syntactic function, at least locally.

ARTICULATION. Subdivision of a semantic space. Further articulation is achieved by type generation and by strategic markedness.

ASSOCIATION. Any motivated relationship. Correlations and interpretations are particular kinds of association.

CHANGE. For music, the consequence of extensive growth (regardless of its motivation or source) that can no longer be accommodated by the hierarchy of principles or constraints of a style, often (in Western style history) resulting in a reformulation of the hierarchy through change in one or more of its guiding principles. Change of style is a theoretical concept as well as a historical reality: since there are so many degrees of change, whether one defines a new style depends heavily on the level of one's investigation and the degree to which such differentiation is useful.

COMPENSATION. The adjustment in other musical entities or surrounding events to accommodate an extreme or atypical occurrence in a particular entity or event. Compensation preserves stylistic principles at a higher level, even when regularities (*see* RULES) are apparently exceeded.

COMPETENCY. In terms of music, the internalized (possibly tacit) cognitive ability of a listener to understand and apply stylistic principles, constraints, types, correlations, and strategies of interpretation to the understanding of musical works in that style. More than a lexicon of types or a set of rules.

CONSTRAINT. A limit on the possibilities of sound and meaning in music, either psychological (affordant), stylistic (emergent), or historical (resulting from a particular historical time, its technology, aesthetics, ideologies, etc.).

CONVENTIONAL. Motivated by habit or usage; understood as part of a style whether or not an iconic or indexical motivation is apparent; symbolic.

CONTIGUITY. Motivation for association based on juxtaposition or immediate contact. For music, the associations of a march draw heavily from its juxtaposition with military and ceremonial events. The "recitative chord" (major triad in first inversion) draws its suggestion of a level of direct discourse from its immediate contact with recitative in opera.

CORRELATION. Stylistic association between sound and meaning in music; structured (kept coherent) by oppositions, and mediated by markedness.

CULTURAL UNIT. "Anything that is culturally defined and distinguished as an entity" (D. Schneider, 1968: 2, as cited by Eco, 1976: 67). Anything a culture conceives as meaningful. May be oppositionally correlated with musical entities, or may actually be created as an interpretation for a musical event or work.

CRUX. The point of expressive focus or greatest intensity in a phrase or gesture. May or may not coincide with the apex; often created by a strategically marked event (dissonant harmony, dynamic accent, etc.).

DECODING. Identification or recognition of correlations whose understanding is so habitual as to appear automatic or transparent (*see* ENCODING).

DESIGNATUM. Peirce's term for an object in a sign relationship; substitute term used in place of "object," since not everything that is signified has an actual existence (e.g., a unicorn). Similar to CULTURAL UNIT.

DIACHRONIC. Saussure's term for the dimension of historical temporality and change in language. Opposite of SYNCHRONIC.

DIAGRAMMATIC. Peirce's term for isomorphism of structure, involving a mapping of corresponding parts regardless of different shape, form, domain, etc.

DISCOURSE. For music, loose term describing the strategic or thematic/topical flow of ideas in a musical work, as in "musical discourse" or "thematic discourse." Differing levels of discourse (or reflexivity of discourse) may be suggested by sudden shifts, or cued by the recitative topic.

EMERGENT. Cognitive (learned) competencies (stylistic and strategic) that go beyond the predictions or expectancies of psychological affordances. In music, a cadence that is not given strong textural articulation may not create a segmentation for a listener relying solely on Gestalt cues. Gestalt cues for affordant listening would favor what Leonard B. Meyer calls "secondary" or "statistical parameters" (1989: 15), and would require dramatic changes in such parameters—dynamic levels, rates of activity, texture, etc.—to define larger sections.

ENCODING. Term for the process by which a musical entity, its markedness, and its correlation become a systematic part of the style, creating a stylistic type.

ENTITY. For music, any process, event, or structure that can be defined oppositionally as a unit. A process at one level may be treated as an entity at the next higher level.

EQUIPOLLENT OPPOSITION. Opposition that "asserts the presence of contrary features"; "A versus B where A = not-B and B = not-A" (Battistella, 1990: 2). *Cf.* PRIVATIVE OPPOSITION.

EXPRESSIVE GENRE. Category of musical works based on their implementation of a change-of-state schema (tragic-to-triumphant, tragic-to-transcendent) or their organization of expressive states in terms of an overarching topical field (pastoral, tragic).

FORMAL SCHEME. Category of musical works based on tonal and/or thematic organization. Formal schemes often have inherently dramatic elements, but they are conceived more structurally and less expressively than expressive genres.

GROWTH. Term for such creativity and change as can be accommodated within the (expanding) levels of a style, without requiring substantial reformulation or reorganization of those levels.

HERMENEUTIC. Originating with methods of interpreting the Bible, and long a part of literary criticism; appropriated in this century by Kretschmar (1902) for musical expressive meaning. Here, the term refers to an interpretive approach to any meaning that goes beyond the purely structural or "syntactic" (implicational, functional), drawing on evidence from any relevant source to (abductively) reconstruct (stylistically guided) strategic interpretations.

HIERARCHY. As applied to a style or a work, organization in terms of levels. As opposed to layers, levels need not be organized in the same way, or according to the same principles (cf. Leonard B. Meyer's "fallacy of hierarchic uniformity," 1967: 96–97). Styles are not strictly hierarchical but have the flexibility of more networklike connections as well.

ICONIC. Motivation for association based on similarity, whether of properties or of structure. The latter, structural variety may also be termed isomorphic or diagrammatic.

IMPLICATION. Stylistic expectation (i.e., coded in the style). Based on Leonard B. Meyer (1973) and Eugene Narmour (1977), the implication-realization model assumes that implications (melodic, harmonic, rhythmic) have expected stylistic realizations. Expressive meaning may emerge and be further enhanced or developed by denials of implication, or by varying degrees of deferral or delay in subsequent realization.

INDEXICAL. Motivation for association based on a dynamic relationship between two entities, whether by contiguity, synecdoche, cause-and-effect, stimulus-reaction, deixis (pointing), or ostension ("showing" of a token to convey its type).

INTERPRETANT. Peirce's term for an idea that the sign-designatum relation gives rise to; an interpretation as it mediates the sign-designatum relationship for some (community of) user(s). Part of his triadic conception of semiosis, the interpretant can in turn be conceived as a sign, producing its own interpretant(s). Thus, semiosis is in theory infinite, but in practice (pragmatically) one can reach a workable limit for a given purpose.

INTERPRETATION. Used in two senses: the act of interpreting, going further than correlation; and the result of that act, an interpretation of (expressive or other) meaning in a work, which result may become generalized as a correlation in the style.

INTERTEXTUALITY. As defined for music (Hatten, 1985), the use of (parts of) earlier styles (pastiche or parody) or identifiable (allusions to) works from the home style or earlier styles to enhance the discourse of a musical work. I have not included uses of recurrent types or events that are formulaic in the home style, since privileging those relationships would lead to a more-radical concept of intertextuality in which the work has existence only as an intersection of a network of codes, discourses, and other musical "texts." That would, in my view, diminish the crucial individuality of an artistic "text," at least for most Western music aesthetics.

INVARIANT. To the extent that this can be determined, the unchanging features or oppositions that define a TYPE. TOKENS have invariant and variant features; the latter provide possibilities for style growth by the emergence new types.

IRONY. For music, the bracketing, reversal, or negation of some portion of a musical discourse, so as to undercut its sincerity, and suggest its intentional extravagance (*see* ROMANTIC IRONY).

ISOMORPHISM. Motivation for association on the basis of similar shape or form (as opposed to similarity of qualities or properties). Stronger form of iconism.

ISOTOPY. From Greimas (1966) and Eco (1979, 1984), as applied to music by Grabócz (1986) and Tarasti (1985). My definition: a higher-level expressive topic that dominates the interpretation of topics and entities in its domain.

LEVEL(S) OF ATTENDING. Conjectural level(s) on which a listener might focus during a first hearing, assuming that lower levels would be more automatically processed and higher levels would require more thoughtful reflection. Although strategic markedness is calculated to create or capture a level of attending, artistic interpretation embraces the complete work.

MARKEDNESS. The asymmetrical valuation of an opposition (in musical structure, language, culture). For musical meaning, markedness of structural oppositions correlates with markedness of (expressive or other) oppositions among cultural units. Marked entities have a greater (relative) specificity of meaning than do unmarked entities. Marked entities also have a narrower distribution, which means that they tend to occur in fewer contexts, and thus (usually) less often than their unmarked opposites. Stylistic meaning in music is systematically secured by correlations of oppositions between musical structures and cultural units, as mediated by markedness values. Other motivations (iconic, indexical) may underlie the history of such correlations, but their coherence in a functioning style is tied to their systematic motivation in terms of correlations of marked oppositions.

MARKEDNESS ASSIMILATION. The tendency of marked entities to occur in marked contexts (Andersen, 1968, 1972; Battistella, 1990: 7). When this principle is applied to music, it means that there will be sufficient redundancy of marked expressive meaning to ensure interpretation of the new (strategically marked) in terms of the old (stylistically marked).

METAPHOR. In music itself, figurative meaning based on the interaction within a functional location of two previously unrelated or separately derived stylistic types. In discourse about music, nonliteral expressive or other predicates appearing in descriptive accounts of musical meaning, used in order to suggest a closer, more authentic interpretation of musical meaning than could be conveyed by literal language alone. The responsible use of metaphorical language is grounded in established stylistic correlations and interpretations.

METONYMY. In music, figurative meaning based on the syntagmatic interaction between two previously unrelated types.

MOTIVATION. Basis for correlation of sound and meaning. Original motivations may be irretrievable, but systematic motivations which must exist for a correlation to remain in the style will involve markedness oppositions. "Convention" often merely implies habit, and thus offers little of explanatory value, since habit alone is perhaps the least efficient means of encoding meaning. If "conventions" imply rules (in the sense of habits of correlation), systematic motivation involves the underlying mechanism coordinating those habits and enabling their efficient acquisition.

PARADIGMATIC. Used to describe relations among classes of entities that may be substituted for one another. If one visualizes a horizontal syntagmatic axis of temporal relationships, then the paradigmatic axis may be conceived as a vertical axis above each slot in a sequence, providing a stack of entities that are defined paradigmatically by their appropriate use in each slot. Examples for music include the class of sonorities that may be used to convey dominant function, or the various doubling tokens for a chord type.

PRINCIPLE. In terms of style, a broad guiding idea, such as symmetrical resolution, balance, or compensation, that can translate into a wide range of strategic implementations, whether or not any particular implementation occurs more than once. Thus, a stylistic principle can be a more helpful concept than a rule in that its greater generality permits interpretation of what might otherwise be misconstrued as an anomaly, when the event is merely an atypical strategic implementation.

PRIVATIVE OPPOSITION. "Opposition between the presence and absence of a feature—between A and not-A" (Battistella, 1990: 2).

REFLEXIVITY. For music, the ability of a work to suggest (musical) discourse about (commentary upon) its own discourse; often implies a critical perspective on that discourse (as in the case of Romantic irony).

ROMANTIC IRONY. Reflexivity of discourse, especially implying an author (persona) projecting above the discourse in order to comment critically upon it. Originated in literary theory with Friedrich Schlegel in 1798, but applicable to earlier writers such as Cervantes and Shakespeare; for music, see Longyear (1970). Often cued by drastic shifts (especially of style or topic, and especially late in a work where there is less chance of a thematic working out or rationalization) or by the recitative topic.

RULE. Generally, an account of a typicality in the style, not to be confused with a prescription for behavior by either composer or listener, other than as a habit of correlation or stylistic interpretation.

SEMANTIC SPACE. Eco's (1976: 125) substitute term for code in characterizing the semantic system of language; a "complex network of subcodes," more like an encyclopedia than a dictionary. For music, the expressive realm of a style, as articulated into topical fields, and further articulated by strategies, tropes, and the like.

SEMIOTICS. The discipline focusing on modes of signification (semiosis), the varieties of sign processes, and the various motivations for signification. As used here, a semiotics of music embraces STRUCTURALIST (stylistic correlations mediated by markedness) and HERMENEUTIC (strategies of interpretation) approaches.

SIGNIFIER/SIGNIFIED. [Saussure: *signifiant/signifié*]. Components of the sign, akin to vehicle/content. For Saussure, the relationship between signifier and signified in language is arbitrary, and signifiers articulate a differential or oppositional field of meaning ("meaning is difference"). The dyadic model of signification lacks the crucial *interpretant*, or interpretive mediation between (in music) sound and meaning, as in Peirce's triadic model.

STRUCTURALIST. Term loosely characterizing any method, especially one dealing with oppositions, concerned with reconstructing underlying, systematic relationships of form and meaning. As used here, structuralism does not imply a formalism divorced from expressive meaning, but the oppositional organization of broader categories of expressive meaning (cultural units). Hermeneutic approaches to interpretation of a work are required in order to tease out more specific meanings.

STYLE. For music, that competency in semiosis presupposed by a work, and necessary for its understanding as a work of music. Competency in interpretation implies an understanding of correlations, and is guided by a hierarchy of principles (ensuring flexibility) and constraints (ensuring coherence).

STYLISTIC REGISTER. For the Classical period, high, middle, or low style, corresponding to contexts of performance and carrying associations based on those locations and audiences. In general, a sociologically oriented level of communication, cued by features associated with degrees of formality as appropriate to various social situations.

SYMBOLIC. One motivation for correlation or interpretation, based on convention, habit, or rule (in the sense of regularity or typicality). Saussure considered the sign to be arbitrary, but it is safer to assume that other motivations (iconic, indexical) involved in the origins of that convention have simply been lost.

SYNCHRONIC. Saussure's term for the system of language at a particular historical moment or period. For music, a synchronic study would be the study of a musical style; a diachronic study would be the study of style change.

SYNECDOCHE. Motivation for correlation or interpretation on the basis of part-for-whole relationship.

SYNTAGMATIC. Akin to syntactic, used to describe relations along a temporal axis. For music, harmonic implication (function) would be considered part of a syntagmatic competency. The syntagmatic axis is not purely formal (syntactic), but may include temporal sequences of topics (expressive genres) or strategic working-out of an idea (thematic discourse).

SYSTEMATIC. Internally motivated and coherent. Markedness is a systematic motivation ensuring the coherence of correlation in a style.

THEMATIC. That which is made significant for a work (strategic), and thus important for its ongoing discourse.

THEMATIC CLOSURE. Resolution of inherent tension within, or conflicts between, themes. Thematic closure is often strategically unique, rather than stylistically prescribed (as opposed to stylistic tonal closure).

THEMATIC INTEGRATION. The process of relating two oppositional themes in a work, usually as part of a strategy leading to some kind of mediation, if not resolution, of their conflict.

THEMATIZATION. The process of making thematic. [An awkward term, admittedly, but useful as a nominalization of a process.]

TOKEN. The physical manifestation (either in sound or in notation) of a stylistic type.

TOPIC. A complex musical correlation originating in a kind of music (fanfare, march, various dances, learned style, etc.; Ratner, 1980), used as part of a larger work. Topics may acquire expressive correlations in the Classical style, and they may be further interpreted expressively.

TOPICAL FIELD. Larger areas such as the tragic, the pastoral, the heroic, and the *buffa* that are supported by topical oppositions.

TROPE. Figurative meaning in music. TROPING involves a species of creative growth that goes beyond the typical articulation of established types and their implied hierarchy. Troping akin to metaphor occurs when two different, formally unrelated types are brought together in the same functional location so as to spark an interpretation based on their interaction.

TYPE. A generalized category or concept. Types can tolerate a range of variation in their manifestation (as tokens) without losing their identity. Specifying precisely the invariant features preserving the identity of a type may not always be possible, since a type is often understood more along the line of "family resemblances" (Wittgenstein, [1933–35] 1958) among its tokens.

UNDERCODING. Term developed by Eco (1976) for one kind of ABDUCTION akin to provisional interpretation of a work in a less-familiar style: "a sort of imprecise coding" when the code is not known, or "the operation by means of which in the absence of reliable pre-established rules, certain macroscopic portions of certain texts are provisionally assumed to be pertinent units of a code in formation, even though the combinational rules governing the more basic compositional items of the expressions [i.e., musical entities], along with the corresponding content-units, remain unknown" (135–36).

USAGE. Motivation by habit. Perhaps the most elementary means of encoding (and least efficient by itself), usage is generally supported by a SYSTEMATIC interrelationship of the new with the old, as well as other kinds of motivation or association.

WORK. For music, a piece, movement, or movement cycle as stylistically reconstructed and competently understood. I have not attempted to specify the musical work as delimited by its notation, or by some limited set of "compliant" performances (Goodman, 1968) or interpretations. In my reconstruction of expressive meaning in musical works of Beethoven, I have been concerned with historical stylistic competency (not competency enhanced by knowledge of later styles) and a dialectic between the reconstruction of style and work (whereby each insight with respect to one contributes to the reconstruction of the other).

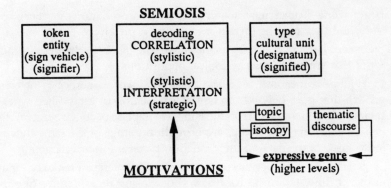

MOTIVATIONS

I. Systematic:

- **Markedness;**

- **Hierarchy of <u>stylistic</u> principles and constraints**

II. Interpretive:

- **Abduction/undercoding;**
  <u>Strategic</u> Markedness

- **Associations via:**

similarity/isomorphism/ diagrammatic/analogy	= <u>iconic</u>
contiguity/synecdoche/ ostention/deixis/cause-effect	= <u>indexical</u>
conventional/arbitrary habit/rule/law	= <u>symbolic</u>

- **Troping:**
  metaphor
  metonymy
  irony

- **Reflexivity of discourse:**
  Romantic irony
  intertextuality

Semiotic terminology.

NOTES

Introduction

1. For important work on the former, see Wallace (1986) and Burnham (1990, 1992). For an illuminating study of the latter, see Neubauer (1986). I consider Eduard Hanslick's ideas in some detail in Chapter 9 because of their influence on current formalist tendencies. For example, Kivy (1990a) considers the first movement of Op. 131 an example of "music alone," whereas my approach to the movement (Chapter 6) reveals a wealth of expressive meaning not accounted for by formal analysis of fugal procedures.

2. Other surveys of this growing international field include Powers (1980), Newcomb (1984b), Lidov (1986), and Hatten and Henrotte (1988). Book-length studies of music semiotics include Coker (1972), Nattiez (1975, 1990), Stefani (1976), R. Schneider (1980), Faltin (1985), Jiránek (1985), Karbusicky (1986), and Tarasti (forthcoming). Book-length analytical applications to specific repertoires include those based primarily on Saussurean semiotics (Noske [1977], Agawu [1991]), Greimasian semiotics (Grabócz, 1986), and Peircean semiotics (Mosley, 1990). Review articles of significant theoretical scope include Lidov (1977, 1980) and Hatten (1980).

3. See Hatten (1989, 1990) and Chapter 10, below, for further critique of recent approaches to music cognition.

I. A Case Study for Interpretation

1. Italicized terms and concepts receive more detailed theoretical treatment in the following chapters, where their further refinement can draw upon exemplification here. Reference to the capsule definitions given in the Glossary may be helpful for the reader who wishes to proceed systematically.

2. I use the term hermeneutics in its traditional sense as a method of interpretation that probes for meaning within literary works. Hermann Kretzschmar (1902) was perhaps the first to appropriate this term for the analysis of expressive meaning in music; it has been revived more recently by Edward T. Cone (1981) and Lawrence Kramer (1990); see also Hatten (1987b). My approach differs

considerably from Kretzschmar's in its grounding in a theory of style, as well as in its proposals for a more rigorous accounting of structural oppositions.

3. Martin Cooper ([1970] 1985: 165–66) speaks of a "momentary shaft of light" and "the voice of a consolation" in countering earlier interpretations of the movement (Lenz [1855], Sullivan [1927]) cast solely in terms of lamentation or despair. Compare the consequent phrase of the first theme in the second movement of Mozart's Piano Concerto in A major, K. 488. The theme is in F♯ minor, and the end of the consequent phrase ascends two octaves with an arpeggiated Neapolitan before dropping back to the tragic register to complete the phrase. The parenthetical Neapolitan expansion in Mozart has an effect similar to Beethoven's. A less extreme example occurs in m. 34 of Bach's Prelude in F♯ minor, WTC II, where the bass shifts up an octave for a one-measure stasis on the Neapolitan. Such earlier (and later—see note 14) uses of similar compositional techniques add an *intertextual* dimension to expressive meaning. Intertextuality is defined and discussed in Chapter 7.

4. I was introduced to this striking term by Walter Robert, Professor Emeritus of Piano at Indiana University, and an inspiring teacher of piano literature.

5. Charles Rosen (1972: 426) and Martin Cooper ([1970] 1985: 166) refer to the figuration as Chopinesque.

6. Alternatively, one might characterize the hymn as more inward and profound in its monumental aspects, and the aria as more external in its giving vent to a public utterance, albeit within the decorum provided by a very formal accompaniment.

7. On the term "accommodate" and its implications for a critique of Schenkerian analysis, see Eugene Narmour (1977: 41–47).

8. Further justification for this interpretation is found in Chapter 2 and in the Appendix.

9. Indeed, Brahms's rather pastoral Second Symphony opens with the same four-note motive (D–C♯–D–A) that appears across the barline (mm. 49–50).

10. Note that I do not specify what is being accepted, nor do I claim to know what the subject of the tragedy is, other than to suggest that it is spiritual (psychological, inner, profound). Music can be exquisitely specific in its tracking of emotional response, without being the least bit forthcoming about the situation that has provoked it. Dwelling on the impossibility of retrieving the latter has, I believe, led aestheticians astray in denying or neglecting an explanation of the former.

As for the intentionality of an emotion, the very consistency with which a composer exploits an expressive "language" (or its stylistic correlations) must suffice to confirm the only intentionality for which we have evidence, in the case of nonprogrammatic works. That we routinely hear Beethoven expressively, in at least a rudimentary way, is evident in the use of labels such as "tragic," "heroic," and "triumphant," or characterizations such as "victory symphony" (Ratner, 1980: 155).

11. Barry Cooper (1990: 52) notes that 1817 was a "depressing year" in which Beethoven "completed virtually nothing of substance," and thus the choice of song text may have a biographical motivation. Nevertheless, I would argue that Beethoven interprets the text with a sense for the positive aspect of resignation, even if abnegation is not the issue here (see below).

12. William Drabkin (1991: 137) lists the programmatic comments Beethoven wrote in the sketches for the Agnus Dei; in Artaria 180, p. 15, the annotation "pacem pastoralisch" indicates a clear connection between the idea of peace and its expression by means of a pastoral topic. Drabkin argues that Beethoven moved from a "naively programmatic" Agnus Dei to a formal design incorporating aspects of sonata and concerto (151–54). I would add that formal design need not be construed as a sublimation of topical and programmatic significance, since form can also enhance the expressive force of a topical expressive genre.

13. See the Appendix for a cultural treatment of this important concept.

14. See Chapter 7.

15. Compare the ascending scales setting and accompanying the "Et ascendit in coelum," from the Credo of Beethoven's *Missa Solemnis*. William Kinderman (1985) analyzes the consistent use of referential sonorities in the Mass, including the association of a specific sonority in a high register with heaven.

16. Brahms, in his Capriccio in F♯ minor, Op. 76, no. 1, heightens the intensity of thematic recapitulation with the same violinistic octave displacements (mm. 54–61) that Beethoven exploits in his recapitulation. For Beethoven, the effect is to integrate the personal expressivity of the aria's texture with the harmonic progression of the hymn. Brahms exploits a more straightforward rhetorical effect as he leads to a minor "arrival six-four" (m. 60) that climaxes the tragic import of the theme. But he allows the light of potential transcendence to shine through with F♯ major through a Picardy third in the codetta (still problematized by mixture), and he also elects the same wide spacing for his closing F♯ major chords as found in the *Hammerklavier* movement.

17. James Webster's (1991) magisterial account of Haydn's F♯ minor symphony (the "Farewell") offers striking parallels, including the "ethereal realm" of a D-major interlude (instead of G) in the first movement that is associated with a "transcendent" resolution into F♯ major at the end of the symphony, over twenty-five minutes later (m. 372). I will trace a multimovement expressive genre in less detail with the analysis of Beethoven's Piano Sonata in A major, Op. 101, in Chapter 4.

II. Correlation, Intepretation, and the Markedness of Oppositions

1. This fundamental dialectic is irreducible despite the hierarchy of styles (Classical style, Beethoven's style, Beethoven's late style) among which one

may shift at various times in an investigation. The work itself is not simply the lowest level of that hierarchy, as implied by Nattiez's "inverted pyramid" (1990: 136).

Only in the twentieth century do we find that a radically novel work may demand a concept of style derived from that work alone. Even in such an extreme case, however, there would be a clear distinction between the stylistic competency presupposed by the work and the actual play upon that competency. Otherwise, one would have to concede that the work has no style in the sense that I conceive it, namely, that there is no generalizable set of principles and constraints guiding compositional choices in the work and flexible enough to embrace unpredictable, but comprehensible, creative strategies. Compare Leonard Meyer's definition of style, as "a replication of patterning, whether in human behavior or in the artifacts produced by human behavior, that results from a series of choices made within some set of constraints" (1989: 3). My use of the term *strategic* is indebted to Leonard Meyer (1973) and Eugene Narmour (1977).

Another way of expressing the difference between style and work is by contrasting the pairs "type/token" and "set/member." The two terms in the latter pair are at the same epistemological level, in that both the set of all members and the individual members themselves could be said to exist at the same level of reality. The former pair, type/token, distinguishes between the abstraction of a type (which exists only in terms of a cognitive category) and its potentially limitless manifestations (as tokens, in various works, whether individually differentiated or not). I apply this distinction to stylistic types and strategic tokens in what follows.

2. For more on Ludwig Wittgenstein's original transitive/intransitive distinction, see Richard Wollheim (1968: 82ff.).

3. I differentiate style growth and change in a manner analogous to the distinction between variation and change in evolutionary theory. A species can undergo a great deal of variation among individuals, but it is only when a subset of those individuals form an exclusive reproductive group that a new species must be considered to have evolved. For musical styles, change is theoretically understood when one can no longer fully understand a style as merely extending an existing style, but must invoke new principles or constraints that significantly alter the hierarchy or system of the previous style(s) from which a new style emerges. For further discussion of this distinction, see Hatten (1982: 129–86); for an example of hierarchical reformulation applied to the development of a new level of harmonic progression in Monteverdi, see Susan McClary (1976).

4. See also Lieberman, *Intonation, Perception, and Language* (1967) and *The Biology and Evolution of Language* (1984).

5. For an example of the problems encountered in accounting for even relatively formal operations and functions by means of a purely surface segmen-

tation, see the extended fable concerning analysis of an imaginary primitive repertoire in Hatten (1982: 136–43).

My critique (1980a) of Nattiez's (1975) "paradigmatic" analysis is that it involved just this type of mechanistic segmentation, based primarily on units defined by repetition and variation. Nattiez (1990) still holds to the validity of "explicit criteria" for determining units at a neutral level of score analysis, before deciding their relevance to poietic (composer, creation) and esthesic (listener, reception) levels of analysis. Whether the explicit criteria have advanced beyond those of the *Fondements* (1975) remains to be seen in his forthcoming volume devoted to semiological analysis. But methodologically I cannot endorse a neutral level, even if the analyst is not neutral, because in my view the expressive significance of an entity must already enter into its identification as a unit. Explicit criteria are not possible even at the level of defining stylistic types, and it is at the level of the style, not the work, that a more structuralist approach is best suited. Furthermore, despite the inevitability of imprecision in terminology and disagreement in analyses, our current understanding of tonality is sufficient to avoid all but the most subtle of disagreements about segmentation. We need not substitute a novel analytical device merely to ensure consistency in segmentation, since the only reliable device would have to have all the competencies of style enfolded into its algorithm—making such an analytical tool more poeitic (or esthesic) than neutral (to say nothing of its impracticality).

Those familiar with Nattiez's *Music and Discourse* (1990) may find a few similar concerns addressed in my study, which was virtually complete before I had the opportunity to review (Hatten, 1992a) his recent semiological project. Although I hold different ideas as to the epistemology and effective methodologies of music semiotics, I admire the intellectual curiosity that has led him to embrace the widest possible range of semiotic influences (including ethnomusicological and twentieth-century compositional sources), and to address a range of important concerns (including a critical examination of discourse about music).

Finally, while I recognize that my analytical approaches would fail his criteria for explicit procedures (since even markedness cannot be mechanistically applied), I trust that there is sufficient "rigor" and clarity in my approach to permit intelligent criticism of its results.

6. Cogan (1984: 123–52) analyzes the characteristics of tone color in terms of a table of thirteen oppositions, drawing on the insights of distinctive features in phonology, as distinguished from phonetics. Although he also describes "archetypal designs," such as the progressive transformation of color from one pole of an opposition to the other (and back), as compositional strategies, he does not invoke the theory of markedness at any point in his study. After completing my own work I did discover a predecessor in Marshall Brown (1992: 79–80). His brief discussion provides an eloquent introduction to the

central concept and shows how it applies to general stylistic oppositions in nineteenth-century music. McCreless (1991) develops an application of markedness to chromaticism, citing an earlier draft of my book for the concept.

7. Battistella claims that "this opposition shows the asymmetry characteristic of markedness," but "it is not apparent whether the best analysis is in terms of equipollent contraries male and female or privative complementarities female and nonfemale" (Battistella 1990: 16).

8. Another explanation for the Gluck example is that of ironic troping (see Chapter 7). This is possible due to the clear cueing of dramatic context.

9. Peter Laki (1985) has pointed out that oppositions of meter (duple vs. triple) or tempo may be more relevant for this distinction in the earlier Baroque.

10. For an interesting expressive interpretation of the *Waldstein*, see Wilfrid Mellers (1983: 108–26).

11. See Andersen (1968: 175) and (1972: 44–45), cited by Battistella, for the origin of this concept; compare its treatment by Shapiro (1983: 84).

12. Unfortunately, there is nearly equipollent opposition between male for doctor and female for nurse in our culture. The popular riddle about the doctor who cannot operate on the boy who has lost his father in an accident because "he's my son" exposes our unwitting bias in this respect.

13. Originally appearing in the Renaissance, the Picardy third was conceived as more closural since the major triad was deemed a more perfect consonance than the minor. Both were imperfect compared to the perfect fifth, octave, or unison, but those open-intervallic cadence sonorities were being replaced by triadic closes. A further, Romantic interpretation of the Picardy third views the resolution as akin to redemption. This interpretation helps support the interpretation of "salvation" for an "arrival six-four" that shifts to major mode, since the effect of mutation is analogous.

14. Other motivations include those based on similarity, contiguity (proximity), and synecdoche (part for whole). See Chapter 10.

15. Richard Strauss drew upon the model of Beethoven's *Eroica* for the heroic ("E♭ and a lot of horns"), but the distant key of D major could be put to the same use (because of the martial associations of trumpets, and since D major is a practical key for trumpets in D). Pastoral major keys for Beethoven range from F (Sixth Symphony) to D (Piano Sonata, Op. 28), and I will argue that the Piano Sonata in A, Op. 101, is pastoral as well. In the high Baroque, G major was popular. Among the examples Herman Jung (1980) gives are Handel's "Beneath the vine, or figtree's shade" from Act II of *Solomon*, 1748; and the chorus from *Israel in Egypt*, "But as for His people, He led them forth like sheep." Even earlier, G minor was a possibility (Vivaldi, Solo Sonata VI; Corelli, Concerto Grosso, Op. 6, no. 8), which supports the thesis that minor vs. major was not marked for tragic until later. Such a variety of keys argues against the inherent qualities of keys. In cases of equal-tempered tuning, there

is no internal difference among keys in the same mode when considered in isolation.

16. Another instance of emphasis on sonority, involving inversion of the V^7, is found in the first movement of Op. 101, which is analyzed in Chapter 4.

17. Compare the discussion in Chapter 10 of Alban Berg's use of white-key clusters in *Lulu*.

18. For a complete analysis of this passage with respect to harmonic ambiguity and implication, see Hatten (1980b). A similar analysis appears in Lawrence Kramer (1984: 60–66).

19. Still another, rhetorical meaning of the initiatory diminished seventh is as a cue for the recitative topic. See the discussion with respect to levels of discourse in Chapter 7.

20. A similar process is worked out in greater detail for cognitive concepts in the fascinating study *Semantics and Cognition* (1983) by Ray Jackendoff.

21. Barry Cooper (1990: 72) notes that for Beethoven a suspension and its resolution sounded simultaneously is "a common mistake in his counterpoint exercises of 1793" that also appears in later works.

22. For more on the interpretant, see the discussion of C. S. Peirce in Chapters 9 and 10.

23. Intertextual relationships (Hatten, 1986) may sustain these markedness values even when the style does not encode them. See Chapter 7 for further discussion.

24. A semiotic analysis of text-music relationships in Beethoven's settings of "Sehnsucht" and other Mignon poems from *Wilhelm Meisters Lehrjahre* may be found in William Dougherty (1989).

25. For more on the concept of the dialogical and on the use of a variety of "voices" in the novel, see Bakhtin (1981). The relevant concept can be made familiar to English readers in terms of the varieties of indirect discourse, by which means the narrator can assume various "voices" (not limited to a simple narrative point of view) for any of the characters, or appropriate various social "discourses" (the means of expression and biases of cultural institutions such as the law, religion, etc.). The novelist can play these various "voices" or discourses against each other, almost the way one can "dialogize" various arguments or perspectives in one's own thought processes. In Beethoven, the dramatization of a kind of "double-mindedness" in the cadential theme of the first movement of Op. 101 is comparable. *Intertextual* uses of other styles (as, for example, in the transition to the last movement of the *Hammerklavier*, see Rosen 1972: 428) can move still further toward the "polyphony of voices" that Bakhtin found so characteristic of the novel at its best.

26. Other displacements that "problematize" significant themes by reversing a scale-degree or chromatic voice leading implication may be found in the main theme of the *Eroica* ($\hat{1}$–$\hat{7}$–$\sharp\hat{6}$!), and in the Florestan motive from *Fidelio* (prom-

inent in the opening of the *Leonore* Overture No. 3, Op. 72a, mm. 9ff., and featuring 3̂–♯2̂–♮2̂!).

27. Roger Kamien (1974) discusses chromatic motives as used thematically in this movement, as well as in the Scherzo and Rondo which follow. His analysis is formal in its orientation, but it goes further than mine in relating still other chromatic events in the slow movement.

28. Lawrence Kramer (1990: 190–203) analyzes this movement extensively in terms of its productive oppositions, leading to an account of its narrative effects. The disturbances of musical discourse are then linked to melancholy as it is represented in literary narrative by analogous disturbances of narrative level and flow.

29. Pierre Bourdieu (1977). See citation in Hatten (1982: 36) of Bourdieu's "strategies of timing" (1977: 6–9). See also Lawrence Kramer (1990: 10–11) on implications of Bourdieu's "habitus" of the social sphere.

III. From Topic to Expressive Genre

1. Kofi Agawu (1991: 26–30) offers a historical account of topics that complements Ratner's. He explores topics as signs for a semiotic analysis of Classical works by Haydn, Mozart, and Beethoven. Unfortunately, there is very little attempt to interpret the expressive significance of these signs; nevertheless, Agawu offers an insightful analysis of their interaction with Schenkerian voice-leading structures and a "beginning-middle-end" paradigm that governs phrase and section construction. For further discussion and critique, see Hatten (1992a).

2. The Fantasy is marked with respect to sonata, even though a "not sonata" formulation might have suggested unmarkedness. Possession of a feature (e.g., sonata form or style) is not a guarantee of evaluation as marked. Of course, one can also characterize an absence positively: "not A" may be defined as a feature, rather than mere absence of a feature.

3. For a discussion of schemata as applied to phrase structure in Classical music, see Robert Gjerdingen (1988).

4. The typological-vs.-processive issue was raised in conversation with Rudolf Arnheim in 1987. My belief is that the theory presented here entails both a competency in recognition (e.g., of rhetorical figures, as in Baroque *Affektenlehre*) and a competency in processing (e.g., of implications and their realizations, as in Meyer's [1973] theory). Of course, expressive interpretation takes place at both stages (identification and processing).

Ultimately, a process may be understood (or hypostatized) at a higher level as an entity (see Meyer [1973: 53, 90] on the alternation of processes and forms in levels of a hierarchy). That entity may then be generalized as a type. Hierarchy, conceived in Meyer's sense, reconciles the potential conflict between claims of temporal process and atemporal type (or entity).

5. Herman Jung (1980) traces the pastoral from its literary roots in antiquity through its musical manifestations in late Medieval, Renaissance, and Baroque styles. Ellen Harris (1980) examines the pastoral in Handel.

For Classical music, F. E. Kirby (1970) treats the pastoral as creating the "characteristic" symphony or sonata. Michael Broyles (1987: 204–205) identifies Beethoven's Fourth Symphony as drawing upon many of the same pastoral devices as the Sixth Symphony (primarily the use of stasis). Ratner (1980) deals with the *musette* and the *pastorale* as topics, without identifying a larger pastoral genre or mode. Allanbrook (1983) goes further, not only identifying the siciliano and various gavotte types as pastoral, but also *interpreting* the pastoral as signifying a "private world" in Mozart's *The Marriage of Figaro*, one that serves to "protect" the relationships of Susanna with the Countess and with Figaro (185).

In his work with nineteenth-century Czech (nationalist) music, Michael Beckerman suggests an interpretation of the pastoral as depicting "the 'eternal present' of the folk as opposed to the dialectical struggle to assert national rights" (personal communication).

6. Paul Alpers (1992) recommends the pastoral be considered a mode, not a genre. I opt for the latter term (conditioned as expressive rather than formal) since "mode" already refers to scale type in music.

7. From his letters, we know that Beethoven was familiar with the Wilhelm Schlegel translation of Shakespeare's plays and with Goethe's literary works, in particular *Wilhelm Meisters Lehrjahre* and Part I of *Faust* (the second parts of *Wilhelm Meister* and *Faust* were not completed in time for Beethoven to have read them). His copies of Shakespeare and Goethe show many annotations in pencil.

8. Gary Tomlinson (1987) underlines the importance of Guarini for Monteverdi's poetics. He emphasizes the mixture of "comic and tragic actions and characters and of magnificent and elegant styles" (20), and traces that fusion to Pietro Bembo's *Prose della volgar lingua* (1525), in which Petrarch and Boccaccio were said to have varied their poetry and prose respectively by such mixings of style. Guarini's motivation, however, was greater realism. Kegel-Brinkgreve (1990: 38) notes the mixture of high and low styles as early as the Idylls of Theocritus (275 B.C.), undoubtedly for similar reasons.

9. Neither Ratner nor Agawu (1991: 26–30) presents topics in a systematically hierarchical way. Description by features and properties drawn inconsistently from different musical parameters and levels is perhaps a less theoretical but necessary first stage in their inventory. Allanbrook (1983: 31–70), however, presents a helpful oppositional classification of dance types by meter, tempo, and high, middle, or low style.

10. Indeed, Ratner (1980: 387) cites an article by Daniel Weber (1800) on comic music in the Classical style in which comedy is classified as the "non-

tragic category," including such types as "mimicry, wit, parody, and artful imitation of musical bungling."

11. The consequence of the unmarked comic is a wider range of content. Interestingly, this greater range of possibility may account for the fact, mentioned in Chapter 2, that earlier attempts to deal with meaning in Beethoven's music (for example, Sullivan [1927]), have typically focused on tragic works in minor keys, such as the *Appassionata*, as opposed to less-specifiable pieces in major, such as the *Waldstein*.

12. See Longyear (1970), Bonds (1991), and Chapter 7, below, for further discussion of Romantic irony.

13. Ratner (1980: 386) cites Johann Sulzer, who ranks levels of comedy as low (farcical, absurd), middle (fine wit, urbanity), and high—"that comedy which approaches the tragedy in content and mood, and where powerful and serious passions come into play" (*Allgemeine Theorie der schönen Künste*, 1774–1779: 212–13). The high category in Sulzer's division recalls the tragicomic category discussed earlier; for the present discussion, the seriousness of high comedy is the relevant factor.

14. Martin Cooper (1985: 156), in discussing the last movement of Op. 101, insists on the "unadulteratedly musical" aspect of its meaning, yet admits such characterizations as "good humour" and "the acceptance and transfiguration of suffering." Lawrence Kramer (1990: 21–71) comes much closer to the spirit of expressive genre intended here, while expanding on its interpretation, in his brilliant analyses of "expressive doubling" in the two-movement piano sonatas of Beethoven. Kramer distinguishes moves toward "transfiguration" (Op. 90, Op. 111) from moves toward "travesty" (Op. 54, Op. 78); the former is "utopian" (low to high) while the latter is "inverted" (high to low style) (37). Kramer's concept goes further than the theory of expressive genres outlined in this chapter, in that for each movement pair, the second movement "tropes" (36) the first as an "expressive doubling," or reinterpretation, of premises, ideas, or perspectives central to the first movement's formal or expressive organization.

Troping is treated in some detail in Chapter 7; the discussion of this fundamental process is primarily at the topical level, but a trope such as "abnegation" has clear consequences for the interpretation of expressive genre, as suggested in Chapter 1.

Since Kramer (1990) and the present work were completed independently of each other, points of correspondence are gratifying and divergences are illuminating. I will note these as they occur. In general, my approach leans more toward the structuralist, his more toward the hermeneutic, yet we share a concern for cultural modeling and a penchant for oppositional analyses. His development of cultural tropes drawn from literature is exemplified by my own approach to *abnegation* in the Appendix. The speculative interpretations of Kramer are well supported by the kinds of evidence he brings to bear, and our approaches are quite complementary, given our mutual concern for hermeneutic exploration.

15. Kerman (1985b: 116) provides several examples of naive, rustic, and "countrified" strains in Beethoven, noting almost as many in minor as in major.

16. Schiller, whose transcendent poem Beethoven adapted for the text of the last movement of the Ninth Symphony, provides a clear account in his aesthetic writings of the Romantic intensification of the pastoral. Nature is viewed in a broader sense, as including natural man and the harmony of the simple or naive poet; by contrast, the sentimental poet seeks to restore that harmonious state without being able ("Sentimental Poetry," [1795] 1884: 291–96). This distinction underlies the difference between idyll and elegy; the elegy laments the loss of nature's harmony, unattainable through art ("Elegaic Poetry," 1884: 303–304). The specifically pastoral idyll, in its presentation of an earlier "golden age" (of youth, as well as of mankind), should be "made, not to bring back man to *Arcadia*, but to lead him to *Elysium*" ("Idyl," 1884: 324). Here again we see the relationship between secular and sacred paradises, with the further infusion of an idealistic moral component, leading from the everyday "beautiful" to the uniquely "sublime" ("On the Sublime," 1884: 135–49).

Halperin (1983: 65–66) emphasizes the oppositional dynamic in pastoral literature between the pastoral world and conventional human society. The "counter-cultural alternative" of a pastoral world thus entails a social critique of the contemporaneous world.

17. For Schiller, the distinction between nature as kindling the flame of poetic inspiration and insipid French wit ("Sentimental Poetry," 291–92) rings a similar change in aesthetic value: "Who does not love [prefer] the eloquent disorder of natural scenery to the insipid regularity of a French garden?" ("On the Sublime," 145).

18. Most of the dance types are written in one of two *formal schemes*, binary or rounded binary.

19. This stylistic trope, or musical metaphor, is a strikingly modern phenomenon as encountered in Beethoven's music (see Chapter 7 for further discussion). As analogous effect is achieved in the twentieth century by composers such as Hans Werner Henze in the use of musical instruments or styles from presumably oppressed cultures to convey solidarity with the victims of oppression. The music is dignified to the extent that its simplicity or artlessness successfully correlates with sincerity.

20. Other helpful accounts of the pastoral in literature include Marinelli (1971), Poggioli (1975), Halperin (1983), Loughrey, ed. (1984), and Kegel-Brinkgreve (1990).

21. Lawrence Kramer (1990: 40–46) interprets this movement in terms of an idyll, drawing on Bakhtin's (1981: 231) characterization of the temporal features of idyllic narrative: "continuity, cyclical movement, and the absence of rigid boundaries" (41).

22. Another way of viewing the admixture of tragic elements in Op. 101 is in terms of Schiller's distinction between naive and sentimental poetry (see note 16). The sentimental poet attempts to regain the lost harmony and simplicity of nature, which is the birthright of the naive poet. The effort can never succeed because man has already split reason from sensation. The sense of loss is ennobled, however, by the longing to achieve a higher integration of mind and nature, not merely to retreat to a former "golden age." Pastoral music in Beethoven can suggest something of Schiller's philosophical elevation of the idea of nature; it is a short step, then, to correlate the tragic occurring in the midst of the pastoral with the idea of loss in Schiller's sense.

23. Certain dance or yodeling figures might exploit less-flowing melodic lines and yet be considered pastoral; see Kirby (1970).

24. Perpetual motion need not correlate with obsessiveness; it is used in the major mode finales of Beethoven's Piano Sonatas, Op. 26 and Op. 54, as an etude topic. Rosen points out that "the chief rhythmic interest of the classical *perpetuum mobile* is focused on the irregular aspects: that is, the rhythmic variety is as great as in any other classical work" (1972: 61); he then contrasts the dynamic tension of a Classical perpetuum mobile with the undramatic use of continuous rhythmic textures in the Baroque (62). Translated into my terminology, perpetual motion would be marked for Classical style and unmarked for Baroque style.

25. David B. Greene (1982: 99–123) distinguishes two cases, one in which "heroism prevails" (the first movement of the *Archduke* Piano Trio in B♭, Op. 97), and one in which "heroism falls short" (the first movement of the *Hammerklavier*, Op. 106). In the latter, "the heroic fanfare generates a harmonic structure that turns out to be at odds with the fanfare itself and consequently deprives the fanfare's return in the tonic of its triumphant character" (121). But the heroism is all the more "profound" in face of nonfulfillment, as opposed to the more "optimistic" or even "idealistic" *Archduke* (122).

26. "The moral law within us, and the starry heavens over us." In the quotation from Kant, these are the two things that never cease to fill the mind with awe. The tie to Schiller's concept of the sublime is clear: nature's vastness elicits recognition of a corresponding (moral) depth within our own being.

27. In an exemplary study, Kinderman (1992) analyzes both symbolic and narrative elements of the expressive progression to transcendence in Op. 110. The qualification of "triumph" as "barely sufficient to counteract powerful forces of dissociation" (145) recalls my distinction above and in the analysis of the slow movement of the *Hammerklavier*. Although I agree that there is less emphasis on "victory" in Op. 110 than in either the Fifth or the Ninth symphonies, the ending is certainly interpretable as an earned (i.e., "willed") spiritual victory, supported by fugal technique and the gradual ascent (registral expansion) to the final cadence.

28. Lawrence Kramer (1990: 32) notes that the "last recurrence [of the

theme] can be experienced as an expressive doubling rather than as a variation." See note 14 above for expressive doubling.

29. I suspect that overly complex arrays would suffer from a distancing effect, if not a law of diminishing returns, and I do not in general find such extremes of categorization very helpful. Simpler models at the level of style are more practical; refinements can then be made at the level of a given work's strategies.

IV. The Pastoral Expressive Genre in Op. 101

1. Kevin Korsyn's dissertation (1983) deals with the first movement's "rhetoric of evasions" (24) and formal compression from a Schenkerian standpoint, with a view toward the organization of the cycle as a whole. Noting the rather late appearance of an authentic cadence in the home key, Korsyn offers an important formal observation about this and other late Beethoven sonata cycles: "the first movement will tend to suppress these foreground cadences, while the finale will tend to emphasize them. Therefore, the proportion between harmonic tension and resolution in the first movement may seem weighted in the direction of instability, in spite of the descent of the fundamental line" (203).

2. See Kirby (1970). The first movement of Op. 101 has never been given the appellation of pastoral, nor does it appear to be a "characteristic" pastoral work like the *Pastoral* Symphony, or even the Piano Sonata, Op. 28, which was labeled pastoral by editors rather than by Beethoven himself. A more intensely personal—psychological or metaphysical—interpretation is called for, and the pastoral element here is distanced even further from nature-painting than is true of the characteristic symphony. Instead of recalling a storm, the subtler style of Op. 101 elicits a personal interpretation of its outbursts as tragic irruptions of the serenity afforded by the pastoral topic.

3. Crabbe (1982: 105–107) cites the influence of Schelling's nature philosophy and the pietist sermons of Christoph Christian Sturm, whose elevation of Nature approaches the pantheist. Among quotes from Sturm's *Betrachtungen über die Werke Gottes in Reiche der Natur* (1740–1786) found in Beethoven's notebooks is the following, which serves as evidence for the intimate connection to be found between an elevated pastoral topic and a transcendent spiritual one: "Nature is a glorious school for the heart. . . . Here I shall learn to know God and find a foretaste of heaven in that knowledge."

4. Personal communication.

5. By, among others, Wilfrid Mellers (1983: 143).

6. Leo Treitler (1980) extends in a similar manner the breadth of the concept "thematic" by observing cases where a relationship between themes is itself thematic (195) and where a kind of thematic process constitutes the thematic idea relating two movements, even though the actual material differs

(198). Dahlhaus ([1987] 1991: 123) observes that Koch implies the individual thematic role of harmonic, rhythmic, and metrical events in their capacity of articulating different affects (Koch [1802: 896ff.]). Dahlhaus also argues that the "underlying idea" or "premise" of the first movement of Beethoven's Piano Sonata in D, Op. 10, no. 3, is a "composed-out contradiction" in which "opposing extremes of divergence and unification" are "compelled to combine" (147).

7. This possibility suggests that there are "deep structures" other than those retrievable by formalist reductions.

8. This is reminiscent of Mozart's similar use of expressive 5–6–5–6 technique in *Don Giovanni*, during Don Ottavio's dramatic recitative in Scene 3, no. 2, mm. 47–48.

9. See Kerman (1982) and Hatten (1987a).

10. For further perspectives on the concept of thematic integration, see Kerman (1966: 303–49), Lidov (1981), Brodbeck and Platoff (1983), Dahlhaus ([1987] 1991: 159–65), Hatten (1987a), Webster (1991: 174–224), and Kinderman (1992). An extended example is discussed in Chapter 6.

11. For other examples of learned-rustic combinations used for humorous effect, see Kerman (1985b).

12. Ratner (1980: 260) considers the fugato to have a dance-derived subject, stemming historically from the canzona, and possessing rhythmic-metric characteristics of the bourrée. Dance features would support my argument for an overarching pastoral genre, although the tragic topic seems to dominate the fugato because of its minor mode.

13. Although the interval is a fifth and not the typical third, the textural effect is similar to that in Handel's Organ Concerto in F major, HWV 295, second movement (Allegro), mm. 43–45. I am grateful to Ken Logan for this observation.

V. The Thematic Level and the Markedness of Classical Material

1. Schenker's title for his voice-leading analysis of the *Eroica* (in *Das Meisterwerk in der Musik* 3) is "Beethovens 3. Sinfonie zum erstenmal in ihrem *wahren Inhalt* dargestellt" (italics added).

2. For an account of inconsistencies between theory and analytical practice with regard to Schenkerian analyses of motivic structure, see Richard Cohn (1992). Carl Schachter's keynote address to the Society for Music Theory (Yale, 1984) provided a superb illustration of how thematic and voice-leading approaches can effectively interact to produce a more sensitive analysis.

3. Patrick McCreless (1991) tackles the more difficult distinction between paradigmatic motivic and syntagmatic tonal functions in the realm of chromaticism.

4. The term *thematic* is employed in two senses: a generic one that refers to

strategic foregrounding (hence, markedness) throughout a work, and a more specific sense that refers to presentational material having the characteristics outlined in Figure 5.1. An easy way to distinguish these two senses is in terms of strategic markedness vs. presentational design. Thematic discourse refers to the ongoing strategic use of ideas. Context should clarify which sense of thematic is intended.

5. William Caplin (1991) defines three formal functions, which he labels presentation, continuation, and cadential (29). His functions "operate syntactically [in that order] at various levels of structure within a work" (28). Their analytical application to expanded first or second theme groups derives from Schoenberg's concept of the *Satz* (sentence) in *Fundamentals of Composition* (1967).

6. Compare the beginning-middle-ending paradigm discussed by Agawu (1991). For a related argument on the interaction of location and function within a formal genre by Schumann, see Newcomb (1987).

7. For specific examples, see Jonathan Kramer (1973), Judy Lochhead (1979), and Leonard B. Meyer (1979).

8. Robertson (1983) explores the consequences of such logical economic motivation for grammatical categories in language.

9. Mozart's fantasia-type passage-work development sections in his piano concerti often use conventional material in modulatory sequences.

10. Leonard Meyer (1982) makes a similar point for Mozart's phrase morphology.

11. For an illuminating account of phrase structure from a Schenkerian perspective, see William Rothstein's (1989) theory, which integrates rhythm, meter, grouping, and tonal structure. Rothstein brings a welcome stylistic sensitivity to his interpretations of unusual phrase structures in Haydn, Mendelssohn, Chopin, and Wagner.

12. Alternatively, one might view hypermetric conflict as a marked feature, in that mm. 18 and 19 are both "strong," upsetting a two-bar alternation of strong and weak downbeats. Note also the potential ambiguity between m. 1 as downbeat or anacrusis for a four-bar hypermeasure.

13. The cadential theme of Op. 13 may compensate for the more processive "theme" occurring at the arrival of E♭ major. A sufficiently stable (closural) theme may be needed to satisfy stylistic or rhetorical demands in very processive second key groups.

VI. Thematic Markedness

1. For a highly complementary analysis of integration in this movement, see Brodbeck and Platoff (1983). Kerman (1966: 305–13) notes several motivic derivations and associations, but emphasizes the dissociative aspect in the coda's "forced wedding" of the two constrasting themes from the beginning

(312). Ratner (1980: 236) speaks of a "collage of unassimilated sections," but he also demonstrates how the Adagio portions of the whole movement can be laid out end to end to make a complete, if miniature, two-reprise form (234–35).

2. A well-known exception is the first movement of Haydn's Symphony no. 92 in G (*Oxford*), where the Allegro begins on a downbeat, but the structural downbeat coinciding with the arrival of tonic harmony is reserved for a magnificent tutti four bars later.

3. Ratner (1980: 236) calls this a "hurdy-gurdy episode." Although that is perhaps its initial topical correlation, I agree with Kerman's (1966: 312) more sensitive interpretation of the section as existing "in a trance."

4. This is an important point in Brodbeck and Platoff's argument for integration (1983).

5. Note the positive contribution of an ascending chromatic bass line in contrary motion that accompanies the D♭ statement of the integrative "second" theme in the recapitulation, mm. 162–64.

6. Ratner (1980: 267) considers the topic to be a "motet without text for strings, a reincarnation of the imitative ricercar of the Renaissance" and notes the later "duet sections à la Josquin."

7. Compare the end of the development section from the first movement of Beethoven's Second Symphony for a remarkably similar (common-tone) modulation involving the same two keys.

8. For an analysis of this aspect of the quartet, see William Dougherty (1985).

9. See Winter (1982: 113–17) for a complete account, with further details on chronology.

10. It should be clear that the reversals analyzed in this book are like Leonard B. Meyer's (1973), the result of the interaction of several richly conceived "parameters," and not like Eugene Narmour's (1990), defined more narrowly and shaped by "bottom-up" implications for reversal of both interval size and direction. Narmour's theory of melodic structure offers a far more finely grained approach to the analysis and cognition of melodic shapes or contours than required for analytical purposes here, but I whole-heartedly support his enterprise: to tease out a wealth of significance from a surface that is often devalued or neglected in reductive theories giving higher priority to harmony and voice leading. Narmour's analysis of the B♯–C♯–A pattern by itself (344) is "(VR)," or "retrospective registral reversal," which creates a particularly strong aesthetic effect. The parentheses indicate "retrospective," V stands for register, and R for reversal (see definition and discussion in Narmour, 1990: 335, 436).

11. Compare this processive expressive interpretation with the more synoptic, typological analysis of the subject head as "pathetic" (Ratner, 1980: 268–69, drawing on Kirkendale, 1966: 137, for the type).

12. Interestingly, the fugue of Op. 135, the famous "Es muss sein," has a similar marked-unmarked head-tail relationship. In fact, the tail (mm. 5ff. of the Allegro, first violin part) is equivalent to a fragment of the tail of the Op. 131 subject.

13. Compare Bach, Fugue in C minor, WTC I, with its structural descent from $\hat{6}$ to $\hat{3}$.

14. Rosen (1972: 447) comments on the static quality of a harmonic sequence occurring after the climax of the last movement of Op. 111: "the long series of tiny harmonic movements that prolong this immense inner expansion serve only as an harmonic pulse and in no sense as a gesture." It is not because a sequence lacks dynamic or gestural capacities that it allows this sense of relative repose, I would suggest, but the fact that the kind of harmonic sequence involved happens to be stylistically unmarked, and that the context in which it occurs undermines its importance as tonal activity in terms of the major climaxes and goals of the movement.

15. Note, however, the impressive leaps that prolong the climax in m. 107 through the descent and into the next crux in m. 113. The culminating effect of these open octaves and fifths is reminiscent of the recapitulation of the first movement of the Ninth Symphony; they may share a rhetorical significance somehow related to the recitative topic (see Chapter 7).

16. The treatment of a permutation of the subject head in the last movement of the quartet suggests that the enigma posed by four tones—$\hat{1}$, $\sharp\hat{7}$, $\flat\hat{6}$, $\hat{5}$—is far from resolved. Beethoven's String Quartets, Op. 132 and Op. 135 (composed the previous year and the following month respectively), both play with permutations of these four pitches, as is well known.

VII. Beyond the Hierarchies of Correlation

1. Theories of troping in language actually have a long history, beginning with Aristotle's four classifications of metaphor (*Poetics*, 21:3) under the general description of "the application of the name of a thing to something else."

Tropes can be either more or less creative. Some tropes create new meanings in the sense of using old names for new things; such meanings quickly become literal. For example, to use such terms as "space ship" and "shuttle" for new vehicles reflects a growth in the range of application for the terms "ship" and "shuttle" (the latter derived from the "back and forth" action of a weaving loom). But there is little figurative gain in the sense of emergent meanings. One has simply metaphorically applied an old name in place of inventing a new one.

More-creative tropes, on the other hand, couple two terms from different domains in order to spark a new meaning from the interaction of their original meanings. An example from Quintilian (VIII, vi: 9), "He is a lion," goes beyond finding a term for a quality (such as courage or strength) and produces an enhancement of meaning, interpreting metaphorically the implausible equivalence created by the copula "is." This interpretation of potential cross-applications between properties of lions and men is not spelled out, need not be consistent from one use to the next, and thus cannot be guaranteed to communicate a literal meaning. Metaphor, then, has the capacity to play more freely within the semantic field established by a language.

2. These and other aspects of Goodman's (and Peter Kivy's) work are reviewed from a broader semiotic perspective, and in a comparative historical context, in Chapter 9. Here, the focus is on their contributions to a theory of metaphor. Unfortunately, some redundancy between the two accounts is unavoidable.

3. Creativity is characteristic of the interaction model of metaphor proposed by Max Black (1954–55, 1977) and further developed by Carl Hausman (1989).

4. The notion of troping is not a new one in music theory, either, but its earlier application in Medieval music was restricted to formal construction. An addition of words, music, or both to the established liturgical chant was labeled a trope. The purely material interpolation might be seen as figural in the sense that the new text or melody served to inflect or enlarge upon the sense or significance of the original, and indeed the Church authorities may have taken a dim view of such interpolations for that very reason. But the troping of meaning was probably secondary to the primary urge of church composers to open up new areas for musical development, while not presuming to an originality unrelated to the canonical chant repertory. Hoppin, in his text on medieval music (1978: 144), observes that "because the elaboration of existing liturgical items was tolerated much more readily than the introduction of totally new ones, troping provided religious poets and musicians with an important outlet for their creative energies." But troping for a Medieval composer was more a matter of adding new material, and any new meanings were likely to be glosses on the original.

5. Marion Guck (1990) and Robert Snarrenberg (1991) have examined metaphors in theoretical discourse. Elaine Barkin and others created something of an art form out of self-consciously "poetic criticism" in past issues of *Perspectives of New Music*. Nattiez (1990) also addresses categories of discourse about music.

6. Peter Laki (private communication) points out that *Humoresque* has "a touch of nostalgia in it, too," thus perhaps undermining the extreme contrast in affect that, for Karbusicky, supports an interpretation of humor. Nevertheless, the intercutting of the two works is humorous in its very artificiality and in the fact that it can be made to work harmonically.

7. For further discussion of the concept of isotopy for literature, see Eco (1984: 189–201). The concept originates with Greimas (1970: 188) as "a complex of manifold semantic categories making possible the uniform reading of a story." Grabócz's isotopies are close to my expressively correlated topical

fields presented in the matrixes in Chapter 3. Their sequence could constitute an expressive genre. See also Tarasti (1984, 1987).

8. Lawrence Kramer's (1990) tropes are more broadly conceived than the ones examined here. They can be cued interpretively by "points of under- or overdetermination: on the one hand, a gap, a lack, a missing connection; on the other, a surplus of pattern, an extra repetition, an excessive connection" (12). For Kramer, the higher-level constraint on tropological interpretation is "the power to maintain a detailed scrutiny of a text that also reaches deep into the cultural context" (15). Since Kramer and I developed our theories of tropes independently (my first paper outlining these constraints was delivered in Helsinki in 1988; see Hatten, forthcoming), our points of similarity and constrast are all the more interesting. Broadly speaking, my interpretation of tropes relates them to the correlations they ultimately transform or (in the case of ironic reversal) deny. Thus, my interpretations are somewhat more cautious, and my tropes are less spectacular than Kramer's. Our different grains of focus are nevertheless quite complementary.

9. That context for language or literature, as Ross Chambers has pointed out (personal communication), may be construed as the context of the surrounding textual discourse or as the "enunciatory" context, the circumstances of its utterance. For music the latter could be viewed as "a perceived discontinuity between the discursive subject and a subject produced negatively, or dissociating himself from the former." This phenomenon will be treated as Romantic irony below.

10. Wayne Booth, in his *Rhetoric of Irony* (1974: 22–24) offers a similar distinction between "additive" metaphor and "subtractive" irony.

11. For more on the problematic interpretation of deception in music, see Deborah Stein (1989), Abbate (1991: 19), and Hatten (1992b).

12. See the important article by Rey Longyear, "Beethoven and Romantic Irony" (1970) for a more detailed account of the historical development and significance of this concept. One of his examples is discussed later in this chapter. My theoretical treatment of irony differs from Longyear's in being grounded in a general theory of musical correlations, troping, and levels of discourse. Bonds (1991) offers historical support for the interpretation of Romantic irony in Haydn, as well, but the comparison is with the English novelist Laurence Sterne.

13. One of the strongest exponents of this concept is Carolyn Abbate (1991), who explores the multiple discursive disjunctions in nineteenth-century tone poems and opera, along with the evidence they give of a narrating voice (19). Her approach goes beyond the reordering of events as expected in a formal genre (Newcomb, 1987) to insist that narrative discourse must somehow set itself apart from other discourse, "which also orders and tropes" (52). By setting a higher standard (48), she constrains the concept so that not every disjunction provokes an interpretation of a narrating voice. James Webster

(1991: 267–87) provides an example from Haydn's Symphony No. 46 in B major of a "meta-musical reminiscence" (284) that meets Abbate's criterion of evoking a past tense in music (Abbate 1991: 54). Webster notes that the recall of a varied reprise from the minuet in the finale constitutes a "second order" reprise, and thus "is not merely a recall, but a *reminiscence*—a re-experiencing, tinged with nostalgia or regret" (284). Lawrence Kramer (1990: 189–203) explores disruptive effects in Beethoven's "La malinconia" movement (from Op. 18, no. 6) to illustrate his strong claim that "instrumental music seeks narrative as a strategy of deconstruction" (189). My concern in this chapter is less with narrativity than with the projection of another discursive level and the Romantic ironic roots of that projection, but see Hatten (1991).

14. Kinderman (1991: 162–63) has noted the topical use of recitative-like structures in Beethoven's instrumental music as a "moment of internalization and reflection" (Op. 31, no. 2) or "a deeply contemplative vision" (Op. 110). Richard Kramer (1992) extends the concept of "narrative shift" (184) in ways that complement the approach in Hatten (1991) and below. Compare, as well, Subotnik (1991: 182).

15. For the concept of persona in music, see Edward T. Cone (1974). The problem of agency in music is addressed by Fred Maus (1989). Both Lawrence Kramer (1990) and Carolyn Abbate (1991) have fruitfully extended the notion of "voice" in music.

16. See, for example, Leo Treitler's analyses in "To Worship That Celestial Sound" (1982: 165–66) and "History, Criticism, and Beethoven's Ninth Symphony" (1980, 195–96), where Tovey's characterization of the "catastrophic return" is complemented by Treitler's reference to "horrifying brightness." Treitler emphasizes another important feature of the chord: its unexpected arrival. This feature may also be understood in relation to the cueing of recitative in that the suddenness of "modulatory" departures by means of a first inversion dominant are characteristic of recitative discourse. Thus, in my interpretation the recapitulatory arrival is neither as catastrophic nor as horrifying, although it is certainly assertive and "hard-edged." The chord's climactically annunciatory force is verified by the summative counterline in the bass, which intensifies, and adds tragic poignance to, the return of the main theme (see especially the line in the cellos and basses, mm. 319–23).

17. Schering (1936: 508) cites W. v. Lenz, who states that Beethoven provided this poetic program in February 1816. Sullivan (1927: 51) cites Schindler as the source for the claim "that Beethoven, in his later years, complained that people were less able to grasp the meaning of music than they were in his young days, and he even thought of giving poetic titles to his earlier works to supply this deficiency in his hearers' imaginations."

18. Andrew Mead (personal communication) suggests that the interruption is thematic for the cycle since the previous movements' discontinuities are also somewhat schizophrenic or irrational. I would also suggest two more prosaic

formal motivations: the melodic inversion (hence, expressive reversal) of the fugato subject from the second movement, and the stylistic convention of a suitably fast ending to achieve sufficient closure for the cycle as a whole.

19. Lawrence Kramer (1990: 14) goes still further in describing the freedom involved in tropological interpretation: "Interpretation . . . cannot be regimented, disciplined, or legislated—at least not successfully. As a practice, it is opportunistic, unruly, and contestatory, inescapably committed to both preserving and appropriating whatever it addresses."

20. For an unmarked example of a German augmented sixth proceeding to vii°7/V, see the third and fourth bars from the end of the third movement of Op. 59, no. 3. Here the two sonorities are involved in a passing chromatic ascent in the bass from $\hat{5}$ to $\hat{7}$, and thus the directionality of the passing ascent overrides the voice-leading implication of $\flat\hat{6}$. The coda in which this occurs, incidentally, is also a transition to the fourth movement, and thus the elaborated fill of an arpeggiated dominant subsumes the expressive effect of the German augmented sixth (here, an incidental sonority).

21. Barthes, *S/Z* (1970). Patrick McCreless, in a paper delivered to the 1987 meeting of the Society for Music Theory, applies equivalents for two of Barthes' codes to the analysis of music. His application is still tied to the formal/syntactic in the sense that his "narrative" code is a Schenkerian analysis, while his "hermeneutic" code consists of pitch events outside the diatonic that suggest a thematic level of discourse.

22. The borrowing of syntagms from the works of major composers constitues an enormous field of investigation in itself. Ellwood Derr of the University of Michigan has been pursuing such hidden and transformed borrowings in the music of Handel, Mozart, Beethoven, and Brahms with remarkable results. His conclusions have led him to a new perspective on the ways composers taught themselves their craft, through compositional modeling at all levels of structure. See Derr (1984) for a representative study.

23. Indeed, Klimowitsky (1978) makes a strong claim for Beethoven's modeling this passage on a Palestrina Gloria that appears among his sketches. His claim is disputed by Brandenburg (1982). When writing out the five-measure Palestrina excerpt, Beethoven altered the Lydian B♮s to B♭s in F major. Whether the Gloria forms an intertext with the quartet movement is not as important as the evidence of Beethoven's considering it as a source piece for the style. The Gloria would certainly carry an appropriate textual message, as well, if its identification were intended.

24. The use of subdominant-directional moves helps create closure partly because of their reversal of the forward temporal direction of moves to the "sharp side" (see Chapter 2 above).

I leave open the question of the extent to which this passage hints at the richer concept of abnegation—perhaps the descent in the right hand is only tinged with regret by the chromatic reversal.

25. For more on this concept in literary theory, with coverage of its major proponents, see Robert Siegle (1986). Carolyn Abbate (1991: 6, 61–118) explores reflexivity in operatic narration (not recitative, but musically-set narrative text that may either prefigure the plot or comment reflectively on past events). Such narration may lead to interesting interpretive results when contradictions among "voices" occur.

26. Conversely, a twentieth-century composer like Stravinsky may use reflexivity to "get outside" the sincerity of earlier styles, emphasizing the artificiality and objectivity of Classical musical discourse. According to Robert Siegle (1986: 9–15), one of the consequences of a concern for reflexivity is the move from a representational or mimetic poetics to a constitutive poetics, one in which "realism" gives way to involving the reader in the understanding and remaking of the very codes that go into the formation of the work itself.

27. There is a still further reflexive possibility. Rose Subotnik's penetrating article "Adorno's Diagnosis of Beethoven's Late Style: Early Symptom of a Fatal Condition" (1976: 250–51) explains how Adorno interprets Beethoven's third-period style as itself a critique of the syntheses attempted in the second-period style. While I do not agree with Adorno's particular analysis, his position demonstrates concern for reflexivity of discourse across a whole *oeuvre*, a higher-level intertextuality toward which Beethoven criticism might ultimately aspire. Such reflexivity could easily be applied to composers like Mahler; consider the way in which his symphonies return to the same basic issues and scenarios, enabling later ones to comment upon earlier ones and to raise the expressive stakes.

28. Abbate (1991: 11, 252–53, note 7) and L. Kramer (1990: 187–88) also invoke Bakhtin, but in opposing ways—Abbate emphasizes the multiplicity of "voices" in opera, while Kramer finds instrumental music to be "monological" (although the "unity of the presiding subject" may be "disturbed," it is "recovered" [188]).

VIII. Analysis and Synthesis

1. A more abrupt move in the coda of the *Hammerklavier* slow movement featured recitative-like diminished sevenths and *Bebung*-like reiterations disrupting the serenity of the elevated second theme in G.

2. Lewis Lockwood (1992) discusses other features of the cavatina as an operatic genre that may have affected Beethoven's compositional choices. The placement of the cavatina as the fifth movement, just before the culminating fugal finale in the original version of the quartet, suggests to Lockwood a formal parallel to operatic practice: "the cavatina in many contemporary German operas often provides a serious, deeply felt lyrical utterance by a major character, who comments introspectively upon a dilemma of the plot and thus deepens the emotional seriousness of the dramatic action as it moves toward

crisis and resolution" (210). Lockwood's formal analysis of sections (213) does not address the issue of an aborted transition, and takes the *Beklemmt* section to be an unproblematic, if short, middle section. Concerning the *Beklemmt* section, however, Lockwood notes Wolfgang Osthoff's (1969) conjecture that it may allude to an opera seria tradition of cavatinas in *ombra* scenes relating to suffering and death (210).

3. Compare other hybrid slow movements, such as those in Op. 7 and Op. 95, where sonata elements are clearly in evidence, but the resulting form is a negotiation between sonata and part form, motivated by expressive considerations.

4. Compare the A♭ "second" theme of the slow movement of Op. 7, originally heard as part of a contrasting B section that then takes on the character of a *Durchführung*, including a false recapitulation. When the A♭ theme is resolved to C in the return section, it satisfies a sonata principle requiring resolution to the tonic of significant thematic material presented in another key. Thus, in this hybrid form the B section comprises both S theme and development portions of a sonata form, but a T (transition) section is omitted.

5. Dahlhaus ([1987] 1991: 234–37) elaborates on motivic coherence in the movement, noting how it creates "unexpected associations between [themes] that were originally disparate" (236). In this way, lyricism and motivic working are seen as compatible rather than contradictory.

6. Compare the more chromatic technique in the first movement of Beethoven's "Ghost" Trio, Op. 70, no. 1, where an introductory gesture shifts to minor mode and an implied German augmented sixth, but it sets up the main thematic entrance on an *arrival six-four*, which restores the major mode and emphasizes the positive emotional expressivity of the main theme.

7. However, Barry Cooper (1990: 203–205) notes that the $\hat{2}$–$\hat{4}$–$\hat{3}$ melodic pattern found in m. 6 appears in the early sketches (*Egerton*, folios 7r and 8r) of a movement in D♭ major that eventually became the *Cavatina*. Thus, the idea of a marked melodic reversal was already present, and Beethoven's later sketches "intensify" the effect by leading up to it more expressively—with an ascent as hopeful as the first three notes of Op. 131 (note the resemblance to m. 5 of the *Cavatina*).

8. My peculiar adaptation of Schenkerian analysis warrants a brief explanation. I have attempted to illustrate a structurally significant expressive event in the theme, but that event is an irreducible surface event, as well. Nevertheless, the integration of phrase-structural and voice-leading "derivations" demonstrates that (in this case) the intensity of the expressive crux is enhanced by its strategic placement within the interpolated expansion of the phrase. The analytical reduction is highly unorthodox in that it presents different levels of voice-leading structure in different measures and preserves phrase-structural derivation (somewhat along the lines of Schenker's [1933] method of measure counting and his [1935: 124–25] concept of phrase expansion).

Rhythmic and dynamic features are also preserved only as needed to illustrate my points. This *ad hoc* reductive technique is nothing more than an unsystematic but helpful illustration of the interaction of expressive and structural features in this passage. Clearly, I have reduced away other expressively significant features already discussed in my verbal analysis of this theme; to that extent reductions can be misleading. But equally clearly, a Schenkerian approach sensitive to phrase structure and rhythm (see, for comparison, the analysis of phrase expansion in Carl Schachter [1987: 40–58] and William Rothstein [1989: 64–101]) can complement, and at times enhance, the kinds of arguments I have made for the expressive significance of a passage. Completely systemizing an analytical reductive technique that could adequately convey the interaction of expressively significant (but irreducible) thematic, motivic, or topical events with structurally significant voice-leading events (as revealed by selective reduction), would appear to be an impossibly difficult task. Thus, such *ad hoc* "perspectives" as found in Example 8.3 should be read as neither consistent nor comprehensive analyses of a single level, but simply as individualized illustrations that highlight particular interactions among several levels of structure.

Having said that, let me emphasize that I am not trying to misrepresent Schenkerian insights into structure (any flaws are my own), but to coordinate them with my own interpretation of expressive meaning. Clearly, there is (or can be) an extensive expressive component to the interpretation of Schenkerian reductions; but as this book has explored, there are other elements of expressive meaning that are not as easily addressed (or have not been) by some applications of Schenkerian analysis. (For a recent approach that coordinates topical and Schenkerian analysis, see Agawu, 1991.)

Finally, I have applied ideas from Leonard B. Meyer's (1973) implication/realization model in even less systematic fashion, but in commonsense ways I trust are readily evident (e.g., "denial" of implication, "reversal").

9. Interestingly, the first violin at the same cadence (mm. 8–9) undermines an expected stepwise descent on the surface with arpeggiation and an escape tone, creating the surface effect of a more chordal close (B♭–G–E♭) emerging from the underlying $\hat{3}$–$\hat{2}$–$\hat{1}$ descent. The bass and the soprano appear to be reversing roles in a way that keeps the authentic cadence "open."

10. The so-called psychological harmony characteristic of the Romantic period has its origins in such marked sonorities (which need not be chromatic), as well as in the troping of unmarked sonorities used in marked contexts. Compare the role of the thematic half-diminished seventh chord in Wagner's *Tristan und Isolde*.

11. Notice that although I have not committed myself to describing a particular tragic import, the interpretation is no less semantic for not claiming a programmatic specificity that would not, in any case, be aesthetically relevant. What Beethoven's music appears to provide is intentionality without a specific object, understood instead in its more archetypal or general applicability to a

class of experiences. The experience here is nevertheless "specified" (via markedness) in its qualification of intensity, extremity, temporal duration, contextual relationships, etc. The paradox of musical meanings that are simultaneously general and specific, or vague but precise, or abstract yet concrete, will be treated in the first section of Chapter 10.

For a similar example, this time of positive (nontragic) insight, compare the reiterated Mm^7 in the slow movement of Op. 95, mm. 149–50 (Example 2.3, further discussed in Chapter 7).

12. Note that repetition here has an opposite expressive effect from what was argued in Chapter 5, where it was a means of thematization, creating strategic markedness and thus greater expressivity. Context is everything. Having already defined the crux, further repetition, especially over a single harmony, only diffuses its expressive intensity. Such flexibility and interaction among elements frustrates any overly systematic account of expressive meaning—even at the correlation level. The potential expressive effect of repetition is encountered again in the interpretation of mm. 23ff., which follows.

13. Neither Hanslick (1854: 34) nor Peter Kivy (1980: 73–77) seems able to resolve the problem of this uncharacteristic musical setting of the text, although Hanslick uses the anomaly to support his thesis of the plasticity and indeterminate nature of musical expressivity in general, whereas Kivy finds the anomaly in a contradiction of broader (correlational) conventions (derived from such oppositions as major and minor). See Chapter 9 for further discussion of their theoretical positions on expressive meaning in music.

14. Compare the mad scenes in Romantic opera (e.g., *Lucia di Lammermoor*), where normal tragic expression is pushed to such an extreme that the protagonist is "overwhelmed," and "inappropriate" music occurs. The dramatic and expressive effect is even more powerful because of the ironic disparity between appropriate and actual responses. Obviously, the effect can be used to enhance the expression of grief even in those instances where the protagonist does not go mad.

15. Note, however, that the I^6–vi with $\hat{5}$–$\hat{1}$ in the soprano might be interpreted as a kind of trope on the deceptive move associated with V–vi, since $\hat{5}$–$\hat{1}$ brings such strong closural (hence reassuringly stable) associations, and the vi undermines a $\hat{1}$ that follows a $\hat{5}$. Another way of understanding the theme is in terms of a reharmonization of the G–C in the bass, as related to the previously thwarted attempts to cadence in C minor. This time, the potential $\hat{5}$–$\hat{1}$ in C minor is integrated with the unrealized harmonic potential of $\hat{5}$–$\hat{1}$ in E♭ major in the soprano. The interpretation suggested is that of an accommodation being reached, which accords quite well with the previous notion of the consoling effect of the passage. Finally, consider the potentially resignational connotations of the melodic drop $\hat{5}$–$\hat{1}$, related to a similar triadic descent ($\hat{1}$–$\hat{5}$, then $\hat{5}$–$\hat{3}$) in the second theme of the *Hammerklavier* slow movement, as discussed in Chapter 1. Note that all of these interpretations are mutually supportive rather

than ambiguating; they each suggest a particular kind of closure that relinquishes only reluctantly, with a poignant sense of tragic awareness and resignation.

Although it might be hard to maintain that a listener could simultaneously be aware of all of these interpretations, they can contribute to a tacit sense of appropriateness for the theme, an "inevitability" that is often commented upon in Beethoven.

16. Consider, also, the expressive reversal of the melodic drop in m. 18 by the drop in m. 23, transforming a dissatisfied protest into a more-resigned acceptance.

17. The leap of a tenth had been thematically appropriated for its heroic impetus in the first and last movements of the *Hammerklavier*, Op. 106. Its use here, like that of the abnegation progression, may appear less focal, but exemplary works such as the *Hammerklavier* may influence the interpretation of similar ideas, even if one might otherwise be reluctant to claim an intertextual relationship between the *Cavatina* and the *Hammerklavier*.

18. This technique is exploited by Tchaikovsky in the waltz movement of the Sixth Symphony (*Pathétique*). Here, the 5/4 waltz sets an exterior dramatic scene and the "trio" of the form (occurring over a D pedal that is now $\hat{3}$ of B minor and a pulsation that marks time like a heartbeat) shifts to an interior, psychological level of discourse, almost as though piece-time were standing still. The "freeze-frame" device, where some characters think aloud in asides unheard by other characters frozen in place, is a similar (if outdated) technique found in plays and movies.

19. Richard Kramer (1992: 178–84) argues that the doubled Gs also enhance the rhetorical and narrative function of the quadrupled Gs which follow, announcing the Ouverture of the *Grosse Fuge* finale. The narrative function is akin to what I have termed a shift in level of discourse; Kramer draws on the distinction in Gérard Genette (1980: 25–26) between story, discourse, and the narrative act in itself. The forte Gs disrupt the world of the *Cavatina* and, for Kramer, render the *Cavatina* "an act of fantasy" (181). While I agree with the interpretation of a narrative shift, I do not read the Ouverture's Gs as a negation, but rather as a displacement to another realm of discourse and another approach to issues at stake in the quartet.

IX. From the Aesthetic to the Semiotic

1. Ironically, Kerman misapplies his criticism to some of the very analysts who have most often gone beyond the prevailing formalism (Edward T. Cone, Charles Rosen, Leonard Meyer, even himself!).

2. See the separate reviews of the Fifth Symphony and the Piano Trios, Op. 70, as edited, annotated, and introduced by David Charlton (1989: 234–51, 300–25).

3. Neubauer's comprehensive survey of major philosophical figures in the ongoing aesthetic argument about expression reveals that their attempts to deal with the phenomenon of instrumental music's autonomy from language—to explore its distinctive expressive "language"—led paradoxically (in my interpretation) to a formalism that made it increasingly difficult to credit expressive meanings as other than "extramusical," and thus less important than purely musical meanings.

But the response to an increasingly "subjective" expressivity or "emotional flux" in music from 1740 to 1780 prompted what I would consider a more promising response from some writers, notably Carl Heinrich Heydenreich, whose *System der Äesthetik* (1790) Neubauer cites in the following summary (159): "Heydenreich observed that emotions endure, have a continuous spectrum of intensity, flip over into their opposite, or shade into adjacent feelings. The signs of passions must therefore be finely graded, sustainable, and diverse—criteria best met by sounds, 'which copy feeling and passion with generally comprehensible veracity and irresistible effect in the heart. No other sign can match them therein, and music is therefore the only art which can copy feelings and passions in the full sense of the word' " (Heydenreich, 166).

4. Scott Burnham (1992: 24) echoes Schumann's point in arguing that the programmatic reception of works such as Beethoven's *Eroica* Symphony by critics such as A. B. Marx do not reveal the "true content" of the work but communicate, metaphorically, the spirit of intense engagement. In his analytical example (the first movement of the *Eroica*) Marx's program suggests the action of heroic myth and offers no less relevant an account of the experience of the movement than more modern, formal-structural accounts.

5. Other recent approaches to Hanslick's essay include Peter Kivy (1990b) and Fred Maus (1992). Carl Dahlhaus ([1978] 1989: 18–41) emphasizes an irony in the evolution of the concept of "absolute" music (see also note 3, above). For the Romantics (Wackenroder, Tieck, E. T. A. Hoffmann) instrumental music attains an "absolute" status in the positive metaphysical sense—it is ineffable and capable of infinite longing, hence more "poetic" than texted music. By the time Wagner (not Hanslick) coined the term in 1846, absolute music is conceived as "objectless" in its expression and thus relegated to a stage in the process leading to reintegration with both word and bodily movement in the music drama (conceived as a rebirth of Greek tragedy). Wagner criticizes Rossini for "absolute melody" in arias "detached from all linguistic or poetic basis," i.e., not expressive of the poetic idea of the text. Instrumental music, on the other hand, evades the stigma of absoluteness to the extent it exhibits characteristics of the dance (recall Wagner's assessment of the Seventh Symphony as an "apotheosis of the dance").

In my critique of Hanslick, I concentrate on the issue of autonomy itself, as a musical value and prescription.

6. Ironically, Hanslick's work ([1846–99] 1950) as a music critic suggests a

rather different picture of his conservative tastes. Hanslick criticizes Brahms (First Symphony) as well as Wagner (from *Lohengrin* to *Parsifal*) for failing his standard of clear melodic structure. Brahms's First Symphony is too complex in its working-out, "at the expense of sensuous beauty (125–28)," while Wagner's endless melody and "tyrannical" leitmotivic design (198) lead to an absence of pure melody. This insistence on clear "tunes" strikes one as naive. For Hanslick, the only successful parts of *Die Meistersinger* are Pogner's monologue, Walther's songs, and the quintet (111–22). Despite his recognition of Wagner's genius in declamation, orchestration, and scenic effects, he remains implacably opposed to Wagner's aesthetic as exemplified by the music drama.

7. Compare Kivy (1990a), for whom "music alone" includes presumably autonomous works such as the fugue in Op. 131. My expressive interpretation of this movement in Chapter 6 provides an alternative to Kivy's resuscitation of autonomy.

8. This idea is best expressed in terms of the composers' intent by A. B. Marx in his biography of Beethoven (1863: 257), with his response to a rhetorical challenge not unlike Hanslick's. I quote the translation from Wallace (1986: 52): "Is not music, by virtue of its inability to indicate things and objects, unsuited for the presentation of objective content? Does not this content lie in the merest superscription and—in your subjective imagination? *Our* subjective imagination?—Let us consider what the pronoun represents: nothing less than all the great composers . . . from Bach and Handel . . . to our own time. They have all known how to find this potential in their art, and have built their life's calling upon it. Or else—if you dare to say it—they have all been fools, who have not understood their own line of work."

9. On the other hand, in criticizing Hanslick's position I cannot assume the absence of musics that might be autonomous in just the sense Hanslick was driving at, although I seriously doubt that any Western style in the nineteenth century would so qualify. The notion seems more prevalent in the twentieth century, and more applicable to the professed aesthetic of composers such as Xenakis. Stravinsky is the most curious example of a gap between his expressively conceived music and his philosophical claims to the contrary (in the *Poetics*).

10. Meyer, in his later book on style (1989: 216), also notes the increasing tendency of Romantic music to emphasize "secondary" parameters (timbre, texture, register, dynamics, duration, tempo) to achieve more-delineated expressive effects. For example, extremes of (high) register, (soft) dynamics, (slow) tempo, stepwise motion, consonant harmonies, and chorale-like textures help to represent "the ethereal and poignant sadness of Violetta's impending death in the preludes to acts 1 and 3 of *La traviata*" (216).

11. This summary account is derived from Goodman (1968: 50–53).

12. The issue of general vs. specific will be dealt with in the next chapter, but for now it should be noted that it is one of degree, not of kind; Langer certainly

indicated more possibilities of symbolization than a generalized "emotive life," and she articulated them more fully than Kivy appears willing to credit (see quote from Langer [1953: 27] above).

13. Wilson Coker (1972) and Deryck Cooke (1959) both fall short in this respect. Coker was one of the first to apply semiotic concepts to music, but his approach is based more on Charles Morris's work (1946, 1964) than Peirce's, and it lacks Peirce's crucial triadic approach to interpretation. I avoid his terms (*congeneric* for internal musical meaning and *extrageneric* for extramusical meaning) since I do not believe any musical meaning to be "external" in that sense (a perspective I share with Lawrence Kramer [1992: 17]). Coker considers congeneric sign complexes as "primary," and as "metaphors" for "secondary" extrageneric meaning (152), but he comes no closer to an ongoing interpretational process.

X. Further Perspectives on Musical Meaning and Cognition

1. See Allan Keiler's (1981a) analysis of Rameau's fundamental bass as a metalanguage in just this sense.

2. Jerry Fodor, in his book *Representations* (1981: 269), makes this important point as a critique of typical experiments in concept learning.

3. Marion Guck (1991) has coined the term "music-literal" to capture these kinds of labels which are ingrained in our very conceptualizations of music. They may vary from culture to culture; thus, I have borrowed Schneider's (1968) useful term "cultural unit."

4. Wittgenstein's ([1933–35] 1960) concept of family resemblances (cited in Chapter 7) is relevant to this argument, as well.

5. See, for example, Coulter (1983), and debate in the journal *Cognition*. A helpful summary of theories of human categorization may be found in Lakoff (1987: 12–57).

6. The prototype (robin) would be an unmarked token of the type (bird); the less prototypical tokens (ostrich, kiwi) would be marked tokens of the type.

7. Russell's (1961) discovery has since been borne out in experiments by Schachter and Singer (1962) on artificial arousal: "Unexplained arousal can be experienced as different emotions according to cognitive circumstances" (60). This point is not unrelated to the phenomenologists' emphasis on intentionality.

8. Interestingly, the sketches show that Mendelssohn's original choice was to have the oboes enter before the clarinets (Larry Todd, 1979: 199). Todd examines the sketches with a keen understanding of expressive motivations, demonstrating, for example, that Mendelssohn subtly disguises the "characteristic" parallel fifths in the outer voices of the opening progression (i–III–v) by a rest in the contrabass in m. 3 (the D is provided by the cello), thereby preserving the "desolate" and "primitive, epic quality" of his original sketch.

9. As indicated earlier, the present study is more concerned with growth in a single style than with style change. Change is theoretically distinguished from growth in that it involves a major hierarchical reformulation of structural and semantic organization. My dissertation (Hatten, 1982) explores various implications of this distinction, which is crucial to the theoretical definition of a style: how much growth can a style accommodate before it ceases to be a useful explanatory construct?

Change, historically, exhibits the same "punctuated equilibria" (Eldridge and Gould, 1972; Gould, 1977) or "functional branch points" (Lieberman, 1984) that have been hypothesized to explain biological evolution. Longer periods of relative stability or consolidation alternate with shorter periods of rapid change, often provoked by unpredictable events. Such a model avoids the problems of historical determinism or "progress" that plague the grand histories of the nineteenth and early twentieth centuries. Change can come from any source, and growth may be motivated in many ways.

10. *Webster's New World Dictionary*, (1974).

11. Drawn from Hatten (forthcoming b). Ray Jackendoff's discussion of type generation in *Semantics and Cognition* (1983: 82) is relevant here: "one can create new [TYPE] concepts at will. One of the simplest ways to do this is to construct, for an arbitrary [TOKEN], a [TYPE] of THINGS LIKE [TOKEN], where likeness can be determined along any arbitrary class of dimensions." The problem remains to justify the process for a given type in a musical work, and that leads to the issue of possible *motivations* (see below).

12. This passage is cited by Max Fisch in his essay "Hegel and Peirce," reprinted in Fisch (1986).

13. The complete couplet is "The moan of doves in immemorial elms,/And murmuring of innumerable bees" ("The Princess," Stanza 3, Part VII, lines 206–207).

14. Actually, I can "hear" the moanings of thousands of cattle smelling blood in the slaughterhouse, even in this unhappy poetic fragment. But I have a personal bias as a poet for the potential of sound-exemplifications, and thus I am more likely to "blow up" such latent potential. That does not mean I consider the line successful poetically!

15. A theory of expression based on salience, or foregrounding, alone would look like Mathis Lussy's (*Traité de l'expression musicale*, 1873), which is forward looking in its concern for "expressive accents" that go against the grain of normative structures, but which is primarily geared toward performance. Lussy's contribution to expressive interpretation is documented in William S. Newman's insightful book on the proper performance of Beethoven's piano music (1988: 174ff.). Newman points out Lussy's debt to Jérome-Joseph de Momigny's *Cours complet d'harmonie et de composition* of 1806. Michael Green (1991) is currently investigating implications of Lussy's ideas for performance practice.

16. The markedness of contrast can be understood either as helping underline markedness already inferrable from more coded aspects (i.e., pitch structure) or as strategically marking otherwise unmarked material.

17. The distinction among Worlds 1 through 3 is Karl Popper's (1977: 38).

18. For a more complete critique of Lerdahl and Jackendoff, with further arguments for a semiotic approach to music cognition, see Hatten (1990).

Conclusion

1. A point on which I agree with Nattiez (1990).

2. For more on neuron-like networks as a model for music cognition, see Robert Gjerdingen (1990).

3. "Semiotic Tropes," plenary address to the conference on Semiotics and Art held at the University of Michigan, 1978. Pertinence refers to the status of distinctive features as opposed to other acoustical properties of speech that are not relevant to the interpretation of phonemes.

4. I am grateful to Karim Benammar, doctoral candidate in philosophy at Penn State University, for this insight.

5. As in Susan McClary (1991) and essays in Leppert and McClary (1987).

6. From a poem by the author.

Appendix

1. *Beethoven's Letters*, J. S. Shedlock (trans.), no. 71, ([1807] 1926: 68–69). Beethoven proposed to Therese von Malfatti, unsuccessfully, in 1810.

2. Book 6, however, is entitled "Confessions of a Fair Saint" and presents an early, Pietist model of renunciation for Wilhelm. Natalie, Wilhelm's ideal love, is presented in the context of the spiritually ideal when we learn that she is the niece of the saint, who recognizes in her the natural spirituality which the saint has had to earn through a long struggle.

3. For Beethoven's references to Indian literature in translation, see his several *Tagebuch* (1812–18) entries, reprinted in Solomon (1988: 265–69).

4. Several references by Beethoven to the concept of (at times stoic) resignation are found in the *Tagebuch* (Solomon, 1988: 246, 254, 262, 268–69, 271).

BIBLIOGRAPHY

Abbate, Carolyn. 1991. *Unsung Voices: Opera and Musical Narrative in the Nineteenth Century*. Princeton: Princeton University Press.

Agawu, Kofi. 1991. *Playing with Signs: A Semiotic Interpretation of Classic Music*. Princeton: Princeton University Press.

Allanbrook, Wye Jamison. 1983. *Rhythmic Gesture in Mozart*. Chicago: University of Chicago Press.

Alpers, Paul. 1992. Literary modes. In *Music and Text: Critical Inquiries*, Steven P. Scher, ed. Cambridge: Cambridge University Press, 59–74.

Andersen, Henning. 1968. IE *s after *i, u, r, k,* in Baltic and Slavic. *Acta Linguistica Hafniensia* 11, 171–90.

———. 1972. Diphthongization. *Language* 48, 11–50.

Aristotle. [350 B.C.] 1967. *Poetics*, Gerald F. Else, trans. Ann Arbor: University of Michigan Press.

———. 1973. *Aristotle's Ethics*, J. L. Ackrill, ed. London: Faber.

Babbitt, Milton. 1972. The structure and function of music theory. In *Perspectives on Contemporary Music Theory*, Benjamin Boretz and Edward T. Cone, eds. New York: Norton, 10–21.

Bakhtin, M. M. [1935] 1981. *The Dialogic Imagination: Four Essays by M. M. Bakhtin*, Michael Holquist, ed., Caryl Emerson, trans. Austin: University of Texas Press.

Barnet, Sylvan; Morton Berman; and William Burto. 1960. *A Dictionary of Literary Terms*. Boston: Little, Brown, and Co.

Barthes, Roland. 1970. *S/Z*. Paris: Seuil.

Battistella, Edwin L. 1990. *Markedness: The Evaluative Superstructure of Language*. New York: State University of New York Press.

Beethoven, Ludwig van. [1790–1827] 1926. *Beethoven's Letters*, J. S. Shedlock, trans. London: J. M. Dent and Sons.

Bell, Clive. 1914. *Art*. London: Chatto and Windus.

Bentley, Eric. 1964. *The Life of the Drama*. New York: Atheneum.

Black, Max 1954–55. Metaphor. In *Proceedings of the Aristotelian Society*, n. s. 55, 273–94.

_____. 1977. More about metaphor. *Dialectica* 31:3/4, 431–57.

Bonds, Mark Evan. 1991. Haydn, Laurence Sterne, and the origins of musical irony. *Journal of the American Musicological Society* 44:1, 57–91.

Booth, Wayne C. 1974. *A Rhetoric of Irony.* Chicago: University of Chicago Press.

Bourdieu, Pierre. 1977. *Outline of a Theory of Practice,* Richard Nice, trans. Cambridge: Cambridge University Press.

Brandenburg, Sieghard. 1982. The historical background to the "Heiliger Dankgesang" in Beethoven's A-minor Quartet Op. 132. In *Beethoven Studies* 3, Alan Tyson, ed. Cambridge: Cambridge University Press, 161–91.

Brodbeck, David L., and John Platoff. 1983. Dissociation and integration: the first movement of Beethoven's Opus 130. *19th-Century Music* 7:2, 149–62.

Brown, Jane K. 1983. The theatrical mission of the *Lehrjahre.* In *Goethe's Narrative Fiction: The Irvine Goethe Symposium,* William J. Lillyman, ed. Berlin: W. de Gruyter, 69–84.

Brown, Marshall. 1992. Origins of modernism: musical structures and narrative forms. In *Music and Text: Critical Inquiries,* Steven P. Scher, ed. Cambridge: Cambridge University Press, 75–92.

Browne, Richmond. 1981. Tonal implications of the diatonic set. *In Theory Only* 5:6/7, 3–21.

Broyles, Michael. 1987. *Beethoven: The Emergence and Evolution of Beethoven's Heroic Style.* New York: Excelsior.

Buck, Ross. 1984. *The Communication of Emotion.* New York: Guilford.

Burnham, Scott. 1990. Criticism, faith, and the *Idee*: A. B. Marx's early reception of Beethoven. *19th-Century Music* 13:3, 183–92.

_____. 1992. On the programmatic reception of Beethoven's *Eroica* Symphony. *Beethoven Forum* 1 [Lincoln, Nebraska], 1–24.

Caplin, William E. 1991. Structural expansion in Beethoven's symphonic forms. In *Beethoven's Compositional Process,* William Kinderman, ed. Lincoln: University of Nebraska Press, 27–54.

Charlton, David, ed. 1989. *E.T.A. Hoffmann's Musical Writings: Kreisleriana, The Poet and the Composer, Music Criticism,* Martyn Clarke, trans. Cambridge: Cambridge University Press.

Cogan, Robert. 1984. *New Images of Musical Sound.* Cambridge: Cambridge University Press.

Cohn, Richard. 1992. The autonomy of motives in Schenkerian accounts of tonal music. *Music Theory Spectrum* 14:2, 150–70.

Coker, Wilson. 1972. *Music and Meaning: A Theoretical Introduction to Musical Aesthetics.* New York: Free Press.

Cone, Edward T. 1974. *The Composer's Voice.* Berkeley: University of California Press.

_____. 1981. Schubert's promissory note. *19th-Century Music* 5:3, 233–41.

_____. 1984. Schubert's unfinished business. *19th-Century Music* 7:3, 222–32.

Cooke, Deryck. 1959. *The Language of Music*. Oxford: Oxford University Press.

Cooper, Barry. 1990. *Beethoven and the Creative Process*. Oxford: Oxford University Press.

Cooper, Martin. [1970] 1985. *Beethoven: The Last Decade, 1817–1827*. Oxford: Oxford University Press.

Coulter, Jeff. 1983. *Rethinking Cognitive Theory*. New York: St. Martin's.

Crabbe, John. 1982. *Beethoven's Empire of the Mind*. Newbury, England: Lovell Baines.

Dahlhaus, Carl. [1970] 1983. *Analysis and Value Judgment*, Siegmund Lavarie, trans. New York: Pendragon Press.

_____. [1978] 1989. *The Idea of Absolute Music*, Roger Lustig, trans. Chicago: University of Chicago Press.

_____. [1980] 1989. *Nineteenth-Century Music*, J. Bradford Robinson, trans. Berkeley: University of California Press.

_____. [1987] 1991. *Ludwig van Beethoven: Approaches to His Music*, Mary Whittall, trans. Oxford: Clarendon.

Derr, Ellwood. 1984. Beethoven's long-term memory of C. P. E. Bach's *Rondo in E♭*, W. 61/1 (1787) manifest in the *Variations in E♭ for Piano*, Op. 35 (1802). *Musical Quarterly* 70:1, 45–76.

Dougherty, William. 1985. An examination of semiotics in musical analysis: the Neapolitan complex in Beethoven's Op. 131. Ph.D. diss., Ohio State University.

_____. 1989. One through two to ten: Beethoven's and Schubert's settings of Goethe's *Nur wer die Sehnsucht kennt*. Paper delivered to the College Music Society, St. Louis.

Drabkin, William. 1991. The Agnus Dei of Beethoven's *Missa Solemnis*. In *Beethoven's Compositional Process*, William Kinderman, ed. Lincoln: University of Nebraska Press, 131–59.

Dreyfus, Laurence. 1987. J. S. Bach and the status of genre: Problems of style in the G-Minor Sonata BWV 1029. *The Journal of Musicology* 5:1, 55–78.

Eckelmeyer, Judith A. 1986. Structure as hermeneutic guide to *The Magic Flute*. *The Musical Quarterly* 72:1, 51–73.

Eco, Umberto. 1976. *A Theory of Semiotics*. Bloomington: Indiana University Press.

_____. 1979. *The Role of the Reader*. Bloomington: Indiana University Press.

_____. 1984. *Semiotics and the Philosophy of Language*. Bloomington: Indiana University Press.

Eldredge, Niles, and Stephen Jay Gould. 1972. Punctuated equilibria: an alternative to phyletic gradualism. In *Models in Paleobiology*, Thomas J. M. Schopf, ed. San Francisco: Freeman, Cooper, 82–115.

Epstein, David. 1979. *Beyond Orpheus: Studies in Musical Structure*. Cambridge: MIT Press.

Faas, Ekbert. 1984. *Tragedy and After: Euripides, Shakespeare, Goethe*. Kingston, Ontario: University of Toronto Press.

Faltin, Peter. 1985. *Bedeutung ästhetischer Zeichen: Musik und Sprache*. Aachen: Rader.

Fisch, Max. [1974] 1986. Hegel and Peirce. In Fisch, *Peirce, Semeiotic, and Pragmatism: Essays*, Kenneth Lane Ketner and Christian J. W. Kloessel, eds. Bloomington: Indiana University Press, 261–82.

Fodor, Janet. 1977. *Semantics: Theories of Meaning in Generative Grammar*. New York: Thomas Y. Crowell.

Fodor, Jerry. 1981. *Representations*. Cambridge: MIT Press.

Frye, Northrup. 1957. *Anatomy of Criticism*. Princeton: Princeton University Press.

Genette, Gérard. 1980. *Narrative Discourse: An Essay in Method*. Jane E. Lewin, trans. Ithaca: Cornell University Press.

Gibson, James J. 1966. *The Senses Considered As Perceptual Systems*. Boston: Houghton Mifflin.

Gjerdingen, Robert O. 1988. *A Classic Turn of Phrase: Music and the Psychology of Convention*. Philadelphia: University of Pennsylvania Press.

———. 1990. Categorization of musical patterns by self-organizing neuronlike networks. *Music Perception* 7:4, 339–69.

Goethe, Johann Wolfgang von. [1795] 1824. *Wilhelm Meister's Apprenticeship*, Thomas Carlyle, trans. Boston: Wyman Fogg, 1901.

———. 1827. Nachlese zu Aristoteles' Poetik. *Goethe's Sämtliche Werke* 38 [Stuttgart, Berlin: J. G. Cotta'sche], 81–85.

Gombrich, Ernst. 1960. *Art and Illusion: A Study in the Psychology of Pictorial Representation*. Princeton: Princeton University Press.

Goodman, Nelson. 1968. *Languages of Art: An Approach to a Theory of Symbols*. Indianapolis: Bobbs-Merrill.

———. 1975. The status of style. *Critical Inquiry* 1, 799–811.

Gould, Stephen Jay. 1977. *Ontogeny and Phylogeny*. Cambridge: Harvard University Press.

Grabócz, Márta. 1986. *Morphologie des oeuvres pour piano de Liszt*. Budapest: MTA Zenetudományi Intézet.

Green, Michael. 1991. Mathis Lussy's *Traité de l'expression musicale* as a window into performance practice. Paper delivered to the Society for Music Theory, Cincinnati.

Greene, David B. 1982. *Temporal Processes in Beethoven's Music*. New York: Gordon and Breach.

Greimas, A. J. 1970. *Du sens*. Paris: Seuil.

Guarini, Battista. [1580–84] 1976. *Il pastor fido* [*The Faithfull Shepherd*]. Richard Fanshawe, trans. 1647; J. H. Whitfield, ed. Austin: University of Texas Press.

Guck, Marion. 1990. Analytical fictions. Paper delivered to the Society for Music Theory, Oakland.

————. (forthcoming). Two types of metaphoric transference. In *Metaphor— A Musical Dimension*, Jamie C. Kassler, ed., vol. 1 of *Australian Studies in History, Philosophy, and Social Studies of Music*, Margaret J. Kartomi, ed. Davis, California: Currency.

Guérard, Albert L. 1940. *Preface to World Literature*. New York: H. Holt.

Guthke, Karl S. 1966. *Modern Tragicomedy*. New York: Random House.

Halperin, David M. 1983. *Before Pastoral: Theocritus and the Ancient Tradition of Bucolic Poetry*. New Haven: Yale University Press.

Hanslick, Eduard. [1854] 1974. *The Beautiful in Music: A Contribution to the Revisal of Musical Aesthetics*, 7th ed. (Leipzig, 1885), Gustav Cohen, trans. New York: Da Capo (reprint of London: Novello, 1891).

————. [1846–99] 1950. *Music Criticism, 1846–99*, Henry Pleasants, trans. and ed. Baltimore: Penguin.

Harris, Ellen T. 1980. *Handel and the Pastoral Tradition*. London: Oxford University Press.

Hatten, Robert S. 1980a. Nattiez's semiology of music: Flaws in the new science. Review article: Jean-Jacques Nattiez, *Fondements d'une sémiologie de la musique* (1975). *Semiotica* 31:1/2, 139–55.

————. 1980b. An approach to ambiguity in the opening of Beethoven's String Quartet, Op. 59, no. 3. *Indiana Theory Review* 3, 28–35.

————. 1982. Toward a semiotic model of style in music: Epistemological and methodological bases. Ph.D. diss., Indiana University.

————. 1985. The place of intertextuality in music studies. *American Journal of Semiotics* 3:4, 69–82.

————. 1987a. Aspects of dramatic closure in Beethoven: A semiotic perspective on music analysis via strategies of dramatic conflict. *Semiotica* 66:1/3, 197–210.

————. 1987b. Style, motivation, and markedness. In *The Semiotic Web 1986*, Thomas A. Sebeok and Jean Umiker-Sebeok, eds. (Berlin: Mouton de Gruyter), 408–29.

————. 1989. Semiotic perspectives on issues in music cognition. *In Theory Only* 11:3, 1–10.

————. 1990. The splintered paradigm: A semiotic critique of recent approaches to music cognition. Review article: Lerdahl and Jackendoff, *A Generative Theory of Tonal Music*; Serafine, *Music as Cognition*; and Sloboda, *The Musical Mind*. *Semiotica* 81:1/2, 145–78.

————. 1991. On narrativity in music: expressive genres and levels of discourse in Beethoven. *Indiana Theory Review* 12, 75–98.

———. 1992a. Review of Agawu (1991) and Nattiez (1990). *Music Theory Spectrum* 14: 1, 88–98.

———. 1992b. Interpreting deception in music. *In Theory Only* 12: 5/6, 31–50.

———. (forthcoming a). Metaphor *in* music. In *Proceedings from the Second International Congress on Musical Signification, Held at the University of Helsinki in 1988*, Eero Tarasti, ed. The Hague: Mouton.

———. (forthcoming b). A Peircean perspective on the growth of markedness and musical meaning. In *Peirce and Value Theory; On Peircean Ethics and Aesthetics*, Herman Parret, ed. Amsterdam: J. Benjamins.

Hatten, Robert, and Gayle Henrotte. 1988. Recent perspectives on music semiotics. In *The Semiotic Web 1987*, Jean Umiker-Sebeok and Thomas A. Sebeok, eds. Berlin: Mouton de Gruyter, 408–29.

Haley, Michael. 1988. *The Semeiosis of Poetic Metaphor*. Bloomington: Indiana University Press.

Hausman, Carl R. 1989. *Metaphor and Art: Interactionism and Reference in the Verbal and Nonverbal Arts*. Cambridge: Cambridge University Press.

Heller, Erich. 1962. Goethe and the avoidance of tragedy. In *The Proper Study: Essays on Western Classics*, Quentin Anderson and Joseph A. Mazzeo, eds. New York: St. Martin's, 463–82.

Hernadi, Paul. 1972. *Beyond Genre*. Ithaca: Cornell University Press.

Heydenreich, Carl Heinrich. 1790. *System der Äesthetik*. Leipzig.

Hoppin, Richard. 1978. *Medieval Music*. New York: Norton.

Jackendoff, Ray. 1983. *Semantics and Cognition*. Cambridge: MIT Press.

Jakobson, Roman, and Morris Halle. 1956. *Fundamentals of Language*. The Hague: Mouton.

Jander, Owen. 1983. Romantic form and content in the slow movement of Beethoven's violin concerto. *The Musical Quarterly* 69:2, 159–79.

Jiránek, Jaroslav. 1985. *Zu Grundfragen der musikalische Semiotik*. Berlin: Neue Musik.

Johnson, Mark. 1987. *The Body in the Mind: The Bodily Basis of Reason and Imagination*. Chicago: University of Chicago Press.

Johnson, Mark, ed. 1981. *Philosophical Perspectives on Metaphor*. Minneapolis: University of Minnesota Press.

Jung, Herman. 1980. *Die Pastorale: Studien zur Geschichte einer musikalischen Topos*. Bern, Munich: Francke.

Kamien, Roger. 1974. Chromatic details in Beethoven's piano sonata in Eflat major, op. 7. *The Music Review* 35:1, 149–56.

Karbusicky, Vladimir. 1986. *Grundriss der musikalischen Semantik*. Darmstadt: Wissenschaftliche Buchgesellschaft.

———. 1987. "Signification" in music: A metaphor? In *The Semiotic Web*

1986, Thomas Sebeok and Jean Umiker-Sebeok, eds. Berlin: Mouton de Gruyter, 430–44.

Kegel-Brinkgreve, E. 1990. *The Echoing Woods: Bucolic and Pastoral from Theocritus to Wordsworth*. Amsterdam: J. C. Gieben.

Keiler, Allan. 1981a. Music as metalanguage: Rameau's fundamental bass. In *Music Theory: Special Topics*, Richmond Browne, ed. New York: Academic Press, 83–100.

———. 1981b. Two views of musical semiotics. In *The Sign in Music and Literature*, Wendy Steiner, ed. Austin: University of Texas Press, 138–68.

———. 1983–84. On some properties of Schenker's pitch derivations. *Music Perception* 1, 200–28.

Keller, Hans. 1957. Functional analysis: its pure application. *Music Review* 18, 202–206.

Kerman, Joseph. 1966. *The Beethoven Quartets*. New York: Norton.

———. 1981. Academic music criticism. In *On Criticizing Music: Five Philosophical Perspectives*, Kingsley Price, ed. Baltimore: Johns Hopkins University Press, 38–54.

———. 1982. Notes on Beethoven's codas. In *Beethoven Studies* 3, Alan Tyson, ed. Cambridge: Cambridge University Press, 141–59.

———. 1985a. *Contemplating Music*. Cambridge: Harvard University Press.

———. 1985b. *Tändelnde Lazzi*: On Beethoven's Trio in D major, Opus 70, no. 1. In *Slavonic and Western Music: Essays for Gerald Abraham*, Malcolm H. Brown and R. John Wiley, eds. Ann Arbor: UMI Research Press, and Oxford: Oxford University Press, 109–22.

Kinderman, William. 1985. Beethoven's symbol for the deity in the *Missa solemnis* and the Ninth Symphony. *19th-Century Music* 9:2, 102–18.

———. 1991. Beethoven's compositional models for the Choral Finale of the Ninth Symphony. In *Beethoven's Compositional Process*, William Kinderman, ed. Lincoln: University of Nebraska Press, 160–88.

———. 1992. Beethoven's Piano Sonata in A♭ major, Opus 110. *Beethoven Forum* 1 [Lincoln, Nebraska], 111–45.

Kinderman, William, ed. 1991. *Beethoven's Compositional Process*. Lincoln: University of Nebraska Press.

Kirby, F. E. 1970. Beethoven's pastoral symphony as a *Sinfonia caracteristica*. In *The Creative World of Beethoven*, Paul Henry Lang, ed. New York: Norton, 103–121.

Kirkendale, Warren. 1966. *Fuge und fugato in der Kammermusik des Rokoko und der Klassik*. Tutzing: Hans Schneider.

Kivy, Peter. 1980. *The Corded Shell*. Princeton: Princeton University Press.

———. 1984. *Sound and Semblance*. Princeton: Princeton University Press.

———. 1990a. *Music Alone*. Ithaca: Cornell University Press.

———. 1990b. What was Hanslick denying? *The Journal of Musicology* 8:1, 3–18.

Klimowitsky, Abraham. 1978. Ein "Gloria" von Palestrina als Modell des "Heiligen Dankgesanges" aus Beethovens Streichquartett op. 132. In *Bericht über den Internationalen Beethoven-Kongress, Berlin, 1977*, H. Goldschmidt, K.-H. Köhler, and K. Niemann, eds. Leipzig: VEB Deutscher Verlag für Musik, 513–17.

Koch, Heinrich C. 1802. *Musikalisches Lexicon*. Frankfurt am Main.

Korsyn, Kevin. 1983. Integration in works of Beethoven's final period. Ph.D. diss., Yale University.

Kramer, Jonathan D. 1973. Multiple and non-linear time in Beethoven's opus 135. *Perspectives of New Music* 11, 122–45.

Kramer, Lawrence. 1984. *Music and Poetry: The Nineteenth Century and After*. Berkeley: University of California Press.

———. 1990. *Music as Cultural Practice, 1800–1900*. Berkeley: University of California Press.

———. 1992. Haydn's chaos, Schenker's order, or hermeneutics and musical analysis: can they mix? *19th Century Music* 16:1, 3–17.

Kramer, Richard. 1992. Between Cavatina and Ouverture: Opus 130 and the voices of narrative. *Beethoven Forum* 1 [Lincoln, Nebraska], 165–89.

Kretzschmar, Hermann. 1902. Anregungen zur Forderung musikalischer Hermeneutik. *Jahrbuch der Musikbibliothek Peters der 1902*, 45–66.

Kripke, Saul A. 1972. Naming and necessity. In *Semantics of Natural Language*, Donald Davidson and Gilbert Harman, eds. Dordrecht: D. Reidel, 253–355.

Laki, Peter. 1985. The idiomatic use of the minor mode in the early Classic period. Paper delivered to the Department of Music, University of Pennsylvania.

Lakoff, George. 1987. *Women, Fire, and Dangerous Things*. Chicago: University of Chicago Press.

Lakoff, George and Mark Johnson. 1980. *Metaphors We Live By*. Chicago: University of Chicago Press.

Lakoff, George, and Mark Turner. 1989. *More than Cool Reason: A Field Guide to Poetic Metaphor*. Chicago: University of Chicago Press.

Langer, Suzanne K. 1953. *Feeling and Form*. New York: Charles Scribner's Sons.

LaRue, Jan. 1970. *Guidelines for Style Analysis*. New York: Norton.

Lenz, Wilhelm von. [1855] 1921. *Beethoven. Eine Kunststudie*, vol. 1, A. C. Kalischer, ed. Berlin: Schuster & Loeffler.

Leppert, Richard, and Susan McClary. 1987. *Music and Society: The Politics of Composition, Performance, and Reception*. Cambridge: Cambridge University Press.

Levy, Janet M. 1982. Texture as a sign in Classic and early Romantic music. *Journal of the American Musicological Society* 35:3, 482–531.

Lewalski, Barbara Kiefer. 1985. *Paradise Lost and the Rhetoric of Literary Forms*. Princeton: Princeton University Press.

Lidov, David. 1977. Nattiez' semiotics of music. (Review of Nattiez, 1975.) *The Canadian Journal of Research in Semiotics* 5:2, 13–54.

_____. 1980. Musical and verbal semantics. (Review of Noske, 1977.) *Semiotica* 31:3/4, 379–91.

_____. 1981. The Allegretto of Beethoven's Seventh. *American Journal of Semiotics* 1:1/2, 141–66.

_____. 1986. Music. In *Encyclopedic Dictionary of Semiotics*, Thomas A. Sebeok, ed. Berlin: Mouton de Gruyter, 577–87.

Lieberman, Philip. 1967. *Intonation, Perception and Language*. Cambridge: MIT Press.

_____. 1984. *The Biology and Evolution of Language*. Cambridge: Harvard University Press.

_____. 1985. Biology and the evolution of language. Guest lecture, University of Pennsylvania.

Lochhead, Judy. 1979. The temporal in Beethoven's opus 135: When are ends beginnings? *In Theory Only* 4:7, 3–30.

Lockwood, Lewis. 1992. *Beethoven: Studies in the Creative Process*. Cambridge: Harvard University Press.

Longyear, Rey. 1970. Beethoven and romantic irony. In *The Creative World of Beethoven*, Paul Henry Lang, ed. New York: Norton, 145–62.

Loughrey, Brian, ed. 1984. *The Pastoral Mode*. London: MacMillan.

Lussy, Mathis. 1873. *Traité de l'expression musicale*. Paris: Heugel.

McClary, Susan. 1976. The transition from modal to tonal organization in the works of Monteverdi. Ph.D. diss., Harvard University.

_____. 1986. A musical dialectic from the Enlightenment: Mozart's *Piano Concerto in G major*, K. 453, movement 2. *Cultural Critique* 4, 129–69.

_____. 1991. *Feminine Endings: Music, Gender, and Sexuality*. Minneapolis: University of Minnesota Press.

McCreless, Patrick. 1991. Syntagmatics and paradigmatics: some implications for the analysis of chromaticism in tonal music. *Music Theory Spectrum* 13:2, 147–78.

Marinelli, Peter V. 1971. *Pastoral*. London: Methuen.

Marx, Adolf Bernhard. 1859. *Ludwig van Beethoven: Leben und Schaffen*, 2 vols. Reprint of the original ed., Leipzig: Adolph Schumann, 1902.

_____. [1863] 1898. *Anleitung zum Vortrag Beethovenscher Klavierwerke*, 3d ed. Berlin: Behncke, 1898.

Mattheson, Johann. 1739. *Der vollkommene Capellmeister*. Hamburg. Ernest C. Harriss, rev. trans. Ann Arbor: UMI Research Press, 1981.

Maus, Fred. 1989. Agency in instrumental music and song. *College Music Symposium* 29, 31–43.

———. 1991. Music as narrative. *Indiana Theory Review*. 12, 1–34.

———. 1992. Hanslick's animism. *The Journal of Musicology* 10:3, 273–92.

Mellers, Wilfrid. 1983. *Beethoven and the Voice of God*. New York: Oxford University Press.

Meyer, Leonard B. 1956. *Emotion and Meaning in Music*. Chicago: University of Chicago Press.

———. 1967. *Music, the Arts, and Ideas*. Chicago: University of Chicago Press.

———. 1973. *Explaining Music*. Chicago: University of Chicago Press.

———. 1982. Process and morphology in the music of Mozart. *The Journal of Musicology* 1:1, 317–41.

———. 1989. *Style and Music*. Philadelphia: University of Pennsylvania Press.

Mies, Paul. 1929. *Beethoven's Sketches*, Doris L. MacKinnon, trans. London: Oxford University Press. [Johnson Reprint, 1969].

de Momigny, Jérome-Joseph. 1806. *Cours complet d'harmonie et composition, d'après une theorie neuve et générale de la musique*, 3 vols. Paris: de Momigny.

Monelle, Raymond. 1992. *Linguistics and Semiotics in Music*. Chur, Switzerland: Harwood Academic Publishers.

Morris, Charles. 1946. *Signs, Language, and Behavior*. Englewood Cliffs: Prentice-Hall.

———. 1964. *Signification and Significance*. Cambridge: MIT Press.

Mosley, David. 1990. *Gesture, Sign, and Song: An Interdisciplinary Approach to Schumann's* Liederkreis *Opus 39*. New York: Peter Lang.

Muecke, D. C. [1970] 1982. *Irony and the Ironic*. London: Methuen.

Muenzer, Clark S. 1984. *Figures of Identity: Goethe's Novels and the Enigmatic Self*. University Park: Penn State University Press.

Narmour, Eugene. 1977. *Beyond Schenkerism*. Chicago: University of Chicago Press.

———. 1990. *The Analysis and Cognition of Basic Melodic Structures*. Chicago: University of Chicago Press.

Nattiez, Jean-Jacques. 1975. *Fondements d'une sémiologie de la musique*. Paris: Union générale d'éditions.

———. 1990. *Music and Discourse: Toward a Semiology of Music*, Carolyn Abbate, trans. Princeton: Princeton University Press.

Neubauer, John. 1986. *The Emancipation of Music from Language*. New Haven: Yale University Press.

Newcomb, Anthony. 1983. Those images that yet fresh images beget. *Journal of Musicology* 2, 227–45.

———. 1984a. Once more "between absolute and program music": Schumann's Second Symphony. *19th-Century Music* 7:3, 233–50.

_____. 1984b. Sound and feeling. *Critical Inquiry* 10, 614–43.

_____. 1987. Schumann and late eighteenth-century narrative strategies. *19th-Century Music* 11:2, 164–74.

Newman, Ernest. 1970 [1927]. *The Unconscious Beethoven*. New York: Alfred A. Knopf.

Newman, William S. 1988. *Beethoven on Beethoven: Playing His Piano Music His Way*. New York: Norton.

Noske, Frits. 1977. *The Signifier and the Signified: Studies in the Operas of Mozart and Verdi*. The Hague: Mouton.

Nottebohm, Gustav. 1887. *Zweite Beethoveniana*. Leipzig: C. F. Peters.

Osthoff, Wolfgang. 1969. Mozarts Cavatinen und íhre Tradition. In *Helmut Osthoff zu seinem siebzigsten Geburtstag*, W. Stauder et al., eds. Tutzing: Hans Schneider, 139–77.

Peirce, Charles Sanders. 1931, 1960. *Collected Papers of Charles Sanders Peirce*, vols. 1–6, Charles Hartshorne and Paul Weiss, eds.; vols. 7–8, Arthur W. Burks, ed. Cambridge: Harvard University Press.

Plantinga, Leon. 1967. *Schumann as Critic*. New Haven: Yale University Press.

Poggioli, Renato. 1975. *The Oaten Flute*. Cambridge: Harvard University Press.

Powers, Harold S. 1980. Language models and music analysis. *Ethnomusicology* 24, 1–60.

Ratner, Leonard. 1980. *Classic Music*. New York: Schirmer.

Réti, Rudolph. 1951. *The Thematic Process in Music*. New York: Macmillan.

Robertson, John S. 1983. From symbol to icon: The evolution of the pronomial system from common Mayan to modern Yucatecan. *Language* 59:3, 529–40.

Rodway, Allan. 1962. Terms for comedy. *Renaissance and Modern Studies* 7.

Rosen, Charles. 1972. *The Classical Style*. New York: Norton.

Rothgeb, John. 1977. Design as a key to structure in tonal music. In *Readings in Schenker Analysis and Other Approaches*, Maury Yeston, ed. New Haven: Yale University Press, 72–93.

Rothstein, William. 1989. *Phrase Rhythm in Tonal Music*. New York: Schirmer.

Rousseau, Jean-Jacques. 1768. *Dictionnaire de music*. Paris: Chez la veuve Duchesne.

Russell, Bertrand 1961. *An Outline of Philosophy*. Cleveland: World.

de Saussure, Ferdinand. [1916] 1966. *Course in General Linguistics*. Charles Bally and Albert Sechehaye, eds., Wade Baskin, trans. New York: McGraw-Hill.

Sax, Benjamin. 1987. *Images of Identity: Goethe and the Problem of Self-Conception in the Nineteenth Century*. New York: P. Lang.

Schachter, Carl. 1976. Rhythm and linear analysis: a preliminary study. *Music Forum* 4, 281–334.

———. 1980. Rhythm and linear analysis: durational reduction. *Music Forum* 5, 197–232.

———. 1987. Rhythm and linear analysis: aspects of meter. *Music Forum* 6, 1–59.

Schachter, S., and J. E. Singer. 1962. Cognitive, social and physiological determinants of emotional state. *Psychological Review* 69, 379–99.

Schauffler, Robert Haven. 1929. *Beethoven: The Man Who Freed Music.* Garden City, N.Y.: Doubleday, Doran.

Schenker, Heinrich. [1920] 1972. *Beethoven: Die letzten Sonaten: Sonate A Dur, Op. 101*, Oswald Jonas, ed. Vienna: Universal.

———. 1930. *Das Meisterwerk in der Musik*, Jahrbuch III. Munich: Drei Masken.

———. [1933] 1969. *Five Graphic Music Analyses.* New York: Dover.

———. [1935] 1979. *Free Composition*, Ernst Oster, trans. and ed. New York: Longman.

Schering, Arnold. 1936. *Beethoven und die Dichtung.* Berlin: Junker und Dunnhaupt.

Schiller, Friedrich. [1772–95] 1884. *Aesthetical and Philosophical Essays.* Boston: S. E. Cassino.

Schneider, David M. 1968. *American Kinship: A Cultural Account.* New York: Prentice-Hall.

Schneider, Reinhard. 1980. *Semiotik der Musik: Darstellung und Kritik.* Munich: Wilhelm Fink.

Schoenberg, Arnold. 1967. *Fundamentals of Musical Composition*, Gerald Strang and Leonard Stein, eds. New York: St. Martin's.

———. [1950] 1975. *Style and Idea: Selected Writings of Arnold Schoenberg*, Leonard Stein, ed., Leo Black, trans. New York: St. Martin's.

Scruton, Roger. 1983. *The Aesthetic Understanding.* London: Methuen.

Seeger, Charles [1935–75] 1977. *Studies in Musicology, 1935–1975.* Berkeley: University of California Press.

Shapiro, Michael. 1976. *Asymmetry: An Inquiry into the Linguistic Structure of Poetry.* Amsterdam: North Holland.

———. 1983. *The Sense of Grammar.* Bloomington: Indiana University Press.

Shapiro, Michael, and Shapiro, Marianne. 1976. *Hierarchy and the Structure of Tropes.* Bloomington: RCLSS, Indiana University; Lisse: Peter de Ridder.

———. 1988. *Figuration in Verbal Art.* Princeton: Princeton University Press.

Sheldon, David. 1989. The concept *galant* in the 18th century. *The Journal of Musicological Research* 9:2/3, 89–108.

Siegle, Robert. 1986. *The Politics of Reflexivity: Narrative and the Constitutive Poetics of Culture.* Baltimore: Johns Hopkins University Press.

Silverstein, Michael. 1976. Shifters, linguistic categories, and cultural description. In *Meaning in Anthropology*, Keith H. Basso and Henry A. Selby, Jr., eds. Albuquerque: University of New Mexico Press, 11–55.

Snarrenberg, Robert. 1991. Writing (Figures) Music. Ph.D. diss., University of Michigan.

Solomon, Maynard. 1977. *Beethoven*. New York: Schirmer.

_____. 1988. *Beethoven Essays*. Cambridge: Harvard University Press.

Staiger, Emil. [1946, 1963 6th ed.] 1991. *Basic Concepts of Poetics*, Marianne Burkhard and Luanne T. Frank, eds., Janette C. Hudson and Luanne T. Frank, trans. University Park: Penn State University Press.

Steblin, Rita. 1983. *A History of Key Characteristics in the Eighteenth and Early Nineteenth Centuries*. Ann Arbor: UMI Research Press.

Stefani, Gino. 1976. *Introduzione alla semiotica della musica*. Palermo: Sellerio.

Stein, Deborah. 1989. Schubert's "Die Liebe hat gelogen": the deception of mode and mixture. *Journal of Musicological Research* 9:2/3, 109–31.

Sturm, Christoph Christian. [1740–1786] 1824. *Reflections on the Works of God, and on His Providence in the Regions of Nature, and in the Government of the Universe*. 4 vols. London: J. Sharpe.

Subotnik, Rose Rosengard. 1976. Adorno's diagnosis of Beethoven's late style: early symptom of a fatal condition. *Journal of the American Musicological Society* 29, 242–75.

_____. 1991. *Developing Variations: Style and Ideology in Western Music*. Minneapolis: University of Minnesota Press.

Sullivan, J. W. N. [1927] 1958. *Beethoven: His Spiritual Development*. New York: Alfred A. Knopf.

Sulzer, Johann Georg. 1773–75. *Allgemeine Theorie der schönen Künste*, 2 vols. Leipzig: M. G. Weidmanns Erben und Reich.

Tarasti, Eero. 1978. *Myth and Music: A Semiotic Approach to the Aesthetics of Myth in Music, especially that of Wagner, Sibelius, and Stravinsky*. Helsinki: Suomen Musiikkitieteellinen Seura.

_____. 1983. Towards a structural semantics of music: Reflections on the logic of musical discourse. In *Semiotics Unfolding*, vol. 3, Tasso Borbé, ed. Berlin: Mouton de Gruyter, 1791–98.

_____. 1984. Pour une narratologie de Chopin. *International Review of the Aesthetics and Sociology of Music* 15:1, 53–75.

_____. 1985. Music as sign and process. In *Analytica: Studies in the Description and Analysis of Music in Honour of Ingmar Bengtsson*. Stockholm: Royal Swedish Academy of Music, 97–115.

_____. (forthcoming). *A Theory of Musical Semiotics*. Bloomington: Indiana University Press.

Tarasti, Eero, ed. 1987. Basic concepts of studies in musical signification: A report on a new international research project in the semiotics of music.

In *The Semiotic Web 1986*, Thomas Sebeok and Jean Umiker-Sebeok, eds. Berlin: Mouton de Gruyter, 405–581.

Thirlwall, Connop. 1833. On the irony of Sophocles. *Philological Museum 2*, 490–91.

Todd, R. Larry. 1979. Of sea gulls and counterpoint: the early versions of Mendelssohn's *Hebrides* Overture. *19th-Century Music* 2:3, 197–213.

Tomlinson, Gary. 1987. *Monteverdi and the End of the Renaissance*. Berkeley: University of California Press.

Tormey, Alan. 1971. *The Concept of Expression*. Princeton: Princeton University Press.

Tovey, Donald F. [1949] 1959. *Essays and Lectures on Music*, reprinted as *The Main Stream of Music and Other Essays*. New York: Meridian.

Treitler, Leo. 1980. History, criticism, and Beethoven's Ninth Symphony. *19th-Century Music* 3:3, 193–210.

———. 1982. To worship that celestial sound: motives for analysis. *Journal of Musicology* 1:2, 153–70.

———. 1989. *Music and the Historical Imagination*. Cambridge: Harvard University Press.

Trubetzkoy, N. B. [1939] 1969. *Principles of Phonology*. Christine A.M. Baltaxe, trans. Berkeley: University of California Press.

Vaget, Hans Rudolf. 1983. Goethe the novelist: on the coherence of his fiction. In *Goethe's Narrative Fiction: The Irvine Goethe Symposium*. Berlin: W. de Gruyter, 1–20.

Wallace, Robin. 1986. *Beethoven's Critics*. Cambridge: Cambridge University Press.

Weber, Daniel. 1800. Über komische Characteristik und Karikatur in praktischen Musikwerken. *Allgemeine musikalische Zeitung* 3:9 [Leipzig].

Webster, James. 1991. *Haydn's "Farewell" Symphony and the Idea of Classical Style*. Cambridge: Cambridge University Press.

Winter, Robert. 1982. *Compositional Origins of Beethoven's Opus 131*. Ann Arbor: UMI Research Press.

Wittgenstein, Ludwig. [1933–35] 1960. *The Blue and Brown Books*. New York: Harper & Row.

Wohlheim, Richard. 1968. *Art and Its Objects*. New York: Harper & Row.

INDEX OF CONCEPTS

Firstness, Secondness, Thirdness (C. S. Peirce), 258–9, 270; as modeling style growth, 260–6
Foregrounding (see Salience)
Formalist aesthetics, 228, 231–5

Galant style, 61, 77–8, 103
Genre (see Expressive genre), 67; classifications in literary theory, 68, 71–4, 283; cavatina, 208, 318–9; fantasy, 68, 304; romance, 69, 216–7
Gestalt perceptual strategies, 34, 237
Ground (C. S. Peirce), 243
Growth of style (see Markedness), 33, 41, 42, 121, 132, 189–90, 257–78, 290, 299, 300, 326
Grundgestalt (A. Schoenberg), 66, 99, 113

Hermeneutic, for music (H. Kretzschmar, E. T. Cone), 2, 10–1, 62–4, 277, 290, 293, 297; as speculative component of music semiotics, 61, 228; as creatively inferential process (see Abduction), 56–63, 297; complementary to structuralist, 63, 228, 279; vs. license, 279
Heteroglossia/multiplicity of voices (M. M. Bakhtin), 202, 303, 315, 316, 318
Hierarchy, 11, 120, 161, 189, 290, 300, 304; vs. network of interpretants, 162, 167

Icon, iconic, iconism (C. S. Peirce), 38, 164, 167, 241, 258, 290
Implication (L. B. Meyer), 11, 18, 41, 56, 275, 290, 303, 320
Index, indexical, indexicality (C. S. Peirce), 164, 242, 258, 290
Integration, 24, 28; by tempo mediation, 134, 141; thematic, 134, 136, 210, 218, 220, 284, 294, 310, 311; topical, 24
Intentionality, 298, 320
Interpretant (C. S. Peirce), 243–4, 262, 290–1
Interpret, interpretation (see Hermeneutic, Interpretant), 4, 9, 33, 55–6, 157, 243, 269–71, 275, 291; importance of context, 321
Intersubjective, 5, 245
Intertextual, intertextuality (see Quotation), 56, 176, 196–201, 276, 291, 317
Invariant, invariance, 50, 53, 291
Irreducible significance of the surface, 160, 278
Irony, ironic (see Romantic irony), 172–4, 291, 315; as higher-order trope, 172, 302; constraints on ironic interpretation, 184–6; dramatic irony, 173–4, 216, 321; metaphor vs. irony, 172–3, 174–5, 186

Isomorphism, 164, 167, 236, 241, 291
Isotopy (A. J. Greimas, U. Eco), 170, 291; in literature, 314; in music (M. Grabócz, E. Tarasti), 314–5; bi-isotopy, 168

Language and music, 233–6, 247–56; varying expectations for specificity, 56, 233, 236, 253–5, 257, 321; vs. referential precision, 236, 251–2; referential fallacy (U. Eco), 252
Leakage, 270–1
Learned vs. innate, 270
Level of attending, 278, 291
Level of discourse, 202, 275, 316, 322
—shift cued by: fermata/cadenza, 180, 200; intertextual contrasts, 199–200; quotation or reminiscence, 176, 199–201; recitative topic, 175–6, 180–4, 208, 316; stylistic shift, 176

Markedness (N. Trubetzkoy, R. Jakobson, M. Shapiro), x, 5, 34–8, 63, 69, 245, 276–8, 291–2, 301–2; asymmetry of oppositions, 34, 36, 245, 262, 276, 302; change of, 39–43; examples from language, 34–6, 39, 44, 62
—examples from music: doubling of tonic triads, 50–6; formal location, 43, 119–20, 268; head vs. tail of fugue subject, 154, 313; intervals, 156, 159–60; key relationships, 43–4; material in Classical style, 115–9, 120–1; phrase construction, 122–6; Picardy third or V^7/iv, 39–43; referential sonorities, 299; sonorities, 46, 159, 214–5, 303, 320; tonal relationships, 159–60; thematic, 117; textural, 115–9, 160
—growth of, 39–43, 260–8
—in other parameters, 267–8
—strategic or thematic, 42, 111, 117–8 133–60, 154, 262
—stylistic, 39, 117
—summary of theoretical principles, 63–5
—unmarked raised (strategically) to marked, 101, 117, 150, 154, 211, 320; unmarked harmonic sequence, 313; unmarked theme, 126–32, 154
—unresolved issues, 65–6
—vs. salience, 42, 64, 267, 278, 279
Markedness assimilation (H. Andersen), 37, 64, 118, 292
Metalanguage, 166, 247, 249, 257
Metaphor: in language, 162–8, 314; in language about music, 314
—in music, 168–72, 292; as non-hierarchical, 172; attribution and speculative models, 169; ironic reversal

INDEX OF NAMES AND WORKS

Eldredge, Niles, 326
Eliot, T. S., 270
Epstein, David, 113–4

Faas, Ekbert, 284
Faltin, Peter, 297
Fisch, Max, 326
Fodor, Janet, 272
Fodor, Jerry, 325
Forster, Georg, 284
Frye, Northrup, 73

Genette, Gérard, 322
Gibson, James J., 286
Gjerdingen, Robert O., 304, 327
Gluck, Christoph Willibald, 36, 302; "Che
 farò senza Euridice," 36, 216
Goethe, Johann Wolfgang von: *Faust*, 73,
 284, 305; *Nachlese zu Aristoteles' Poetik*,
 283; *The Sufferings of the Young Werther*,
 282; *Wilhelm Meister's Apprenticeship*, 56,
 281–6, 303, 305
Gombrich, Ernst, 167
Goodman, Nelson, 163–7, 236–42, 249, 295,
 314, 324
Gould, Stephen Jay, 326
Grabócz, Márta, xv, 168–9, 291, 297, 314
Green, Michael, 326
Greene, David B., 308
Greimas, A. J., 291, 314
Guarini, Battista, 305; *Il pastor fido*, 74
Guck, Marion, xv, 314, 325
Guérard, Albert L., 72
Guthke, Karl S., 73, 83

Halle, Morris, 269
Halperin, David M., 307
Handel, George Frideric, 80, 317; Concerto
 for Organ in F major, HWV 295, 310;
 Israel in Egypt, 302; *Messiah*, 233; *Solomon*,
 302
Hanslick, Eduard, 229, 231–6, 247, 276, 297,
 321, 323, 324
Harris, Ellen T., 305
Hausman, Carl R., 314
Haydn, Franz Joseph, 83, 103, 112, 304,
 311, 315; Sonata for Piano in C minor
 (1770), 119; Symphony no. 45 in F♯ minor
 (*Farewell*), 299; Symphony no. 46 in B
 major, 316; Symphony no. 92 in G major
 (*Oxford*), 312
Hegel, Georg Wilhelm Friedrich, 144
Heller, Erich, 284
Henrotte, Gayle, 297
Henze, Hans Werner, 307
Hernadi, Paul, 71–3, 253
Heydenreich, Carl Heinrich, 323

Hjelmsley, Louis, 165
Hoffmann, E. T. A., 229–30, 323
Hoppin, Richard, 314

Jackendoff, Ray, 1, 272, 303, 326, 327
Jakobson, Roman, 167, 245, 269, 277–8
Jander, Owen, 69, 216
Jiránek, Jaroslav, 297
Johnson, Mark, 163–4
Jung, Herman, 70, 80–1, 302, 305

Kālidāsa: *Sacontalá*, 284
Kamien, Roger, 304
Kant, Immanuel, 86, 308
Karbusicky, Vladimir, 168–9, 297
Kegel-Brinkgreve, E., 305, 307
Keiler, Allan, 325
Keller, Hans, 247
Kerman, Joseph, 122, 186, 229, 250, 307,
 310, 311, 312, 322
Kinderman, William, xiv, 86, 299, 308, 310,
 316
Kirby, F. E., 305, 308, 309
Kirkendale, Warren, 312
Kivy, Peter, 164, 240–3, 255, 314, 319,
 323–5
Klimowitsky, Abraham, 317
Kleist, Heinrich von: *Prinz von Homburg*, 73
Koch, Heinrich C., 208, 310
Korsyn, Kevin, 309
Kramer, Jonathan D., 311
Kramer, Lawrence, xiv, 10, 279, 297, 303,
 304, 306–8, 315–8, 325
Kramer, Richard, 322
Kretzschmar, Hermann, 290, 297
Kripke, Saul, 251

Laki, Peter, 302, 314
Lakoff, George, 44, 162–3, 325
Langer, Suzanne K., 236–41, 324–5
LaRue, Jan, 115, 119
Lenz, Wilhelm von, 298, 316
Leppert, Richard, 327
Lerdahl, Fred, 1, 272, 327
Levy, Janet M., 14
Lewalski, Barbara Kiefer, 71–2, 75
Lidov, David, ix–xi, xv, 297, 310
Lieberman, Philip, 33, 300, 326
Liszt, Franz, 15, 97, 168, 282
Lochhead, Judy, 169, 311
Lockwood, Lewis, 220, 318
Logan, Ken, xv, 310
Longyear, Rey, 184, 186, 293, 306, 315
Loughrey, Brian, 307
Lussy, Mathis, 277, 326

McClary, Susan, 169, 300, 327
McCreless, Patrick, xv, 302, 310, 317

Sullivan, J. W. N., 3, 298, 306, 316
Sulzer, Johann Georg, 306

Tarasti, Eero, xv, 291, 297, 315
Tchaikovsky, Peter Ilyich: Symphony no. 6 in
  B minor, Op. 74 (*Pathétique*), 322
Tennyson, Alfred, 82, 263, 326
Theocritus, 82, 305
Tieck, Ludwig, 323
Todd, R. Larry, 255, 325
Tomlinson, Gary, 305
Tovey, Donald F., 185, 316
Treitler, Leo, xv, 309, 316
Trubetzkoy, N. B., 245, 277
Turner, Mark, 163

Vaget, Hans Rudolf, 283
Verdi, Giuseppe: *La traviata*, 324
Virgil, 82
Vivaldi, Antonio, 83

Wackenroder, Wilhelm Heinrich, 323
Wagner, Richard, 46, 223, 235, 311, 323;
  Lohengrin, 232, 324; *Die Meistersinger*,
  281, 324; *Parsifal*, 324; *Tristan und Isolde*,
  320
Wallace, Robin, 230, 297, 324
Weber, Daniel, 305
Webster, James, 299, 310, 315
Winter, Robert, 145–50, 312
Wittgenstein, Ludwig, 163, 295, 300, 325
Wohlheim, Richard, 300

ROBERT S. HATTEN, Associate Professor of Music Theory at The Pennsylvania State University, is the author of numerous articles and papers on music semiotic issues. He is also active as a pianist, poet, and librettist.